TIQ SLO'W: The Making of a Modern Day Chief

Mary Louise Contini Gordon

AMETHYST MOON
PUBLISHING

TIQ SLO'W, The Making of a Modern Day Chief

©2013 Mary Louise Contini Gordon

An Amethyst Moon Book
Published by AMETHYST MOON PUBLISHING
P. O. Box 87885
Tucson, AZ 85754
www.ampubbooks.com

First Edition 2013

Available in these formats:
Paperback: ISBN 978-1-938714-17-7
eBook (epub): ISBN 978-1-938714-18-4
eBook (mobi): ISBN 978-1-938714-19-1

Library of Congress Control Number: 2013947414

Front cover photos:
Charlie Cooke, Age 12, Newhall, CA, c 1946, 1947 (Santa Clarita Valley Signal)

Charlie Cooke Sherman Oaks, CA, August 8, 2002 (Photo by Phil Bedel)

Boney Mountain, Satwiwa, Newbury Park, CA, March 20, 2013 (Author's photo)

Back cover photo:
Charlie Cooke, Acton, CA, February, 2009 (Author's photo)

TIQ SLO'W: The Making of a Modern Day Chief

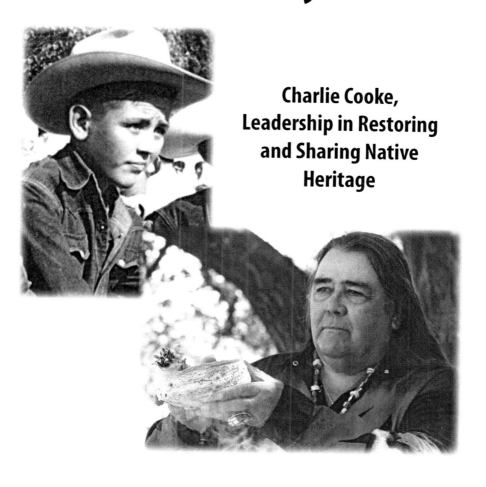

Charlie Cooke,
Leadership in Restoring
and Sharing Native
Heritage

Dedication

To our elders
Wherever they came from in the world,
To bring alive the past in the present
To form our future.

Especially for Grandma Frances Garcia Cooke
And Grandma Rosaria Cultrona Contini

Foreword

by Joe Edmiston, FAICP, Executive Director, Santa Monica Mountains Conservancy, Natural Resources Agency, State of California

In the 1970s there was growing recognition that conservation of the Santa Monica Mountains was of both statewide and national importance. This coastal range that had once so ably sustained generations of Chumash and Tonga was threatened by explosive population growth and haphazard development. It was about the time when the Santa Monica Mountains Conservancy was established by the California Legislature, in 1979, that I met Charlie Cooke. Calm, respectful, and absolutely implacable in his dedication to Native American values and to bringing those values into the mainstream culture, Charlie professed what became our guiding principal: to listen to the land. "Let the land dictate the use." Today, some 30 years later, these mountains adjacent to one of the greatest metropolitan areas in the world still support a diverse and healthy population of wildlife, including mountain lions, bobcats, golden eagles, and steelhead. Charlie Cooke, Hereditary Chief, kindred spirit, has blessed the land that has sustained these populations, and shared its blessings with the people who have come to these remarkable mountains—from schoolchildren to one of our presidents.

Map 1: Overview of Major Locations in the Story
(Courtesy of independent cartographer James
Mansfield and NPS cartographer, Brendan Clarke)

Bakersfield

5

99

58

101

Santa
Maria

VANDENBERG
AIR FORCE BASE

Lompoc

101

Solvang

Point
Conception

Santa
Barbara

1

101

Pitas Point

Ventura

Ojai

Lebec

ANTELOPE
VALLEY

EDWARDS
AIR FORCE BASE

14

Lancaster

Palmdale

5

LOS PADRES
NATIONAL FOREST

Santa
Clarita

14

Acton

Newhall

ANGELES
NATIONAL FOREST

SANTA SUSANA
MOUNTAINS

PICO
CANYON

Channel Islands
(North)

San Miguel

Santa Cruz

Santa Rosa

Anacapa

Oxnard

Thousand
Oaks

SAN FERNANDO
VALLEY

101

Burbank

118

Pasadena

SANTA MONICA MOUNTAINS

Malibu

Los Angeles

110

El Segundo

5

Long
Beach

Santa
Barbara

Catalina

San Nicolas

Channel Islands
(South)

San Clemente

P A C I F I C   O C E A N

7

Preface

Why this story matters

Charlie Cooke's story is important from both historic and leadership perspectives. Both Native Americans and the general public came to respect him as a leader of causes that would shape the Southern California landscape and change the mindset of its peoples.

From an historic perspective, he is important in Southern California indigenous history and heritage because he helped find, protect, and bring it back to life. Some of it had been lost. He rose up out of strong dedication and deep-seated respect to take a determined stance at every opportunity he saw to be a voice for those that had been silenced in the past, whether they were Chumash, Yokuts, Tongva, Tataviam, Kitanemuk, Vanyume, Kawaiisu, or one of the many other Native peoples of Southern California. In the process, he not only was a factor in raising awareness of their here-and-now existence, but he was also a major influence in creating and promoting National and State Park lands and their Native programs.

From a leadership perspective, his work over decades demonstrates many characteristics of effective leaders. He found a cause that was sparked by a **defining moment** as happens with many leaders, and then he developed as a leader **through his experiences, in spite of his circumstances**, and **through mentorship across boundaries**. Early on he developed **personal credibility** by constantly learning and then openly sharing his knowledge. As he began to see opportunities for his people, he became a **visionary**. He demonstrated a special **ability to work with multiple perspectives**. He **communicated frankly** with humor and humility. He listened closely with the keen **sensitivity to hear the unspoken**. Very importantly, he **motivated others through sincere involvement**.

The leadership and historic perspectives intertwine. Charlie's style is one of influence. While he had positions of note, he had no actual authority in many of the situations in which he found himself and yet he was and continues to be effective. Charlie Cooke is an everyday husband, father, and worker. Although there is some dispute, written record, oral tradition, and DNA results suggest that he is at least Chumash, Tongva, Tataviam, Vanyume, French, and German. Perhaps, more importantly, he is an effective leader even when groups are splintered and opposing each other. Family history makes him an hereditary Chumash chief, again disputed by some, but more importantly, he exemplifies what it means to be a chief. This book peels back his leadership, his chiefness, because it defies being put succinctly. You know there is something special when you work with Charlie, see him presenting to a crowd, talk with him, or just walk with him.

Bob Chandler, National Park Service, Santa Monica Mountains National Recreation Area superintendent in the early 1980s, remembers his quiet leadership in elevating the general awareness that the Chumash existed and still do. People were more concerned with the land and what the National Park Service might do with it and with opportunities for themselves. There were few if any advocates for recognizing the Chumash other than Charlie Cooke and one or two others.

Dr. Kote Lotah, Chumash Medicine Man and Spiritual Leader, says Charlie is like a drop into water, the ripples get bigger and bigger. His leadership kept awareness of California Indians alive in political and traditional arenas and made Indian lives palatable. In the past Indians hid their heritage, fearful of how they would be treated. He gives people of all walks of life a sense of being part of the land. His very persona is part of his achievements. He takes charge in a way that everyone benefits. He has insights before the page is turned.

Phil Holmes, National Park Service Anthropologist says that Charlie is a citizen of the universe. He sees wide and far. Charlie stood on a hill in Newbury Park and looked over the majestic expanse where his ancestors once lived. He saw it as an opportunity for all peoples. His vision became Satwiwa, the only outdoor NPS venue in the United States devoted to sharing with everyone the culture and spirit of Native Americans from all the 50 states.

How this story was researched and written

In peeling back what made Charlie so effective and why he gave untold hours to his heritage and to the parks, I, the author, talked to American Indians, State and National Park Service officials, anthropologist/archaeologists, curators, archivists, scientists, elected officials, community activists, and Charlie's family and friends. I visited sites with Charlie, searched archives, consulted published and unpublished documents, and drew from my involvement with Charlie's activities starting in the late 1970s. The exact facts (names, dates, places) were lost due in part to how California Indians were treated just a few generations ago. Time also erased exact dialogs. The spirit of the events, though, was passed on and became part of Charlie. Thus, in the first chapter names and dialog are created based on research into the times to reveal this spirit. In subsequent chapters, dialog is based on what Charlie's associates, family, and friends told me, what was documented, or in a few cases what some people remembered. I checked dialog sections with their sources and made changes as indicated.

There is the issue of how American Indian history told by archaeologists, anthropologists, and historians tracks with that of local Indian oral history. Where relevant, both perspectives are presented as legitimate input.

In addition, there is some disagreement within and among park service personnel, anthropologists, and indigenous peoples themselves regarding usage of the terms *Native American* and *American Indian*. *American Indian* prevails until people in the story start to use the term *Native American*. In this story, *Native American* refers to indigenous people throughout the United States and its territories before European contact, while *Indian* refers to original peoples in the first 48 states and to some in interior and southeast Alaska. Charlie, however, with his inclusive attitude, and others used the terms interchangeably as the reader will see in quotations and paraphrases.

The narrative is interspersed with inserts from interviews usually at the ends of chapters but not always. The inserts are paraphrases unless otherwise noted; paraphrases were checked with their sources. The first insert from an individual (after this preface) includes name, title, and the date of the interview, email, or other communication. Afterwards, the citation includes the name only, unless the date or other information is different. A number of individuals who are part of the story went on to positions of significant responsibility, summarized in an appendix.

Many people gave input to this story. They are acknowledged at the end where their contributions can be better appreciated.

In sum, Charlie Cooke's story is an ethnographic biography integrated with the Native American, park, and civic histories in which Charlie was embedded. It follows the leadership path he grew into; unveiling the cooperative networks he formed as he went along, adding fuel to the Native American resurgence of the time, to the emergence of state and national parks, and to related environmental causes.

While the reader may notice a novelistic flair, this biography is based in fact. It takes the reader on a road back in time based on stories from those who were on Charlie Cooke's path. It takes you into the mind and will of TIQ SLO'W, a very special man, who exemplifies what it means to be a good human being and an effective leader. To many, Charlie is what it means to be a chief.

Contents

PART ONE, FOUNDATION: Background history, childhood and youth, early Indian leadership

If you think about the past, you know it is related to the present and future. Charlie was a hero to me when I was a child. I remember Charlie visiting our house about fifty years ago after he came home from the service. I was about ten, but right then I knew he would represent our family in Indian affairs. I was in awe of that. I looked up to him. Growing up in Pacoima with a Latin surname, people assumed we were Mexican; but my Grandmother Mary made sure we knew we were Indian. She got that from her mother, Charlie's Grandmother Frances.

Charlie went on to represent us in an intelligent way. He does research. He knows what he is talking about. I always knew he would become our chief. (Ted Garcia, Jr., Chumash, Tongva, Tataviam, Vanyume, Current Chumash Chief, June 19, 2009)

Map 2: Highways through Santa Monica Mountains and loop introducing the story (Courtesy of James Mansfield)

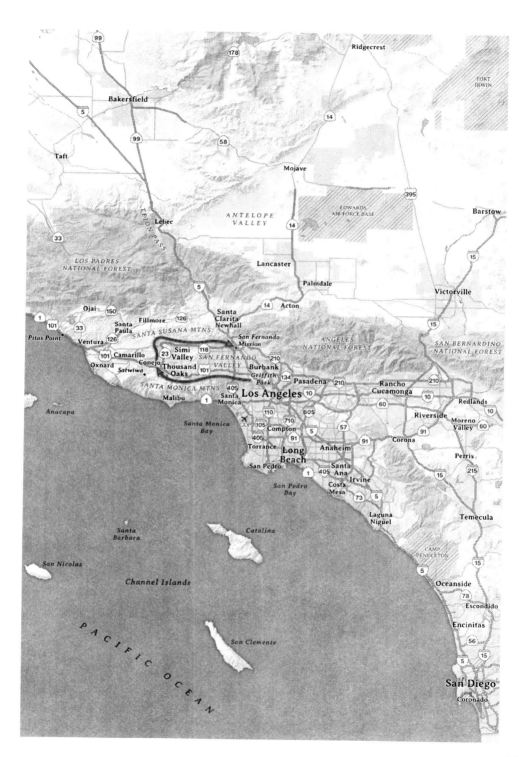

Chapter 1: Just Imagine

"You are Indian and don't you forget it!" The strong voice shook loose a slat or two on the old, frayed, wooden shed.

This is the story of Charlie Cooke, a Native American Chief known to many as TIQ SLO'W, a man who by many counts could not exist. But here he is: a cowboy, a ranch hand, a rodeo champ, an Air Force Korean War veteran, a regular husband and father, and an everyday working American. This is a story of ironies—of a man whose ancestral lands were taken and, in some cases, ravaged, of a man whose culture was almost obliterated. It is the story of this very same man who worked tirelessly to preserve these ancestral lands for posterity—for his descendants and those of the very people who took lands from his forbearers. He worked in construction inadvertently dumping cement that would obscure some of his heritage and then used what he had learned in the process to bring it back to light.

The mountain scene

Rolling hills and mountains with magnificent rock outcroppings, dotted with yucca, prickly pear, scrub oaks, and other native Southern California plants: It's the early twenty-first century and that's your view as we wind together through canyon roads and then zip along the freeways between Los Angeles and Santa Barbara. Imagine yourself at the wheel as we drive through the landscape that Charlie affected. You might very well think to yourself, "What beautiful vistas and natural recreation areas!"

Now rolling hills and mountains dotted with precariously perched hilltop homes, and now valleys with grand shopping centers and sprawling industrial parks: That's also your view on our way west in our sporty California car on the busy 101 Freeway. Now it's stop and go, stop and go, stop and go. You notice a cement truck parked up a mountainside ready to pour for a development project, but you also see untouched hillsides in the midst of building after building.

We are on our way through the Santa Monica Mountain Range. We are coming from Griffith Park, which is the largest municipal park in the United States. It overlooks Los Angeles from a mountaintop on the eastern-most edge of this range. Griffith Park is only one example of urban, recreational, and wilderness settings co-existing in these mountains. It is behind us now, to the east, as far east as the Santa Monica Mountain Range goes. We are headed to the far west of this range to a place with the Indian name, Satwiwa. We are traversing an expanse to which Charlie dedicated himself over many years. We drop down and skim along the southern edge of the large San Fernando Valley for a while and then climb back into the mountains. The range is inland at this point, but it parallels the coast. Proximity to the ocean still matters to today's residents, although now mostly for recreation. We are descending to a small, high valley, known as Conejo.

Finally we wind off the 101 Freeway at the Borchard Road exit in Newbury Park, which is part of the City of Thousand Oaks. We are at the western-most end of the Conejo Valley, a high valley nestled in the Santa Monica Mountains about half way between Los Angeles and Santa Barbara. We pass a small strip mall and then turn left onto Reino, what used to be a country road, but nowadays it sports commercial buildings for a mile or so and then becomes Potrero Road, which is still rural. The new buildings disappear as tall grasses and wide, low woodland trees take over. We pass a residential area that has been there since the late 1960s dated by some wood shingle roofs, now outlawed in this high fire alert region.

A large, white, rocky bluff rises into view as we make our way on this sunny California day with a 98-year-old woman, whose ancestors came from Italy. Still at her age, she loves outings. She is sitting comfortably up front, saying the same things she says almost every time she comes down these roads because it has bothered her ever since she moved here thirty years ago, "To think, the Indians lived here; they walked where the houses are; they picked berries; they sang their songs right here among these hills. What happened to them? They are all gone now."

But are they? There is an echo in those hills and it bounces off the bluff. "You are Indian and don't you forget it!"

Figure 1: The bluffs also known as Boney Mountain in the distance (Author's photo, 2013)

This story takes place on land and sea: the land along the Southern California coastline, the nearby inland mountains, the coastline itself, and the serene Channel Islands not too far off the coast. Today this area glitters with the wealthy, the movie stars, the tanned beach crowd, and the daring surfers slapping the world-renowned Malibu waves. They, too, are part of the story.

This is an area one can drive, ride on horseback, hike, swim, surf, sail, and picnic right in the midst of a populated area but hidden from urban sprawl. We drive under a wooden arch that says Rancho Sierra Vista/Satwiwa. We stop at this national park site in the shadow of the bluffs and sit at some outdoor tables to eat sandwiches. We spend some time just gazing at the scenery and then we take the spunky 98-year-old back to her home nearby.

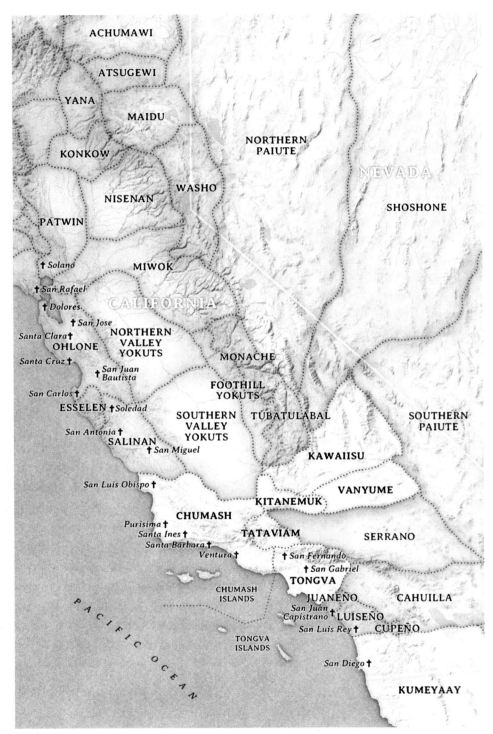

Map 3: California Indian Tribal and Mission areas
(Courtesy of James Mansfield)

The mission influence

Now it is a few days later. We are driving the 118 Freeway through the Santa Susana Mountains to the San Fernando Mission, the seventeenth of the twenty-one mission churches founded by Spain and their Franciscan padres, this one in 1797.

We stand in the central courtyard in front of the stucco church and then wander out where crops such as wheat, corn, and other vegetables and fruit formerly grew. On the edges we see descendants of native, wild plants that were here along with the crops in those mission days. There are bushes, large and small, such as wooly blue curls eventually cultivated as rosemary, toyon, sage, yucca, laurel, California lilac or ceanothus, and choke cherries. There are clusters of the evergreen coast live oak. Blue jays flutter and the woodpeckers tap in the trees. A ground squirrel scurries by and then a rabbit hops into view. In a time past we might have seen a red-tailed hawk or a golden eagle.

The wild plants and the animals softly rustling among the live oaks take us back to another era. Although the area is now a quiet, serene historical site, we can imagine the bustling of over two centuries ago. By 1819 the San Fernando Mission had its best year with 11,000 cattle, 8,000 sheep and 2,300 horses and fields of agriculture, all worked by the Indians who lived within its confines. The padres did not take a formal census of the people attached to a mission due to the ebb and flow of the population as people came and went, but we can glean from writings that there were over one thousand Indians at the San Fernando Mission by 1812.

Before the Indians entered the missions they ran freely among the streams and waterfalls, hunted and gathered without fail from the abundance in valleys and mountains, fished in the ocean, felt the spirits when looking down from high mountains over pristine vistas, and experienced the exhilarating adventure of the tomol, a sturdy boat used to trade with the islands off the coast.

Now the mission courtyard is a manicured green lawn with benches for visitors, a fountain, and steps up to the church. We sit on the steps where it is shaded for a while on this midafternoon. Certainly, it looked different in the late 1700s and early 1800s of the mission days. We notice an old wooden table close to the church entrance.

For those who know Charlie and a little of the history of this place, this is a scene that could play out in their minds. The names are fictitious but the people and what happens among them are based on what is known about the California missions under the rule of Spain. It is around 1810.

An Indian couple is crossing the courtyard and coming into view. They could be in their thirties. They look strong, but tired. In just the few moments they take to cross the courtyard, they notice women huddled together making baskets from reeds, men and women around a large wheel spinning rope, and a young woman carrying candles that look newly made. They notice tilled fields off to the side with people harvesting crops. They see some soldiers walking the grounds. They see big pots steaming in the distance. They see a woman who has her wrists and head in holes in some wood.

They step off to the side, a little distance from the bottom of the steps. You hear them talking with what sounds like stuttering. There is something odd about these sounds. It seems a natural part of their speech rather than a sign of stress, although the woman's eyes are filled with tears. They have their two sons with them, who seem to be about thirteen and fourteen years old. They have other older sons who are not with them since they have found work on a ranch nearby.

A young Franciscan padre, Juan, is sitting at the table at the top of the steps, talking with a middle-aged Indian man and woman. An older padre, Marcos, is with Juan. Marcos is the religious leader at the mission. While Juan continues to talk with the middle-aged couple, Marcos looks down the steps and watches the approaching couple and their two boys. He has seen these people before. He knew they would eventually come to stay since the man's grandparents were already here.

The man is pleading with his wife, "We need to join my family here…"

"We will lose our ways."

"Their cattle overrun our lands. You know we cannot gather enough to eat any longer. We will learn how to grow food and work with the animals their way, and then we can leave."

His wife looks at him with a big question across her already aging face.

He assures her, "Don't worry. We will go back and visit our families still in the mountains and in time they will come too—just like Grandfather and Grandmother came."

The family moves closer to the steps, the man with resolve, his wife just following, his sons looking around at the buildings and the people working. Padre Marcos goes off leaving Juan, who oversees the work at the mission. Juan is finishing with the middle-aged couple while the newcomers hesitate at the bottom of the steps. The man at the table answers Juan's question about his family's ancestry. He tells the padre that he was born near what is today the Los Encinos State Park area in the San Fernando Valley. He says that his wife is from a different group, one that lived closer to the ocean. Today we would say that he was Tongva and his wife, Coastal Chumash.

Suddenly, there is laughing and running in circles! A small boy clutching a deer hoof rattle is chasing a slightly bigger boy, probably his older brother. They are running by the steaming pots. The woman carrying candles grabs them, takes the rattle, and sends them back where they came from, to the mission school. This distracts Juan just as he starts to write a note about the middle-aged couple in an inventory book he keeps. He enters the husband and wife as though they both were born in the same area.

Soon Juan will send his inventory to the Santa Barbara Mission. A padre there might forward it to the Franciscan Offices in Mexico City. If this inventory book makes it without being discarded, as some were, someone a few generations forward might interpret his note as Tongva and Tongva alone, even though his wife was from a different group, making proof of ancestry from other California Indian groups difficult for their descendants later on.

Marcos returns and takes the Tongva couple into the church. A few minutes later, the family at the bottom of the steps starts up. Juan notices strong backs, a sign of the capable workers the mission needs. After some greetings he asks, "Where do you come from?"

This family speaks enough Spanish to know what's being asked but not enough to respond with more than a few words, "Over there," the man points to mountains in the northeast, toward the area of today's Antelope Valley. Immediately he turns to his wife and translates Juan's question and his own response. Padre Juan knows that several Indians at the mission come from that area, but not all from the same village or linguistic group. "Who do these people belong to?" he wonders.

"Ah," the Padre notices the native tongue. He thinks to himself. "These are the people that the coastal Indians say stutter. They are right." And then back to the family, "You will have food and a place to sleep in exchange for your work here."

Juan looks at the two young boys. One of them is gazing at a young girl headed their way. Juan quickly redirects his gaze by pointing in a different direction, "Unmarried men live over there." Then he smiles at their parents and addresses the husband specifically, "You know your grandfather is here. I have sent for him."

Just as Juan expected, Padre Marcos returns with an elderly man. The man is trying to wipe his hands on a clean part of his tanning apron.

Wise Eagle tearfully embraces his grandson and granddaughter-in-law. They call him by his Indian name. The padre puts his hand on the grandfather's shoulder. "We call your grandfather Manuel. He is doing a fine job making saddles in that workshop over there. You will all need Christian names once you are baptized."

27

This padre liked to suggest names early, planning for baptism right away. "For now, Geraldo is a good name for you and for your wife, Elena. Your older son—Francesco and the other, Eduardo."

The older son thinks to himself, "Francesco, baptized? I won't be here long enough."

After some more talk the family moves off with their grandfather, who removes his apron. Grandma stands up from the basket huddle and comes to join them. It is almost dinnertime.

A young Indian girl comes up the steps to the table. She's about thirteen, marriageable age. In today's parlance, she is inland Emigdiano Chumash.

The padre talks to her in a disciplined monotone without looking up, with Marcos again off to the side. Juan wipes his brow. He has been inventorying newly arrived Indians off and on today and is tired. The padres travel to areas outside the mission regularly so that they always know what is happening all around them. There was a deadly outbreak of disease not too long ago that killed children in close-by areas. They are certain that the girl's family pushed her to come to the mission, fearful of losing her. Her parents reasoned that since the padres there did not get sick, the mission would be safer for their daughter.

"I am from over there," The girl points north and inland, in the general area toward what later became the San Sebastian Reservation (after the missions closed) and then the Tejon Ranch near today's Mt. Pinos and Frazier Park. She speaks some Spanish, more than the family before her.

The Padre monotones from a memorized script: "You will get food and a place to sleep in exchange for cooking, cleaning, and planting crops. Your Christian name will be Maria. You will stay in the unmarried women's quarters." And then he looks up to see resiliency on Maria's face. He motions to a woman off to the side. "Signora Dorina will be like your aunt. She will be near you all the time until you marry." Out of the corner of his eye, he sees Francesco lingering. He half scowls to cover his amusement and then motions for him to move along.

"You start working in the field tomorrow morning," he tosses the comment toward the young Indian. But Francesco has lingered just long enough to catch Maria's eye and to hear her whisper as she walks by, "Don't forget that you are Indian."

She says this to herself in her native language but hoping to be overheard. Francesco answers with what was on his mind in his own language, "I am going to work with animals, not crops." And his eyes follow Maria to her quarters. Signora Dorina notices all of this.

A few hours go by. The sun starts to set. *Gong! Gong! Gong! Gong! Gong!*

Gong! The large church bell rings for dinner. Francesco and Eduardo come out of their quarters and walk toward the same large steaming pots that had caught their attention when they had arrived. They are already dirty from checking out the animals.

"So we get the food for the men, until some new boys come," Eduardo says resigned to the chore.

"I don't think our bowls will hold enough, brother. Grandfather said to come around later. He caught a rabbit and Grandmother roasted it."

An elderly woman scoops some *atole* into Francesco's bowl and then Eduardo's. Padre Marcos stands by approvingly. Both young men look at the cooked barley and recognize it as native food they have eaten before. They turn to leave but see Maria approaching with a bowl of her own. Eduardo smiles and moves on, leaving Francesco just enough behind. As she approaches, Francesco smiles and starts to speak but freezes. He doesn't know her language. Quickly, he realizes that she probably knows some Spanish, but—too late. He freezes again as Padre Marcos starts lashing at him for breaking a mission rule—trying to talk with an unmarried, unchaperoned woman.

"You must obey our rules. Do you want the soldiers to have you whipped and have her put in stocks like that woman over there? I can only plead with the soldiers so much and then they will enforce the will of Spain. They are always here. They live in their quarters on the edge of this mission. They will make sure that you behave in a way that our Spanish King Joseph would approve. Get that *atole* back to the men's quarters before I take it away." The boys scamper. Then he turns to Maria and tells her the women's version of the same thing adding that he is going to make sure Sra. Dorina knows to watch out for these two bad mannered, new stutterers. Where is Dorina anyway? As he turns, he sees her walking toward him from the other pot. Dorina whispers to him, "I don't miss anything. I see the way that older one looks at all the women. Marry him soon."

This was how Francesco learned that at the mission a young man does not spend time with an unchaperoned girl. But Dorina was either not as observant as she proclaimed or too busy with her own work, so the next afternoon he talked to Maria behind some trees. As the year went by and the corn grew they found themselves holding hands behind tall stalks. They saw each other at church every morning. Maria sat with her friend Leticia. Padre Marcos thought Dorina was such a dependable chaperone that he put Leticia under her charge as well.

Maria would glance at Francesco right during the services and then Maria and Leticia would stifle some quiet giggles. Dorina prayed. After church Maria, Leticia, and Dorina would walk out together. It always seemed that

Leticia meandered right by Francesco so Maria had to follow, and Leticia started talking so Francesco had to respond. Once the conversation started, Leticia backed away. In time, he was talking only to Maria with Leticia and Dorina right there, of course, listening to their every word. Dorina smiled through her sternness now and then, but not when Padre Marcos walked by.

Another harvest came and went. One day Dorina stopped Padre Marcos and engaged in what seemed to be a very serious conversation in halting Spanish. Francesco could hear Leticia's name being mentioned. He knew what he had to do as long as he was on mission ground.

Amen, Amen, Amen. Morning prayers were over and everyone was scattering for breakfast. Francesco waited at the door of the church. He had practiced what he was going to say in Spanish over and over with his brother.

"Padre Marcos . . ."

"Francesco, hurry along before there is no food left."

"Padre, Padre, uuummm, could I have your permission . . ."

"Francesco, I know that you have eyes for that young lady who works with the basket makers. What's her name, Leticia?"

"No, no Padre, I do not."

"It matters not whether you deny it. Thanks to Sra. Dorina, she is already promised. I have made arrangements for you to marry Maria."

"Oh, Padre Marcos . . ."

"Pray on it my son. You will learn to love her."

But before any marriage could take place, Grandfather Manuel died. The priest entered the date in the death records, one of three pen and ink registries: baptism, marriage, death. As was customary, Manuel was buried in the European-style cemetery out the left door of the sanctuary. The priests had divided the half-moon plot into quarters. After the funeral Mass, Manuel was buried in a quadrant that still had space.

Several months later, Francesco and Maria were first baptized and then married with supposedly no say in the matter—another arranged intermarriage among the six tribes at the mission: Chumash, Yokuts, Tongva, Tataviam, Kitanemuk, and Vanyume. This time it was Maria, a young woman from the tribe that lived inland and on the coast—later known as Chumash, with Francesco, from the seemingly stuttering tribe—that came to be known as Tataviam.

Francesco started a tradition of horsemanship in his family. Despite Maria's whispers of defiance, as time went on, the Mission Indians lost their identities as well as their native names and become known as Fernandeños. The missions closed by 1834 and the Indians scattered. Many worked on ranches in the area but remained connected to the mission, and, in fact, went there regularly.

Mission ancestors

The imaginary scene segues to the real scene at the mission today. Still sitting on the steps, we spend a little time talking about Charlie's family. According to San Fernando Mission records combined with Charlie's family lore, years after the mission was closed, in 1884, a baby girl was born right inside the deteriorating mission chapel. She came with DNA traces of several mission tribes. Her father and mother had her baptized with the Christian name, Frances. If she had not been baptized, the padre would not have scribed her name in the baptism records, which later would have raised questions for herself and any descendant about being a bona fide Mission Indian or even an Indian.

Like many of the Mission Indians, her family continued to come to the mission for church services and various gatherings over the next generations, even after it closed. That's how Frances ended up being born on a church bench. That's how Frances met Fred, a strong young American Indian man whose family had taken on the cowboy life and livelihood.

We wander into the church. Which one? Which bench? It would not have looked like this, polished and clean. About 1860, sometime after the mission closed, the Butterfield Stagecoach used the chapel as a stable. The mission went through other indignations such as being a hog farm. Finally it was restored as a church in the 1940s. Today it looks well-kept and thriving.

Figure 2: Courtyard, Mission San Fernando (Author's photo, 2010)

Back outside, we look for the cemetery. Behind the church, we see a few gravestones. Where are all the rest? We are definitely on the old cemetery grounds, although it looks like an ordinary grass lawn. Even though records state that 2,425 funerals were held at the mission between 1798 and 1852, no plot book remains making it impossible to know exactly who and how many people were buried here. To complicate matters, while these grounds were intended as an Indian cemetery, Europeans were also interred here. In addition, some Mission Indians chose to be buried in their home territory. There is a monument dedicated to the over 2000 American Indians who had been buried at this mission. Are Charlie's ancestors memorialized by this nameless monument? Where are they? As the quadrants in the cemetery filled, the priests had the bones moved to a charnel house and then started over, and then over again. At one point all the quadrants stayed empty; the burials stopped. And the charnel house? Its location remains a question.

Figure 3: Memorial to Native Americans Interred at San Fernando Mission 1797-1852, (Author's photo, 2010)

Mission records and artifacts

More wandering: by the old workshops, by the padres' quarters, and then a stop at a glass door. There's a see-though sign, "Archival Center." This center holds some information about Indian families, but it's not complete. Especially a few centuries ago, Indian people kept their history orally through stories passed down over generations.

<u>Charlie's Grandma Frances Garcia Cooke</u>: Family oral tradition makes Frances the daughter of a chief, Isidoro Garcia, son of Santiago. She can be found in mission records, but other family members are not so easily located. Family charts, submitted to the Bureau of Indian Affairs as part of the process to certify the degree of Indian blood, place Isidoro in Sacramento at his birth, married in San Fernando to Josephine Leyvas, and dying in Oxnard. But another set of charts, prepared by an anthropologist who reconstructs Indian family histories from historical records, lists him as baptized at a Stockton church on his birth date and married to Josefina Leiva; yes, spelled differently. More confusing, family records place Isidoro's father, Santiago, in Stockton at birth, but the other record places him in Sinaloa, Mexico. Some say Santiago never lived in a mission and at some time lived in what today is Acton, north and inland, near the Antelope Valley.

TIQ SLO'W Family Tree

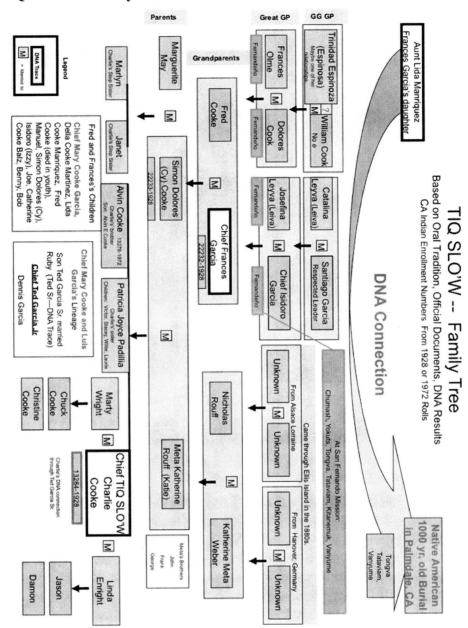

Sources: 1) Cooke family documents and oral history, 2) Interviews and documents from non-family sources. The sources sometimes differ, especially in regard to Charlie Cooke's Chumash ancestry and his hereditary chief line. In such cases, family history takes precedence on this chart summarizing information the family gathered over decades. Numbers are California Indian Enrollment numbers.

Not all sources routinely traced an Indian family's migrations. Perhaps this family migrated north and south as was the custom with some. The spelling of surnames was not always consistent in historical records leaving a question regarding whether the spellings are in error or they represent different families.

Grandpa Fred Cooke: What about Fred? His mother, Francisca Olme, had lived at the mission. She married Dolores, yes spelled that way. Somewhere back in the line before him, the family had taken the surname Cook. Their son, Fred, married Frances; and they had eleven children. They both lost their Indian names and exact heritage, but Frances hung onto Indian pride and spirit for the both of them and added an *e* so the *Cooke* name would be distinctive.

Artifacts outside the Mission: Names and records aside, unless they were on reservations, the Indians as Indians started to fade into oblivion as they blended into towns burgeoning all over California, leaving behind a trove for collectors. With no laws to stop them, builders built over Indian sites and collectors raided grave sites and other suspected stashes of what they considered relics. Some collectors, such as Howard Arden Edwards, were adventurers who thought they were saving important artifacts. Mr. Edwards homesteaded 160 acres in Antelope Valley, an area that had been the territory of the Serrano, Vanyume, Kitanemuk, Tataviam, and Kawaiisu peoples. There he built a home on what he named Piute Butte (named for the Paiute Indians but spelled in his own way). In 1933, he started to invite the public to view displays right in his home. His collection spanned Piute Butte in Arizona, New Mexico, the California Coast, and the Channel Islands off the coast. While his 1930s displays were intriguing, they lacked the American Indian cultural context, which had been lost, of course. Time and a descendant of Mission Indians would help correct this.

What does any of this matter to Charlie's decades of leadership? The artifacts? The Mission records? Time would tell.

A 21st Century Native American voice in the mountains

But back to our mountain tour. We find ourselves on the freeway again, heading toward Newbury Park, winding off a tight exit. We feel the centrifugal force as we round the exit, slowing to stop. There are so many curves to navigate in this up and down landscape. We look at the hillsides studded with new housing developments as we drive down Borchard Road. As we turn onto another road, we notice that some of the hills ahead remain untouched, just basking under the noonday sun. Why? We drive on. Gigantic, pointed, stone bluffs, shining white, jetting out of the mountaintop toward the sky! Volcanic rock frozen in upward momentum! They consume our view. We make a few more turns. There is an Indian program today below those bluffs, which the locals call Boney Mountain, in a natural bowl called Satwiwa.

Under those huge jetting stone faces, there is today a son of chiefs, a seasoned man with deep seated Indian pride and spirit handed down over generations. We lower our windows on this lovely California day. There's a swish of the wind, but we take it as a voice among the yucca, prickly pear, scrub oaks and the rabbits and coyotes scampering here and there as we drive on. We get to Satwiwa in time for one of the many events where a native culture has regained its lost voice through Frances and Fred's grandson:

> People think there are no Indians in California—that they are all on the Plains, New Mexico, or Arizona. But guess what? California has the largest Indian population in the country. How did that happen? They moved here. But many were here: Chumash, Yokuts, Tongva, Tataviam, Kitanemuk, Vanyume. These were the people who built the San Fernando Mission and are sometimes called Fernandeños.

> It is important to grow the Native American community through recognizing and sharing Native American roots. We are sharing our culture and traditions, with all people, not just ourselves.

> Peace is related to our values of sharing and preserving resources. And let's not forget the importance of children—and balance. If we are one sided, everybody loses. Let's stay in harmony with Mother Earth.

> When you become part of a development, you become the people of that land. The problem is people in developments don't know anything but the street they live on. They don't walk around. Get out there and feel the land! (Charlie Cooke, Elder and former Chumash Chief, May 16, 2009)

And as we move on to Charlie's actual life story starting with childhood— we begin to hear from those who know his effect on the surrounding landscape and its people.

> His story is important because people think he couldn't have existed in modern times—that natives are here but not really as natives interested in their background and culture. Charlie is proof that such a person does exist— devoted to maintaining culture. (Dr. Chester King, archaeologist, May 12, 2009)

The general public is still surprised that local Indians are still here today. Charlie is an institution in Southern California. Wherever I go in the anthropology world, people know Charlie—whether it is a powwow, a basket-maker gathering, or people just chatting. They know of him even if they do not know him. (Bryn Barabas Potter, anthropologist, July 16, 2011)

Chapter 2: Don't You Forget, 1940s, 50s

The wind is blowing as two brothers race their horses home through a valley. It is a Saturday in 1946 in Newhall, a town inland and north of the San Fernando Valley. Newhall is tucked between the eastern edge of the Santa Susana Mountains and the westernmost edge of the Angeles National Forest. It is brown, hilly ranch land much of the year. But now it is spring. The creeks are flowing and the birds are building nests in the scrub oak and greasewood trees all around. The two preteen boys had been helping out all day on the nearby Newhall Ranch owned by Atholl McBean. Atholl is a San Francisco businessman and Henry Newhall's grandson-in-law. Dad, Cy Cooke, is a polo horse trainer for the McBeans.

The boys are just having a little fun racing their horses between brush and rocks down a gentle hill to home, a one-room house in the Atwood subdivision of Newhall. The house is one of about forty scattered over three hundred acres. Dad bought it for $1200 then added a lean-to bedroom with cellophane windows for the two boys, an outhouse, and an outdoor shower. Only about ten houses in this subdivision had indoor plumbing. Other than cold running water in the kitchen sink, this is not one of them.

Experiencing the land's bounty

"Look, look," shouts Charlie as he jumps a small anthill. "Look, there's white sage. Grandma says it is good for headaches."

Alvin crosses over to the smoother side of the hill and then kicks his horse with his heels just enough to signal him to go faster.

Charlie stays his course. "Look there, cherries! We'll have to—come back—and pick them in summer." Charlie chops up his sentence as his horse turns to avoid a rock and then sprints to overtake Alvin's horse.

"I win," Alvin laughs as he dismounts.

"Okay, this time." Charlie smiles, scratches his leg, and points behind them, "Hey, did you see all that mugwort right back there?"

"Have you got poison oak again?"

"Yeah, a little. Grandma told me mugwort is a cure. "

"I know. I know."

"How come you never get it, Alvin?"

The boys continue bantering as they walk their horses through the barbed wire chain link fence that corrals the pasture. The owners had allowed the Cookes to use some of the land near the house for grazing. That way they did not have to pay the county to disc it for fire prevention.

"How do the old people know so much about plants?" Charlie wonders somewhat to himself.

"I'm going to wash up. I'm hungry and tired from helping today."

"You just need to grow, Alvin. Eat a lot at supper."

A ranching childhood

Nine-year-old Alvin proudly patted the white star on the forehead of his bay horse. Trail was his mom's and a son of the famous Man-of-War. Then he sauntered to the outdoor shower under a backyard elm tree. During the winter, the family used an old galvanized bathtub with cold water mixed with some from a boiling pot on the stove. But now he took the hose to spray his hands and feet, enjoying the tepid water from the sun-beaten coil. Clean enough, he ran inside.

Charlie spent a little time with Old Jim, who had been his trusty partner at the Newhall Ranch all day this day. Charlie was quite a horseman even at eleven, but no wonder! He and Alvin were both riding on their own at three. They had a way with horses and other animals in general.

Figure 4: Alvin front and Charlie behind at the Mojave Rodeo, (Courtesy of Alvin Cooke, c 1942-43)

Charlie meandered by an old shed, scratched his back against its rough wood, and then leaned against it for a few minutes. After such a busy and physical day, Charlie needed a moment. The boys had a lot of fun in their young lives, but also many responsibilities. Their days were full of chores, chores, and more chores, of lessons about the land all around them, of some mischief here and there, and of experiences that built family pride:

At five Charlie was living in Leona Valley on a 500-acre ranch owned by the Rouffs, Mom's family. It was bounded by a horizon of hills rolling into mountains. Dad met Mom, Katy Rouff, when he had been a cowboy on that ranch and bragged ever since that she was the first woman roper at the Bonelli Stadium in Saugus, not too far from their land.

Every afternoon Mom and Dad sent him out on Birdie to round up the fifteen or so cows grazing near their house on Grandpa Nicholas Rouff's land. Birdie was his first horse. She was thirty years old when he started riding her. He sat tall and proud on his old horse, dwarfed by the family's 500-acre ranch. His dog, Chubby, a Border Collie, usually ran alongside, breaking away barking and circling the cows. Sturdy little Charlie bounced on Birdie, both moving together to edge the plodding cows into the steeply-roofed wooden slat barn that Grandpa Rouff had built. Chubby barked and circled, circled and barked. Birdie knew what to do. She was old, slow, but certainly experienced. As they got to the barn, Charlie jumped down off Birdie. With a swoosh and a bang, his little frame swung the big doors shut. This chore always ended with a hug for Chubby who barked with pride. Well, other than closing the doors, Chubby did do most of the work.

After dinner, it was time to milk the cows. There was Charlie with his family in the barn. Night after night he pulled out his trusty but worn metal bucket and milked the same cow, except one night. Oops, Grandpa Fred found him outside playing with some kids who had a new rubber car. Grandpa's way of disciplining was a stern scolding. "Why weren't you separating cream like you were supposed to?" Charlie never forgot this incident and never skipped out on milk duty again.

But there were rewards. When he was still five, Atholl McBean's chauffeur drove up to pick up Charlie and Chubby to take them for ice cream. This happened about once a week.

When Charlie was seven, the cow had a calf, Charlie's pet calf, Nellie. In the morning he let the cows out and then rambled down the old gravel road to the one-room schoolhouse not too far from home. After school, he rode Nellie. *Clunk, clunk,* sway, hold on! Nellie was like a dog to him except that he rode her like a horse. And he still rode horses. Birdie was gone, so now he and Alvin were riding his mom's horse, Trail, and a little Shetland pony, Blue.

Just out playing, Charlie and three other boys found a nest of ten baby rattlesnakes by a well in a neighbor's vineyard. Fascinated, there they were the next day and the next. A month went by. One day, at dusk, Dad rode up and stopped suddenly. He had been riding in the area looking for the boys for a while. Still astride his horse, he whirled his rope, aimed it down at the ground quickly, and hit the mama snake. Her head popped off. Charlie went to bed that night without listening to his favorite radio show, *The Lone Ranger*.

Still at the age of seven: It was 1941 when he overheard, "We're moving. We lost the ranch because of poor investments." Cy started working for owners of other ranches between 1941 and 1945. The family moved to at least six rentals in that time.

Charlie took his old milk bucket and Nellie to wherever his father landed a ranch-hand job. Still chores, chores, chores; well, usually. On Saturdays, he and Alvin would go with friends to the matinee at the American Theater in Newhall, built for the town in 1941 by Western movie star, William S. Hart. One particular Saturday, on their walk home, the group came across an elevated liquid gas line and decided to walk on it for a while. Finally, they jumped off and walked through a carrot field. It was late. They had lost track of time. Oh, oh, they heard a pick-up. It was Dad. Charlie and Alvin hid down in the carrots; then they ran off. Too late; Dad saw them. No matinees for a month!

By this time, Charlie was eight. Nellie was so big that she had to lie down so Charlie could get on and ride her. One day that same year, Nellie fell off a cliff and died. "Someone shot Nellie," little Charlie said to himself. "She wouldn't fall off a cliff."

He milked cows for a while longer but soon did more riding and roping. He roped his milk bucket, bushes, stumps and even Alvin on occasion. He missed sometimes, but less and less. Already at nine years old, he was roping on his father's horse, Old Jim.

Ever since he was nine years old, he had been helping his dad with horse shoeing. He learned to crank the forge just right to get the shoe just hot enough. If the fire were to get too hot and sparkling, the shoe would burn up. His father did not have to tell him to be careful and to do things right; he could see the need.

As Charlie and Alvin got older, they helped as ranch hands wherever their father was employed. The boys saw the importance of responsibility along with being good neighbors as youngsters. It was obvious to them that animals and crops need constant care and besides Dad wouldn't put up with any slacking. Dad had for a long time been telling Charlie and Alvin about native plants, how they can be food and medicine. Dad learned that from Grandma Frances who learned from her mother, who in turn learned from her mother, going at least as far back as Candelaria, who lived in the 1800s by traditional values. Charlie would play with that chain in his head now and then. Candelaria was a great, great aunt through marriage or even a great, great, great. She was a midwife, whatever that was. She was there when Aunt Mary, Dad's sister, was born.

In 1945, when he was ten Dad broke Pal, Dale Evan's first horse, a beautiful palomino. Along with other work, Dad was training horses for individuals. In a few years Dale Evans would marry Roy Rogers and star with him on his TV show, but Charlie did not know that yet. He was simply proud of his Dad's skill with horses.

Dad told him about the movies he worked on, usually as a wrangler, handling the saddle horses. In 1946, when Charlie was eleven, Dad was actually on screen riding horses in *Duel in the Sun* starring Gregory Peck.

Not too long ago, he helped Dad heat up some water in a bucket, steep some sage, and then soak Old Jim's foot. Jim wound around mounds and jumped over rocks effortlessly today.

Small childhood experiences had started to cement family pride, a sense of adventure, a sense of responsibility, and knowledge about the land. As he continued to lean on the shed, a tumbleweed bumped him across his knees. A breeze touched his face. He looked up to see a hawk circling. Was it a red-tailed hawk? He had heard some of the older folk talk about how they were a good sign. A group right in front of him was chattering away, but he hardly noticed. He watched the tumbleweed roll toward the trail he had made with Old Jim. There he noticed food and water, not just brush and rocks. He noticed yucca and wondered what it would be like to roast the bulb at the base of the stalk for food or weave its fibers into cordage as the Indians who had lived in these hills had done. He looked over at a large clump of green and knew water was nearby. Dad had told him that if you know enough about what's on the land, you can survive on your own in these mountains. He sensed that he was beginning to understand all the lessons his dad had been teaching as they worked and rode together in the hills. Leaning more deeply against the shed, he could hear, see, and feel his childhood all around him on the valley floor and in the hills. He knew his way around these hills for sure.

He lingered a few moments more watching flowering plants as they swayed slightly in the wind. He saw a rabbit scurrying and someone in the distance riding across the field. He could see a lot of detail even far off. In fact, a few days ago when he was walking along the highway with his dad,

"Hey look, Dad, those are our German neighbors coming on down the road in that old pick-up truck. I like that truck."

"What old truck?"

"Right there, up the road?"

"I don't see any old truck."

"Well. Okay, Dad. You'll see. When's the next rodeo? Can I go?"

"Keep practicing your roping. Look there—choke cherries. Let's come back and pick some later when they're ripe. So your grandma can make some jam."

"Okay," Charlie said still thinking about the rodeo.

"Oh, I see it. You're right. Those are our German neighbors. How could you see so far off? You have the eye of an eagle!"

Grandma, Grandpa, and the stranger were still talking. Charlie's grandparents, Fred Cooke and Frances Garcia Cooke, had come from their home in the San Fernando Valley and were in no hurry. They were staying for dinner tonight. Charlie looked over to see his horse safe in the pasture. A job well done today! They worked well together, Charlie and Old Jim. Old Jim was his dad's rope horse. Charlie hoped to be a champion roper like his dad someday soon.

Figure 5: Cy Cooke on a rope horse (Courtesy of Linda Cooke, no date)

Figure 6: Meta Katherine Rouff Cooke (Courtesy of Alvin Cooke, c 1932)

Figure 7: Leona Valley, Rouff barn (Author's photo with permission from Rebecca Haugen, 2010)

Discovering heritage

The afternoon was waning at the Newhall Ranch. The chatter from the group livened up. He noticed that his grandparents were with a fellow who looked and sounded different. "Not one of us," he thought. "Just visiting." They were just chatting at the end of the day.

"So, Fred, with a name like Cooke, where do you come from? What are you? Mexican? Indian? Or what?"

No sound from Grandfather Fred for a few moments and then, "Mexican!" Charlie could feel the glare from Grandmother Frances bouncing right off the loose slats of the shed. He straightened up.

"Odd with a name like Cooke." And the visitor turned and left.

Charlie relaxed and slumped a little against the shed wondering, "Was he Mexican and why did it matter? And what about that name, Cooke?" And then he heard Grandmother Frances booming at Grandpa Fred. Her voice shot out in an emphatic burst as she marched away, "You are Indian and don't you forget it!"

Grandpa Fred followed, looking at his feet as he hurried along, absorbed in justifying himself. Grandmother Frances focused straight ahead as though she didn't hear anything he said. Charlie was amused. He loved his grandparents and found them charming; he found his grandmother especially wise. He walked back to the pasture to talk to Old Jim for a few minutes. He had heard that Indians still had a bounty on their heads. He wondered softly to Old Jim what that meant and if it had anything to do with what he had overheard. Old Jim grazed on, not paying much attention. Charlie took that as a hint and went off to wash up.

Mom was taking some salad out of the old icebox as Charlie burst through the only door to the house. Everyone else was already seated and eating. Baby sister, Patricia Joyce, was banging a cup. Charlie slipped in next to his dad. Mom sat down next to the baby.

"Boys, Saturday I'm practicing at an arena in Salinas. The next rodeo is coming up soon. You both come and watch," and with that Cy Cooke gulped down some potatoes.

Charlie and Alvin were both excited about watching Dad practice. Dad was a roping champ; what better teacher? Maybe they'd get a chance to rope a steer, not just bushes and buckets. As exciting as that was, Charlie had something else on his mind. "Dad, how did we get the name Cooke?"

Grandma Frances intervened, "Well, Charlie, rumor has it that there was a Lt. William Cook in the area. He was in General Fremont's regiment. People say Fremont was mean to Indians. Lt. Cook treated the Indians well so one of the men in the family back in the 1800s took his name."

"Not so," retorted Grandpa Fred. "Our name came from an English settler who married my great, great grandma—not sure what her name was."

Frances looked at Fred and thought to herself, "In one version of the story, he didn't marry her, even though Fred's father, Dolores Cook, was born to the settler and his wife—or woman."

And then out loud with some frustration, "You see what has happened? We lost our history! We really can't tell for sure. But the way I heard the story, Charlie, a man a few generations back in the family took Lt. Cook's name—spelled with no *e* by the way. I added the *e* after I married Grandpa here. You know some say we even had Indian relatives along the coast, far from here—Chumash maybe." Then Grandma Frances more glared than spoke. "None of this really matters. You are Indian."

"But what about Mom and Grandma and Grandpa Rouff?" Charlie dared to ask right as Patricia Joyce finally dropped her empty cup to the gray, concrete floor. Somehow it didn't break.

Cy Cooke was hungry after a long, hard day. "You tell them, Katy," he said to his wife who had left the table to wash the baby's cup.

She started her answer, "My family is German and Alsatian."

"Al—say—chun?" Alvin struggled to say the word.

Katy picked up a tea kettle off the cast iron grill on the old galvanized butane stove and carried it to a table of dish pans. She had adapted to a house without running hot water. She poured boiling water from the kettle into one of the pans and rinsed the cup. Then she continued her explanation.

"Alsace has gone back and forth between France and Germany since the world wars. Right now it is French, but long, long ago it was Celtic. It was taken over and renamed a number of times, like lands that were Indian— the Spanish, the French, the English! I want you boys to find out everything you can about your heritage, including your Indian heritage," she added as she sat down.

"Heritage?" Charlie wrinkled his forehead.

Grandma Frances joined in, "Who you are, where you come from."

Alvin was listening too. He had heard about Grandma Frances making sure that every Indian she knew got on the Indian rolls.

She continued, "There were lots of treaties with other Indians, but that Senate over there in Washington never approved any with us here in Southern California so we are not recognized as Indians yet in Washington but we are here in California."

Grandma Frances had started the enrollment movement in her local area back in the 1930s so at least the state would recognize and document her people as California Indians, give them back their identities, and make them eligible for government funds.

"Now you, Cy, stop pretending you are Mexican every time you go to the liquor store." And with that Grandma Frances firmly put down her fork and looked straight at her son.

"You are Indian and don't you forget it!" It felt like she was looking out the window at every ranch hand across the whole valley. After the missions closed, many of the Indian men became cowboys and lived on rancherias, places set aside on ranchland for them and their families.

Grandma Frances was killed in an auto accident later that year, but Charlie continued to hear her voice—though subdued for a while by Junior Posse parades and escapades, by roaring cheers as he darted down the football field, by the pounding hoofs of his horse bursting onto rodeo arenas, and by the thundering engines at Air Force bases in the United States and overseas where he served as an airplane mechanic during the days of the Korean War.

Figure 8: Frances and Fred Cooke (Courtesy of Alvin Cooke, 1946)

Teenage years

Charlie became the typical youngster in some ways but also became more tied to the earth even as the country was steadily urbanizing in the post-

World War II years. Starting in junior high school, Charlie and Arvin rode with the Junior Posse. They would ride for 20 miles or so practicing for the day when they would have a real search-and-rescue effort. Newhall was quiet and safe so posse activities were centered on performing at rodeos and parades, except for one time.

In 1947, when Charlie was twelve, a desperado escaped from San Quentin Prison. The authorities expected him to be in Pico Canyon, near the Newhall Ranch. Sergeant Smith, the deputy sheriff, was sure that Charlie knew every nook and cranny in Pico Canyon so asked him to ride along to help find the desperado. Charlie knew there was a house in the canyon. The sergeant, another deputy, and Charlie rode until they got near to the house. He slid off Old Jim and started making his way quietly toward the house, keeping low, carefully placing every footstep, and noticing anything that could give him away in his surroundings: a rock he could tumble, a branch he could snap, a trap he could trip. When he got close, he crouched down in the brush and watched. And there he was: the desperado out front in the clear California daylight, talking with his wife! Charlie crept away, staying low as he back-tracked, making no more sound than any animal moving through the brush. Finally, he reached the deputies and whispered what he had seen. They made the arrest and Charlie remained a silent hero.

Figure 9: Left to right: Charlie carrying the Newhall Flag, Taylor Powell, US Flag, Joe Ferris, CA Flag, Alvin on white horse at back left, Junior Posse event, (Santa Clarita Valley Signal, c 1947-48)

Charlie played on basketball and football teams at William S. Hart High School. He was president of Future Farmers of America there too. He planned and led FFA meetings. He needed a calf for his project so cleaned corrals at the Ferndale Ranch to pay for it. The work itself was no problem but there was something about one area on the ranch that gave him an unsettled, spooky feeling. The ranch foreman told him to dump manure back in the pasture, but he just couldn't do it. He negotiated another area for dumping.

Charlie became a better and better rider and roper. Both boys warmed up Dad's horses for rodeos. At one such event he found himself talking to a rodeo contractor who sometimes hired his dad to handle stock for him.

"You gonna start roping soon, Charlie?"

"Hope so"

"That dad of yours is a fine roper. A real champ! You'll have to work hard to beat his time."

"Yeah, I know."

"And that soak he makes with sage for horses, it works!"

"Well, he's Indian and learned it from . . ."

"Indian!" The contractor scoffed at the idea.

It did not feel good to be ridiculed. No wonder Grandpa Fred said he was Mexican! Charlie said nothing, not yet. The truth was that at this point, he could not have said much about his heritage. Charlie knew he was Indian and had mission background, but he was not sure what kind or what tribe or whatever the right way of naming it was.

The start of rodeo days

Finally, at age sixteen Charlie entered his first rodeo competition in Salinas, California, as a team roper with a high school friend, Bud Corwin.

Not too long after, he and Bud roped again at the Saugus rodeo. They did okay, but didn't win. Charlie started entering some events just for fun such as wild cow milking at the Newhall/Saugus Rodeo. The goal was to rope and milk the cow as fast as possible. Of course, you had to rope the cow first and then one team member called the mugger (not Bud) had to hold the cow, but the mugger fell down. Oh well—still an interesting experience.

They graduated from high school in 1953 and Bud went on to national championship competitions. Charlie went off to Lackland Air Force Base in San Antonio for basic training. Then at Chanute Air Force Base in Illinois, he became a squad leader responsible for 20 airmen.

Figure 10: Airman Charlie Cooke, USAF, (Courtesy of Linda Cooke, c 1954)

Early leadership

"Charlie, that new guy is not carrying his load in KP." Charlie's guys had been assigned to kitchen patrol, often assigned to junior enlisted men.

"Why do you say that?"

"See these potatoes," another airman pointed to a large bowl with his paring knife. "He was supposed to help peel them. Do you see him here?"

"Where is he?"

Both airmen shrugged their shoulders. Charlie started watching and noticed that indeed the young fellow they were complaining about was nowhere to be seen when there was work to do. Charlie talked to him about carrying his load, but to no avail. Still he hoped to make a dent in his behavior. Eventually, his fellow soldiers confronted the slacker, which did not go well. He pulled a kitchen knife on his accusers, but backed down and ran off. Now Charlie had to step in. He was done giving the man chances so he reported him to his superiors. The fellow was removed and did not return to the squadron.

After Chanute, Airman Cooke worked as a mechanic on a variety of aircraft. While he was waiting in San Francisco to board a ship to the Philippines, he took the time to call an old man who had been so nice to him in his youth.

"Oh, hello, Mrs. McBean."

"My dear Charlie, how are you?" Charlie smiled at her very classy way of talking. "I will tell Atholl that you called. He's not here right now. He will be so very happy that you phoned us."

Charlie went to the Philippines, Okinawa, and then on to Edwards and McClelland Air Force Bases in California. One day he got a letter from Jesse, a high school friend. He sat in his Air Force bunk reading something like, "Well, Charlie you must have made an impression on my great uncle, Atholl. After you called and talked to my great aunt, he told my stepdad some nice things about you. My stepdad is that same boy, Bobby Newhall Cheeseboro. He was born with a pitched pelvis. Your dad helped him walk better by riding your mom's horse. Anyway, Uncle Atholl told my stepdad that when you get out of the service, you can work at any of the companies he controls and that he'll send you to college. He thinks you're smart. That figures since you skipped fourth grade."

Finding the cause

Back home from the service in 1957, Charlie was feeling that he was a man of the world. He started partying in the evenings. He found himself riding and roping again on weekends or whenever he could. Soon Mr. McBean's offer faded from his mind. Beyond roping and riding, he quickly became absorbed in an interest that had been bubbling inside for many years.

Alvin had become involved in California Indian causes. Charlie joined the effort being led by Aunt Mary Garcia, now the extended family's hereditary leader. Aunt Mary had married Luis Garcia, no relation to Aunt Mary or to her mother, Frances Garcia Cooke, just a common name passed down through the missions. Grandma Frances had been the family leader, and before that, Great Grandpa Isidoro, her father. Grandma Frances was gone, but her daughters, Aunt Mary and Aunt Lida, were in the area. He visited them often. Aunt Mary's little grandsons, Ted and Dennis, listened in on the conversations. Charlie heard his aunts echoing Grandma Frances, "Don't forget, don't forget, don't forget . . ."

His grandparents, especially his Grandmother Francis, instilled in him his sense of heritage. Making a living became secondary to his real purpose in life—heritage preservation. (Dr. John Johnson, curator, Santa Barbara Museum of Natural History and anthropologist, August 18, 2011)

Dad, Cy Cooke, and his brother, Uncle Izzy, were proud of being Indian and talked to us about it. So did our aunts. Our grandparents were "civilized" by the mission system. We learned a lot about our heritage by moving around. (Alvin Cooke, Charlie's brother and first partner in Indian heritage restoration, January 26, 2010)

The Chumash went underground and took Spanish names. I asked Charlie how he got his Cooke name. He told the family story: A Lt. Cook was a nice guy and treated the Indians well. His great grandfather took his name. Twenty years after Charlie told me this story, I came across Lt. Cook's name in an account about Fremont. (Clay Singer, anthropologist/archaeologist, July 9, 2009)

From what I heard from Charlie, he was proud of his dad's roping and riding. He also learned a lot about the land and plants riding with his dad. But his dad did not make a big deal about being Chumash. In fact, it may have been his mother who sat him down to tell him he was Chumash. Above all, he revered his Grandmother Frances. He showed me her grave in a small, hardly accessible cemetery in the mountains. (Phil Holmes, NPS anthropologist, April 26, 2009)

Charlie sees people as friends, and he accepts everyone. Maybe this comes from his cowboy background, or his mixed cowboy/Indian background, like Will Rogers, who had Cherokee heritage. Will Rogers said, "I never met a man I didn't like." What a wonderful way to live! Charlie is sort of a Will Rogers. (Bryn Barabas Potter, anthropologist, July 16, 2011)

Chapter 3: Bucked Off and Back On, 1950s, 60s, early 70s

"Mom, I'm sorry I wasn't here to help when you and Dad split up."

"Well, that's a few years now. It was just a parting of the ways. Alvin was here to help me with your sister."

Charlie had spent four years in the Air Force and then came home to the Newhall area in 1958. Mom was getting ready to trade the one-room house and its one-quarter acre for a modern two-bedroom place.

"Where is Patricia Joyce? It's getting dark."

"You sister's out in the barn with the horses, like you at her age."

"Where's Alvin, with her?"

"He's off to an Indian meeting in Compton. You ought to go with him next time."

Reconnecting with the Mission and with Indian rights

So after working at a gasoline service station all week, Charlie started going with Alvin to Compton on weekends. Sam Kolb, an elder Indian, was calling these meetings. His people had lived at the San Luis Rey Mission and became known as the Luiseños. Many of them now lived on the Rincon Reservation, in Pauma Valley, California. Like many Indians whose families had lived at the missions, Sam could not be sure about his ancestry except that he was from at least one of the tribes at the mission, perhaps Kumeyaay. Regardless, he was passionate about getting all Indian people interested in their heritage. For several years, he held monthly meetings in Compton. Sometimes the Cooke brothers were the only ones there.

At a meeting in 1958, Sam asked, "Alvin, Charlie, weren't your ancestors from the San Fernando Mission?"

"Yes, in fact, Grandma Frances was born there."

Some time passed. Cy Cooke had remarried, this time to Marguerite May, who wrote the *Beverly Hillbillies* song. Charlie had two new stepsisters, Janet and Marlyn.

Charlie started working on a GM assembly line and the brothers kept going to Sam Kolb's meeting every month.

"We need to organize a San Fernando Mission Band for anyone with Indian ancestors from that mission. You two boys get the people together and I'll come talk to them."

Many Indians at the San Fernando Mission had come from the Newhall area. So Sam came to Newhall near where the Cooke brothers lived and where together they started organizing American Indians in the area. Sam was not from any of the Indian groups who had lived at the San Fernando Mission and Charlie and Alvin did not yet know the details of their ancestry; but like Sam, they were beginning to think about the importance and preservation of Indian heritage in general.

In 1958, Charlie and Alvin went to a property rights meeting in Los Angeles. The topic was land that had been taken from American Indians. No action came from this meeting. However, it was a cog in the wheel of their work trying to make a wrong right. It would take years.

Fernandeño leadership

Since Grandma Frances had passed away, Aunt Mary had been the leader of her extended family of Indians whose ancestors had lived in the San Fernando Mission. She did not feel that she could be active enough anymore to maintain that position. For one thing, neither she nor her husband, Luis, could drive and the country was now one of roads and automobiles. She called some family members together in 1959, including her son, Ted, Sr., along with Alvin and Charlie. The small group agreed that Charlie showed the most interest and dedication to their Indian heritage and also had a strong interest in caring for the extended family. So they made him their leader.

Charlie started bringing together people in Newhall who had records of ancestry at the San Fernando Mission. In 1960, about thirty Indian people all came together to form the San Fernando Mission Band with Charlie and Alvin as founding members. Charlie was elected president of the Band. Similar to the San Luis Rey Mission where Sam Kolb came from, and where the Indians were referred to as Luiseños, Indians from the many tribes who lived at the San Fernando Mission became known as Fernandeños. In 1968 the brothers started calling meetings for people of Indian descent to inform them about their rights and to enroll them on the California Indian Land Settlement Roll. Enrollment would make them eligible for land payments and give them State recognition for their Indian ancestry.

In 1954 there were about 37,000 people on the rolls in California. When the rolls closed in December of 1971, there were 90,000 enrolled as California Indians. But the closing of enrollments was not the end. The enrollment process remained the family link to their ongoing pursuit and protection of Native American heritages and rights whether their own or those of others. While Charlie was making good strides on the Indian front, he was struggling in his personal life.

A rough period

"You're fired!" It was 1961. Charlie was now working in Castaic at Union Oil making $22 a day, okay money for that time. He had been with Union Oil since 1959, moving up the career ladder fast. He started as a roustabout, then was shortly promoted to do machine repair. He had been recognized for how smart he was, even given the work of a chemist, but his work started deteriorating. He had married Marty Wright in 1958, moved to a house in Newhall, and had two children, Chuck and Christine, but it just didn't work out. The struggles affected his work life so much that he lost his good Union Oil job.

After the divorce, Charlie bounced around, living with various friends in the San Fernando Valley. He worked in Santa Barbara at Southern Pacific Milling Company for a while in the sand and gravel yard. He shoveled gravel from the pit. He drove gravel and sand in pit trucks to stockpiles. Next he partnered with a cousin in a pickup and delivery laundry operation. It was the early 60s and things were changing all around. Wash 'n Wear made its debut and put the laundry operation out of business.

Next Charlie went to work in an oil field in Newhall driving a truck. He was living in Piru at the time, a very small, unincorporated area. It was near enough to the San Fernando Valley so that he drove into the Valley partying here and there in the evenings.

Some evenings he got together with ranch and rodeo guys. One such time in 1962 he went to the Santa Anita Racetrack in Arcadia, California, and struck up a friendship that was to have a big impact on him. He met Jerry Van der Vanter. Jerry had a sister who was an accomplished horsewoman and the queen of the California Rangers, a group of young riders.

But first, he met Penny Benton, a high fashion model, when he was going from one Valley nightspot to another. He married her in 1963. They moved to a house in Tarzana, an area in the Valley. In 1965, Charlie started driving a cement mixer truck for Wagnild Ready Mix. The work deepened his knowledge of the hills and valleys as did the ranch work he did now and then on weekends. He was still a skilled rider and roper, and he had not lost his love for the ranching life and its wide-open spaces.

He worked as a weekend cowboy rounding up cattle, roping and branding them on Southern California ranches not too far from the San Fernando

Valley, in growing towns along the 101 Freeway like Simi and Agoura. He worked in Cheeseboro, Las Virgenes, and Palo Comado Canyons, all in the Santa Monica Mountain Range. Bob Hope owned much of Palo Comado and leased the land to run cattle. Charlie and his cowboy buddies worked those cattle.

Rodeo: life lessons in the arena

It was 1965. *Clang*, a gate opens a chute, letting go of a thundering steer. A cowboy charges out the other chute chasing the steer and ropes him firmly around the horns. Got him! He's the header. Without missing a beat, he turns his horse slightly forcing the steer to kick up his back heels. This all happens so fast that the audience barely notices his partner, the heeler, on another horse. With perfect timing, the heeler ropes the back heels. Got him! But the steer kicks the rope off and hobbles his great weight toward the other end of the stadium. No score. This was team roping, a cowboy skill that had moved from the ranches to the rodeos, and then back to ranches again.

Charlie and his partner are next. They are competing in a jackpot event at a ranch in Oxnard, California, a city on the coast about 60 miles north of Los Angeles. All the cowboys competing tonight put money into a pot for this ranch event. These events often started in the evening and went all night. Now Charlie is waiting for the 1000-pound steer to dart out. He knows he has to wait for the steer to trip the barrier in the ground that opens the chute. If Charlie and his horse move out a split second too early, he and his heeler will suffer a ten-second penalty. He is worried. His horse, Idaho Mail Man, is skittish. It rears up but Charlie manages to hold on. "Dad told me to get rid of this horse," Charlie says to himself.

The jackpot had started when it was still daylight, and now it is close to midnight. They are all tired. He looks over to see how his partner is doing. Everything is calm over there. Suddenly Idaho Mail Man rears up again and falls over backwards. Charlie grabs the rail and jumps down to the ground. Idaho Mail Man stumbles up, gains his footing, and darts through the chute. Charlie runs after him, catapults back on, and rides him off to the side. He feels that he disappointed his partner, but there will be another chance. It's okay, they signal to each other, knowing they have a chance to do better next time. Later that evening they compete in another jackpot event. They rope more successfully this time, but still no great winnings.

A clue about Chumash ancestry

His marriage to Peggy Benton ended amicably in 1967—no children, no hard feelings. All this time Charlie was trying to find himself. One thing he knew about himself for sure, he was a worker, and usually a good one. Again, he moved among friends in the Valley, but this time he was more focused, especially in regard to American Indian heritage and the environment.

That same year, 30 people from Charlie's extended family on the Cooke and Garcia sides came together at the Newhall Ladies Center to renew and verify the San Fernando Mission Band leadership. Charlie was again elected president.

Also about 1967, a group of lawyers started to meet about forming a legal services group to help American Indians with issues such as land settlements. Charlie attended one of these meetings where he met Jack Forbes, a professor of Native American studies at UC Davis. Jack had lived in Southern California at one time. He had taught at what was then California State College at Northridge. He also had been an ethnographer for Ventura County which was one county north of Los Angeles. Based on what he knew about Indians in the Ventura County area, he thought that Charlie might be Chumash and told him so.

Charlie had known he was of American Indian descent, but the missions had gathered Indians from different tribes. This was a strong clue that he had the blood of the seafaring, peaceful Chumash who had occupied some of the prime real estate in this country, along the Southern California Coast and into the majestic Santa Monica Mountains, an area fast losing its serene beauty to loud and imposing construction. His rumbling cement truck was unwittingly contributing.

Separate advocates for the land

Three women who were living in Santa Monica Mountain communities, not too far from the San Fernando Valley, noticed the ongoing scarring of the landscape. They saw and heard the mixer trucks rumbling up and down canyon roads. They slowed their nimble cars as they came up behind long flatbed trucks puffing up windy, narrow inclines loaded down with large bulldozers and other earth moving equipment. Maybe they passed cement mixer trucks like Charlie's. They watched buildings appear, chopping up the majestic ridgelines. They did not know each other yet, but they all were thinking their own versions of, "Progress, okay, but with sensitivity and respect for these breathtaking, cliff hanging mountains."

Separately, they took up the fight to save the Santa Monica Mountains. Jill Swift started working with the Sierra Club and with her homeowner's association in Tarzana, a city in the San Fernando Valley, off an exit on the 101 Freeway. Sue Nelson was living in the Pacific Palisades, a residential area in a canyon that rose to cliffs then wound to the shore along Pacific Coast Highway. She formed and became president of the Friends of the Santa Monica Mountains and Seashore. Margot Feuer, who was living in Malibu further north on the Coast Highway, started working with her local Sierra Club. Dave Brown, who was teaching History at Valley College in North Hollywood, was also pushing to protect the mountains. He too was working with his local Sierra Club. They had the Santa Monica Mountains and its coastal area covered, but were not working together yet. They would eventually join with other forces to save the mountains.

Rodeo: loss and life changer

It's 1968. The announcer introduces the next team ropers over the loudspeaker and tells those right behind, in rodeo parlance—those in the hole, to be ready to take position. The team is out after the steer.

Charlie Cooke and Jerry Van der Vanter move into position and watch. "Oops," Charlie says, "he's going to miss." He was right. The header's throw was a fraction too slow and too short. Charlie watches and listens for his steer to crash through the chute. Charlie pats Blue. He had taken his father's advice and traded Idaho Mail Man in 1965 for a horse that ended up with a heart murmur. Bad trade! He traded again this time for an Appaloosa, but the beautiful leopard spotted horse did not take to roping, and in fact would fall down running. He traded again for Blue and hit the jackpot.

Figure 11: Charlie on Blue (Courtesy of Linda Cooke, 1972)

Charlie has team roped on many ranches branding and doctoring animals expertly, but now speed as well as accuracy matters. This is another event held at a local arena, this one in the San Fernando Valley. These are the kinds of events he enters with Jerry. Jerry and Charlie had roped together for about a year now. Your partner is everything. Ropers are a brotherhood. If your partner misses, you know that next time you might miss. The horse also matters. A quick double pat to Blue, and a little more waiting!

Charlie sees the steer break through the chute and in a split second, he's out after him. Charlie is a consistent header. He ropes the steer securely around the horns and turns his horse, forcing the steer into position for the heeler. Jerry expertly ropes the hind feet as Charlie turns his horse to force the steer down. Done fast and tight, but probably not fast enough! Dad Cy Cooke was a rodeo champion. In his day, eight to ten seconds was good enough, but now, for an average size arena, you have to rope the head, heels and immobilize the steer in about seven seconds to have any chance of winning. Charlie and Jerry know their time was not great today.

But all was not lost. Jerry invited Charlie to his house, and there was his sister from his mother's second marriage. Linda Enright was in a corner of the grassy back yard watering plants looking trim in white shorts and a black top. She was an accomplished horsewoman with lots of trophies and ribbons. But what Charlie saw that day was a sweet, good-natured young woman who was also quite attractive. It was love at first sight.

A month or so later, Charlie invented an excuse to go to Jerry's house and asked Linda to the Western Dance in Chatsworth at Giovanni's. The more time he spent with Linda the more he found her to be a good-hearted soul. Linda found him to be a good guy with the added bonus of being a handsome, rugged cowboy with a twinkle in his eye. And to cement it all, they shared an interest in horses. Linda started going to roping events with Charlie and Jerry.

Within six months, on October 9, 1969, they eloped to Gardnerville, Nevada. They came back to live in a house in Chatsworth near Linda's home in the Valley, but soon moved to Simi Valley trailering their horses. Linda's mother said they were not really married, so they married again in a Mormon church the following February in Chatsworth, starting a marriage that has lasted for over 40 years. Jason came first and then their other son Damon. For a long while horses were also part of their family. Linda and Charlie rode and groomed the horses together, Linda cheered Charlie on at his rodeo events, and Charlie rooted for Linda at her western riding competitions. What Linda did not know at the time was that she and the boys—and the horses—were going to share Charlie with his passion for Native American heritage. What Charlie may not have realized was that Linda was the stabilizing influence he needed.

Figure 12 (left): Linda Cooke with equestrian awards, all won the same day, (Courtesy of Linda Cooke, 1968)

Figure 13 (right): Linda, Blue, roping event in Camarillo, CA (Courtesy of Linda Cooke, 1975)

Alcatraz: listening and learning

A year before the wedding, in 1968, George Dukes, professor of law at UCLA, had recommended Charlie as a board member for the newly formed California Indian Legal Services Board (CILS). Charlie had become so active with Indian causes that Mr. Dukes had heard of him. Charlie became a board member and would remain so for many years. Establishment of the board coincided with a ground swell of the American Indian Movement, also referred to as AIM. The occupation at Alcatraz was part of that groundswell.

In 1971, after a CILS meeting in San Francisco, Charlie and his brother, Alvin, decided to add an unplanned trip to Alcatraz Island being occupied by American Indians. He sought out and met AIM leaders at a hotel, who told him what he needed to do to get to the island.

"Stay low. Don't let anyone see you," warned the fishing boat skipper as they bounced in the waves from Fisherman's Wharf to Alcatraz. Once on Alcatraz, Charlie talked to some of the one hundred American Indian college students who had been occupying Alcatraz since 1969 and to some others who were there to support them. He knew Alcatraz was no longer a federal penitentiary and the Indians there, with mainland support, wanted permanent possession of it. But what else? He heard things like:

"We have a right to our tribal ceremonies and religious practices."

"Our languages are dying. We need to keep them alive."

"Some tribes have been recognized by the Federal Government but not all."

"Our Indian environments are being ruined."

Charlie's trip had nothing to do with CILS. He just felt he had to be there. After a few days he left and went back to his family and job driving the cement truck but with a keener eye toward the land that his truck rumbled over and the issues that were coming to the forefront of Indian consciousness. By some counts, while the Indians did not gain possession of the penitentiary island, the Alcatraz occupation from November 20, 1967, to June 11, 1971, had raised awareness and awakened new-found respect for American Indians. Charlie had been there!

More exploration of family ancestry

Not too long after, in that same year, he went to several California Indian Legal Services meetings with Jack Forbes and Dave Risling, who were both professors of Native American Studies at UC Davis. One topic at these meetings was a new university. The professors set up DQU (Deganawidah Quetzalcoatl University), also in Davis, with a focus on indigenous peoples. This started Charlie's association with universities, including UCLA where he later spoke on preservation of Native American heritage and culture.

Charlie was still trying to understand the history of the indigenous people of Southern California and how he fit in. At one of the CILS meetings in the late 60s or early 70s, Professor Forbes gave him several books on the topic, which Charlie devoured. Charlie started piecing together what he learned from the books and from family stories handed down over generations to put back together what had been lost during the Mission Era. When he took over the family leadership role from Aunt Mary in 1959, he did not know who he really was and neither did many other Fernandeños. Now he suspected he was Chumash, but what else? After all, a Fernandeño could be from one or from a combination of several different Southern California tribes. He talked to relatives who led him to other relatives. By talking with them all, learning where their ancestors had lived in the vast

Southern California area, and absorbing the history of the area from his many scholarly contacts, he began to piece together the past.

Early monitoring guidelines for burial sites

In 1972 he started working for Livingston Graham Rock and Ready Mix in Santa Paula, deep in a Ventura County Canyon, driving a large mixer truck through mountains and valleys every day. He was to strike up another important and long-lasting friendship there with a weigh master who would eventually became a medicine woman and fierce supporter of all his heritage work.

Around the same time California started building Interstates 5 and 15, two north/south highways. During the massive project, workers struck Indian burials. Some 300,000 indigenous people from many different small tribes had lived the length of the state prior to European contact. By some estimates they had dwindled to 16,000 by 1900. Vincent Ibanez, who like Charlie, came home from serving during the Korean War, met up with people like Sam Kolb, started rediscovering his heritage, and became involved with Indian issues. Vince, like Sam Kolb came from one of the tribes who had lived at the San Luis Rey Mission. (Collectively these people are referred to as Luiseños.) Vince was from the Pechanga tribe, in fact he was a Reservation Pechanga, which meant he was a federally recognized Indian—not the case with other Luiseños. By 1972, aware of burial issues up and down the state, Vince was trying to place Indian observers along the length of each of these highway construction projects. The plan was for observers to monitor the construction to make sure Indian burials and artifacts were treated in accordance with Indian beliefs. He needed someone who knew Central and Northern Indians. He had heard of Charlie's work in Sacramento with CILS and of his work in other parts of the state. A number of Indians told Vince that Charlie was very knowledgeable about Indians up and down the state so he called on him to help.

One day, Vince and Charlie were with a group trying to settle a burial issue at the Sacred Pechanga Eagle site along the I-15 about one hundred miles south of Los Angeles near Escondido. Vince had involved Charlie as an advisor. In four hours the Pechangas and the California Department of Transportation (Caltrans) agreed to put a deep protection layer over the burials and then proceed with the highway work, but there was a lot of conversation in the process that raised a red flag about leveling the playing field between the Indian observers and Caltrans with their archaeological consultants.

"We can't do that because the law says . . ."

"That's not the way we do things in archaeology."

"What is the history of this site? How do we know?"

After the four-hour session, an elder looked Vince in the eye then turned his head to give Charlie a similar look. "Someone needs to start teaching the younger generation how to be involved in saving sites and heritage. There is a lot they need to know."

Vince stepped up and started the Native American Observers Training Association with some funds from the Department of Labor. The training included fieldwork and classes with elders, university archaeologists, lawyers, and experienced Indians such as Charlie and Vince. The observer training experience would come into play again and again off many freeway ramps up and down the state.

For a short time in the early 70s, Charlie delivered cement for foundations of luxury condominiums being built across from Los Encinos State Park in the San Fernando Valley. He heard rumors from work crews that there was a Native burial ground nearby. He looked around. It made sense that there would have been an Indian village here since there was an artesian well and an abundant source of food. He looked up into live oaks, some that were several hundred years old and wondered what it must have been like when they were seedlings, but he could not stay much longer. He needed to get back to the Livingston Graham plant for more cement—cement which would ironically lead him to an even greater awareness of sites to be saved, including this very site. The cowboy was showing signs of turning into a leader of his people and a crusader for their rights.

He is a rugged guy, a real cowboy. He doesn't just wear the hat. (Damon Cooke, Charlie and Linda Cooke's son, August 5, 2009)

Charlie was never on a reservation. Reservation life is different from what he experienced. His father was a horse trainer and shoer. Cowboys like his father, have disappeared. He had to look for another job to survive so he became a truck driver. He had a normal life with a wife and children along with Native American activities. He tried to combine the two life styles: modern world and ancient world. (Linda Cooke, Charlie's wife, May 16, 2009)

He is a genuine cowboy, a genuine teacher, a genuine Chumash, a genuine leader, a genuine good guy. He is a teacher with infinite patience. Charlie seems to have a profound knowledge of where he fits into the world, and is comfortable with that. He seems very balanced. With Charlie, it doesn't seem to matter who you are, where you come from, or what your background is. Acceptance is a word that seems to go with Charlie. Friendship is another one. (Bryn Barabas Potter, July 16, 2011)

I have taken over Charlie's CILS position. Charlie was significant in developing the role of CILS in representing Indians throughout California. (Reginald Pagaling, Chumash, Santa Ynez Reservation, CILS Board Member, Voice Mail of May 2, 2012)

At one point, Native Americans all over the place finally decided they had had enough of being looked down upon. They decided to take charge of their own history and culture. They picked anthropologists to work with them . . . They learned from archaeologists the value of the material they were discovering and vice versa. (Dr. Lowell Bean, ethnologist, professor emeritus, California State University Hayward, February 15, 2012)

Chapter 4: Taking Up the Staff, 1960s, 70s

Alvin moved to Idaho in 1971, but Charlie continued the work to resurrect Indian heritage. Besides Vince Ibanez, others who would become Charlie's allies in his heritage efforts were starting to emerge around native preservation. Some were anthropologists and archaeologists. Some were from state and national park systems. Some were politicians. Some were community activists. Some were Indians who suddenly realized or stood up for who they were. A few were rich and famous. Eventually, they would all converge. A few would cross Charlie's path close to the time he officially took up his Native American leadership role along with its symbolic staff.

The early network: anthropologists

In the late 60s, Clay Singer was taking notes in his UCLA class when he heard something like, "For some of the California tribes, there are no real Indians, so forget it! And if any say they are Indians do not consult them in your work. They are too far removed from what really happened."

In 1970, Clay finished his MA in anthropology and went overseas to work with that advice stored in his memory, but never comfortable with it. Clay was in France until 1973 and then led an excavation in Peru in 1975. When he got back to the United States later that year, the American Indian Movement (AIM) was growing. In 1970, the old law that had established a bounty on American Indians, allowing their capture dead or alive—the law that Charlie wondered about when overhearing his grandfather deny he was Indian—had finally been removed from the books. This was another sign that the attitudes toward Indians were changing. Clay was poised to work well in this changing environment.

Also in the early 70s, Lowell Bean was working on his Ph.D. in anthropology at UCLA where one of his professors told him something like, "There is no Indian culture left out there. You are wasting your time." On the other hand, his Ph.D. chair, cultural anthropologist Wendell Oswalt, supported his endeavors with Native Americans.

In the winter of 1970, Chester King, a Ph.D. candidate at UC Davis, was working at the UCLA Archeological Survey, an institution that supported and kept records of Southern California archaeological sites. He was working on the Pitas Point collection. Pitas Point was on the coast along the proposed 101 Freeway route through Ventura County near Carpentaria. Excavations there revealed a Chumash Village which existed there some eight hundred years ago. The village provided the most information to date regarding the organization of mainland Chumash.

Not only was Chester increasing his technical and cultural knowledge, but he was also observing the start of a shift in attitude. Students at the UCLA institution were writing bylaws for the Society for California Archaeology (SCA). They included a section stating that archaeologists would respect Native American concerns and issues. At the time some academics conveyed through actions, if not words, that archaeologists should control native sites, artifacts, and burials. Chester would not see Native Americans regularly monitoring sites with possible burials or artifacts for a few more years.

The early network: Indians

Kote Lotah had spent his childhood with his Barbareño Chumash grandparents and elders. He had learned about his heritage from them including the medicine ways and his duty as a warrior protector. He joined the Navy in 1962. By 1970 he had served in the Cuban crisis and had done four tours in Vietnam, one as part of a special operations unit. These combat conflicts taught him survival skills, self-reliance, and to be wary. He returned home to Santa Barbara with several medals, where he took up a new fight. In 1971, he joined AIM and by 1972 had started organizing the Chumash in the Santa Barbara area to reclaim their heritage and rights. The Chumash movement quickly spread to adjacent areas. He also delved deeply into native medicine and ceremonies on his journey to become a medicine man and spiritual leader.

John Dawson had Apache ancestry from New Mexico. He was the first director of Indian Center West in Culver City, California, opened around 1970. Indian Center West served as a community center and magnet for Native Americans of many ancestries who had migrated to the Los Angeles area. By the mid-1970s, John Dawson was thinking about forming an All Nations drum group.

Sallie Cuaresma, of Cherokee and Creek ancestry, started working at Indian Center West in 1979. Also, she volunteered at many Indian events, an example of many who gave continuously to the resurgence and preservation of Indian heritage.

The early network: civic leaders and developers

Vicki Goldschlager had just moved back to Thousand Oaks in 1970. She immediately became heavily involved with city and county issues around oak trees, open space, slow growth, and other environmental concerns that would intersect with some of Charlie's causes.

Bob Lewis, an attorney, had just finished his service with the Army. In 1976 he moved with his wife and two sons to Newbury Park right across from historic ranch land threatened by development. His idea of Indian history in the area was from his grade school days when he had learned about the Pueblo Indians. He would soon encounter Vicki.

Rad Sutnar had emigrated from Czechoslovakia with his family as a youngster after World War II. While still in his old country he read Carl May, Jack London, and Thomas Seaton from whom he gathered some knowledge about Western Indians and about the environment. By the time he made his way to the West Coast, he was an architect, and planner specializing in large developments. While cordial, he would not always agree with the likes of Vicki or Bob unless it had to do with preserving history.

The early network: the National and State Parks

Bill Ehorn was finishing up his assignment as the chief of planning at the National Park Service Midwest Regional Office. He was in Omaha, Nebraska, way inland. He'd soon be out to sea off the coast of California.

Under the St. Louis Arch, Bob Chandler was gaining experience with urban issues and making a reputation as a visionary. The Jefferson National Expansion Monument in St. Louis was part of the National Park System but different from the norm since it was an urban park. When he arrived in 1979 as the first superintendent of the Santa Monica Mountains National Recreation Area, straddling the coast from Los Angeles to almost Santa Barbara, he found himself amidst mountains dotted with urban centers and with a lost history buried over their expanse. But he was prepared with the experience and skills to create an unprecedented cooperative partnership with state, county and city agencies, with private landowners—and with the Indians of the area.

Way up in Alaska, John Reynolds was already working for the National Park Service in 1972. He was leading a team that resulted in the creation of the Bering Land Bridge National Preserve celebrating the migration of peoples to North America. This assignment resulted from the passage of the Alaska Native Claims Settlement Act in December 1971.

Phil Holmes had planned to compete in gymnastics, but an injury changed those plans. He worked his way through college by tutoring math. In 1971 he went to graduate school at California State Northridge in anthropology and then did stints as a handyman and an LA County welfare eligibility technician. He had just started to study computer science when he saw an ad for a job with the National Park Service.

Dan Preece had held increasingly responsible posts with California State Parks leading him to the role of the executive secretary of the State Parks Native American Advisory Board where he would begin his association with Charlie as the 70s became the 80s.

Charlie's network expanded many fold from these few. So many more people from various walks of Charlie's life continually crossed his path influencing him and he influencing them.

Laws coming into play

The 1970s saw the beginnings of laws affecting the environment and Indian cultural concerns, which went hand in hand. By this time, the use of the term *Native American* had emerged, in some circles meaning all peoples who before European contact inhabited what became the U.S. and its territories. It was meant to be more respectful, addressing the fact that Native Americans are not from India and recognizing their pre-contact heritage. AIM leadership and others, however, preferred the term, *American Indian*, for at least the indigenous peoples of the Lower Forty-Eight and those in Alaska who are not Eskimo or Aleut. After all, anyone born in the U.S. is native to this land, but not necessarily of American Indian descent.

Charlie and some of his cohorts often used the terms interchangeably. The laws themselves used both terms. Several of these laws came into play as Charlie continued on his journey to preserve Native American heritage. Many just band-aided the surface of the disrespect paid to Native Americans but they were a start.

The California Environmental Quality Act (CEQA) passed in 1973: This act required public agencies to identify, avoid, or mitigate significant effects of their actions on California land. This included Native American sites. This act required that Native Americans be consulted but not necessarily included in land development projects. However, it soon became standard practice to include them, especially after famed ethnologist, Dr. Lowell Bean, urged archaeologists at their various meetings and one-on-one to include Native Americans at archeological sites. Dr. Chester King started doing so by 1975.

The California Native American Historical, Cultural, and Sacred Sites Act passed in 1976: It allowed the state to conduct archaeological surveys on proposed construction sites. Under most conditions, it also prohibited severe or irreparable damage to any Native American sanctified cemetery, place of worship, religious or ceremonial site, or sacred shrine located on public property. Charlie would be working with Clay Singer and others on construction sites, and not as a cement mixer driver.

The California Coastal Act passed in 1976: This act protects and maintains the overall quality of natural and man-made resources in the coastal zone, including archaeological and historic resources. In 1982, the Coastal Commission adopted guidelines for reviewing archaeological projects. Charlie and his cohorts would eventually get involved on the coast due to this act.

The American Indian Religious Freedom Act passed in 1978: This federal act protects the rights of American Indians to practice their traditional religions and to the access of their sacred sites. When Charlie heard that this act had passed, his reaction was, "What took so long?"

The Archaeological Resources Protection Act, 1979: It required a federally issued permit to excavate Indian sites and notification of any affected tribes of archaeological investigations that posed harm to any location of Native American religious or cultural significance. This act did not require direct Native American control of or involvement in the excavations, but gave a boost to that practice already started in Southern California. Vince Ibanez involved Indians in excavations to protect their culture back in 1972.

Finally:

The Native American Graves Protection and Repatriation Act (NAGPRA), November, 1990: This federal law requires federally funded institutions to consult with Indian tribes or individuals prior to removing Native American remains or artifacts and to consult with them regarding disposition, often reburial.

Charlie and his cohorts had interjected themselves, working with public and private landowners to respect indigenous ancestral burials, acting on the principles of NAGPRA and other such laws, before all of them were passed. For example, in the early 1970s, prior to any of these state and federal laws, Kote Lotah, soon to ally with Charlie, had been involved with re-internments at Hammond Meadows in Santa Barbara. In the 1980s, an old amateur archaeologist had found the bones of about 20 Indians when digging his cellar for his house. Charlie heard about this through the grapevine. The amateur archaeologist turned the bones over to Charlie who stored them at a State Park site until Kote was able to re-inter them at Hammond Meadows in the late 1980s.

The medicine man and the chief

By the second half of the 1970s, Charlie was vice president of the Candelaria American Indian Council, originally formed to preserve local American Indian culture. Coincidentally, the center was named after Charlie's great, great aunt through marriage, also the same person who had been the midwife at Aunt Mary's birth. Candelaria had done a lot to help native California peoples. By now, Charlie knew she had been Chumash.

A man Charlie did not know walked into one of Candelaria Council's open board meetings, held in Oxnard along the coast, sat down and listened. Charlie noticed the intensity in his eyes.

At a break, the two started talking.

"Where are your people from, Charlie?" Kote Lotah was studying the Candelaria vice president.

"From many places. Some of my relatives are from around Pitas Point."

"I have some ancestors from Limuw."

"Oh, Santa Cruz Island." Charlie recognized the Chumash name for one of the Channel Islands—this one about twenty-five miles off the Ventura coast.

Kote added that he belonged to the Point Conception and Ventura Coastal Band, and that some other ancestors had lived in what is now Montecito. He told Charlie he had spent some of his childhood on the Santa Ynez Reservation where there were only four families at the time. Then he got to today.

"I have been studying native ways and medicine for years with Grandfather Victor. Do you know him?" Kote was using the term for an esteemed elder as many Native Americans did.

"Of course, Sky Eagle."

"He helped me see my true purpose when I came back from Vietnam."

"I served during the Korean war." Then Charlie lightened up a bit. "I am your elder, I guess."

Kote smiled.

"And your name? Is it Chumash?"

"Yes, Kote Lotah means black obsidian."

"Volcanic glass, important to the Chumash as a cutting edge."

Almost immediately, Charlie and Kote formed a bond. Not too long after, Kote called a meeting at Wagon Wheel Junction, a business and restaurant complex in Oxnard, between the Conejo Valley and Santa Barbara. About ten people of Chumash descent met in an office there. Most were of the Owl Clan. Only Charlie and one or two others were from the Eagle Clan.

"Some Ventura County government officials . . ." One of the group started, hesitated, and then stood up. "They are saying we Chumash are extinct."

"I wonder if some developers want us out of the way?" Charlie mused.

"We do protest when they try to move our ancestor's bones," another real, live Chumash commented.

"We need a leader, a chief," one woman declared, looking at Kote, her son.

Madlyn Hall Guevera had been active in the Santa Barbara area for a while promoting Chumash culture, somewhat as a matriarch. The ancestral Chumash had been a society with both male and female chiefs.

"In the Chumash way, power is shared by a number of leaders," Kote looked over to Charlie.

Charlie noted the determined intensity in Kote's eyes. Kote continued, "You be the chief, Charlie, a WOT."

Charlie had done enough investigating and learning to know that a WOT was the village chief who had the political responsibility.

Grandfather Victor stepped in. "A WOT, the one that makes strong relations among other chiefs. You are already making relations everywhere in the area. Most of us here are Owl Clan, but we have no one ready in Owl Clan to be our WOT. Kote is our spiritual leader."

They were using the term clan to refer to a kinship group that was a smaller part of the area's Chumash people. While this may not have been a term or societal unit of ancestral Chumash, Kote and Charlie, in their belief that culture adapts, were using the term to refer to groups in their own lifetimes.

"We need to join forces in this fight," Kote said directly to Charlie.

Charlie asked, "You mean the fight to make sure our heritage is respected, past and present?"

"And our graves and scared sites." Kote's sternness took hold again.

"And that we are alive" the matriarch emphasized.

Kote said, "You will have some ceremonial roles too, but I will keep the spiritual ones."

Rationale for declaring Charlie as chief

Some more talk and the group concluded that according to their collective family history, Charlie was a Chumash chief. With Grandfather Victor's blessing, they named him their Owl and Eagle Clan chief. In actuality, this was, very likely, a role he would have inherited had the missions and other effects of European contact not intervened. Also, in actuality, the inheritance of a chief's role for Charlie and for other possible Native American chiefs was muddled.

As was the case with many Mission Indians, Charlie's family did not know tribal details about all of their ancestry. So the chief's role had passed down in the family as a Fernandeño leadership role; first from Isidoro Garcia to his daughter, the spunky Grandma Frances Garcia Cooke, then to her daughter, Aunt Mary Cooke Garcia, and then to Frances's grandson, Charlie Cooke. For Charlie, his family, and many who concluded that he was the right person to be the Chumash chief now in the late twentieth century, his role was valid and hereditary.

Charlie quickly stepped in as hereditary chief. Soon officials and newspapers in Ventura and Los Angeles counties started referring to him as the chief of the Southern Chumash, perhaps not fully understanding that a traditional Chumash chief at first European contact led a small village group. Of course, times had changed substantially since first contact with Europeans. There was no Chumash village, just Chumash descendants scattered over Southern California, and a leadership void waiting to be filled.

An Indian cultural center debate

"We need to join forces in this fight," Kote had said meaning that they needed to work together making sure that the general population would see the Chumash as a living, contributing part of the population.

One of Charlie and Kote's first stands together was at a government meeting. The Candelaria Council decided that they should start a Chumash Cultural Center connected with the movement to preserve the Santa Monica Mountains. Around 1979, Charlie went with Jessie Roybal, a Creek and president of Candelaria, and two park commissioners to a Santa Monica Mountains Comprehensive Planning Commission meeting at Taft High School in the San Fernando Valley. There were people from many Southern

California areas. The discussion got contentious. Charlie listened and considered the points of view he was hearing, but then the discussion turned one-sided.

"The Center will not be in Ventura County."

"Why not? We have the Tongva and Chumash people in that county. Both have important histories in the Santa Monica Mountains area."

"Hmm, this is about tax money. Proposition 13 lowered property taxes in California. The Santa Monica Mountains cross over several counties. There won't be enough to go around," Charlie reasoned to himself. Proposition 13 had passed in 1978.

Kote Lotah was there, sitting and listening to the arguments back and forth. At a break:

"Charlie, remember how I said we need to stand together in our different roles."

"This situation is a good opportunity. Let's see how the rest of this goes."

The meeting was degenerating. It became clear that the Planning Commission was going to exclude Ventura as a Chumash Cultural Center site so Charlie, Kote, and two commissioners walked out. Charlie maintained his calm as he banded in exit with his Ventura brethren. That calm would matter later, when even those opposed to each other's views would regroup around this issue.

An Indian name and staff

Around 1978, Charlie decided he wanted to take on a Chumash name. "Can you really see who those people are so far down the road?" he remembered his father asking and then exclaiming, "You have the eye of an eagle!"

"Eye of the Eagle! That's it."

In time, Kote made a chief's staff for Charlie from an oak, the tree of life. He carved a power stick with feathers at the top: eagle, hawk, and owl; three of the four Chumash power birds. No condor feather since it is the last feather the chief earns, at his death. Also, at the time condors were on the brink of extinction. When he handed the staff to him, he told him,

"Cut a notch for every accomplishment; you decide what matters."

"It'll be about our people."

"Charlie, do you know the story of how the Europeans got here?" Kote always had unusual stories, almost parables.

"Columbus. Or is this a trick question?"

"In clay jars."

"Oh, yes, that story. It's a little confusing, but I get the idea. Tribes here caught the first Europeans and put them in jars."

"Yes, and they put the jars in a cave. They were in the cave for so long that the people turned white and their minds went blank. The tribes sent them to the East where all life comes from, and gave them sticks so they could write things down because they were forgetting. Then they came back here."

"This time with Columbus."

"Or before. Now they are the Young American Tribe."

"Kote, I can see why you are a spiritual leader. What this story means is that we need to remind the Young American Tribe that they too have responsibility for the land and to educate them about it." Kote and Charlie shared concerns for the future, but expressed them differently.

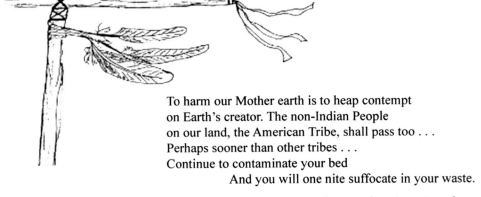

To harm our Mother earth is to heap contempt
on Earth's creator. The non-Indian People
on our land, the American Tribe, shall pass too . . .
Perhaps sooner than other tribes . . .
Continue to contaminate your bed
        And you will one nite suffocate in your waste.

Figure 14: Drawing of staff and verse 1 of 3 of poem by Kote Lotah
(Courtesy of Dr. Kote Lotah, late 1970s)

Charlie started notching soon thereafter. Charlie and Kote understood the long history and role of coastal and near inland Indians. Kote and Charlie took their complementary but individual fights for Chumash ways, respect, and recognition up and down the canyons, into the urban environments tucked in between, and out to sea.

Charlie and I were both struggling to bring awareness about Native Americans in Southern California. We were taught not to call the Europeans who came here the white man, but rather the Young American Tribe who is everyone here and now. Like our ancestors, now their ancestors are buried here and are their seed. We need to educate them. We both want to share our ancestral ways for the good of Mother Earth and all her children. Charlie brings the legal and political aspects. I bring the medical and spiritual. That's why we started working together. We are on the same path, not one in front or behind, but side-by-side. (Dr. Kote Lotah, July 16, 2009)

Charlie and I were recognized as Native Americans because of our skin color. Chumash on the Santa Ynez Reservation are recognized as a people; but the San Fernando Mission Chumash, which we are part of, are not . . . Regarding property in Southern California: it takes a war to get a treaty. There were no wars in Southern California [of large military action, and no treaties were ratified by the Senate] . . . Our traditions still need to be remembered: dances, languages, burial rites, crafts such as baskets, the tomol, and our monetary system. (Alvin Cooke)

As an Apache, my story is so different—a contrast. Some Chumash people hardly knew where they came from—were thrown in with Mexican Americans or Latinos and grew up in that environment. At the time Charlie starting being active with Native American issues, very few people knew anything about the Tongva and Chumash. Back then, very few people believed they still existed and were still living. Now you readily hear about the ancient people of this area—past and present. (John Dawson, Apache and first Director of Indian Center West, November 8, 2011)

Charlie's the real thing. Charlie knows a lot about his family history, that one branch lived in the Santa Barbara / Ventura area for thousands of years. The Chumash are an ancient linguistic group, Hokan speakers; so his family goes way back. (Dr. Alex Kirkish, May 29, 2009)

Culture adapts. Culture is not a static piece. Charlie understood this. (Phil Holmes, April 4, 2011)

PART TWO, HONORING THE PAST: Early activism on behalf of ancestral sites and the environment

From the time I met him, I thought he was a great tribal man. I was proud to share his involvement in preserving our sites and culture. Charlie was involved as a Native American long before that became fashionable. (Mati Waiya, Chumash and Executive Director of Wishtoyo Foundation, May 16, 2009)

Map 4: Southern California Coast and Islands
(Courtesy of James Mansfield)

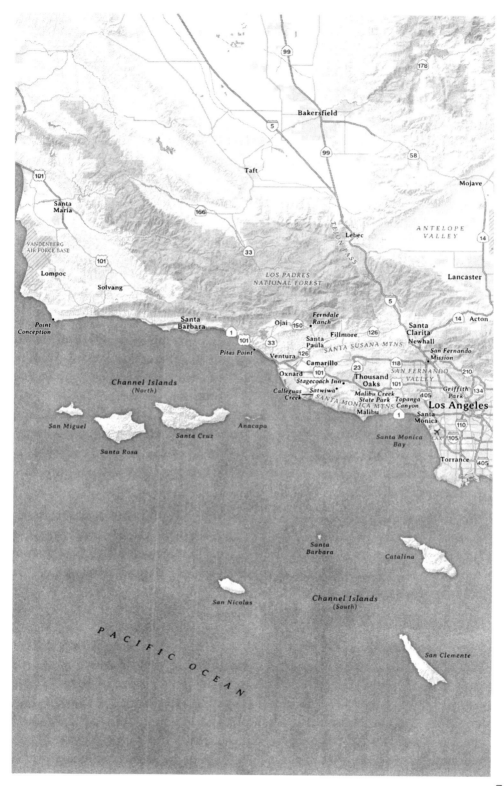

Bakersfield

99

178

5

Taft

58

Mojave

101

Santa
Maria

166

ANTELOPE
VALLEY

VANDENBERG
AIR FORCE BASE

101

Lebec

14

Lompoc

Lancaster

LOS PADRES
NATIONAL FOREST

Solvang

33

Point
Conception

Santa
Barbara

1

101

33

Pitas Point

Ojai

150

Ferndale
Ranch

Fillmore

126

Santa
Clarita

Santa
Paula

SANTA SUSANA MTNS

Newhall

14

Acton

5

San Fernando
Mission

Ventura

126

Channel Islands
(North)

Oxnard

Camarillo

101

118

Stagecoach Inn

23

Thousand
Oaks

SAN FERNANDO
VALLEY

210

Calleguas
Creek

Satwiwa

101

Malibu Creek
State Park

Topanga
Canyon

Griffith
Park

134

SANTA MONICA MTNS

405

Los Angeles

San Miguel

Santa Cruz

Anacapa

Malibu

1

Santa
Monica

110

Santa Rosa

Santa Monica
Bay

LAX

105

Santa
Barbara

Catalina

Torrance

405

San Nicolas

Channel Islands
(South)

San Clemente

PACIFIC OCEAN

Chapter 5: Making a Mark at Sea and on Land—and the Teachings of Elders, 1974-79

Rolling hills and mountains with magnificent rock outcroppings, dotted with yucca, prickly pear, scrub oaks, and other native Southern California plants, and then more rolling hills and mountains. A large rocky, white bluff shining in the distance. That is what Charlie, Linda, and their two boys see as they drive along, again trailering their horses, Blue and Grouch, behind them. They had lived in the San Fernando Valley and then the Simi Valley. Now they were moving on to the Conejo Valley.

The white bluffs overlook Newbury Park, part of the City of Thousand Oaks, a Ventura County town in the Conejo Valley not too far from the coast between Los Angeles and Santa Barbara. For a long time Thousand Oaks was so small that as you drove by at night, you didn't notice it. Hardly any lights! But now more and more lights popping up on ridgelines, on the slopes, and across the valley floor!

The Cookes moved to Newbury Park in 1975 so Charlie would be closer to his job. He was now driving his rolling cement mixer truck up and down canyon roads close to the Conejo Valley, in the Santa Monica Mountains. On the ocean side, the mountaintops become sheer drops to Pacific Coast Highway along the shore. Anyone driving in this area at the time could see a lot of building going on for the rich and famous on cliff tops and ocean fronts on what was once the prime real estate of the seafaring Chumash. At this same time, interest in both the environment and native California peoples was growing.

The Santa Monica Mountain Range has one of the highest concentrations of archaeological sites in the world. The Channel Islands, right off the Southern California Coast, also are ridden with archaeological sites. Native American history was waiting all around Charlie, on mountains, in valleys, and on islands out to sea.

Island ancestors

Bill Ehorn looked out the window of the small airplane as it took off for San Miguel, an island owned by the Navy, twenty-six miles out at sea off the coast at Point Conception which is in the Santa Barbara Channel. Half way he could see dolphins breaking the surf. As the plane got closer to San Miguel Island, he could feel the strong winds that enveloped this island and see its effects on the choppy waters below. The plane bounced back and forth on this summer day in 1974, before Charlie had moved close to the coastal area.

Bill had recently arrived as the new superintendent of the long-neglected Channel Islands National Monument, which at the beginning of his tenure there, consisted only of the smallest islands, Anacapa and Santa Barbara. He was anxious to see San Miguel. He had heard about its magnificent resources.

Through the fog on San Miguel Island: The plane was over land. Bill looked down. Through the fog, he could make out the 817-foot Green Mountain with lush, tall grass and rock outcroppings here and there. He thought he saw a fox running across the hillside. He looked for the National Marine Fisheries Research Station even though he knew it could not be in sight. A few bumps and the plane landed in the dry lakebed west of Green Mountain. A wave good-bye to the pilot and he was on his own.

It was summer, but still cool on this island. He clutched his jacket as the wind pushed him back and forward. He fought to pull his hood back on his head and tighten the lace under his chin. The fog made him feel wet. He looked up to see some brown pelicans soaring out to sea and then he started his two-mile trek to the Research Station above Point Bennett, famous for its wildlife. The sand on the dry lakebed shifted right under his feet as he wound back and forth up its inclined shore onto a small hill. Finally, he was off the lakebed, making his way through tall, waving, green grass left from ranching days. He tripped over dark, soft soil.

"A midden, little garbage heap, left here long ago," he noted to himself.

Up and onward.

Another midden and another.

"Mortars, pestles, shells, more shells," he chanted to himself as he came across them. "Hmm, I need to talk with some Indians about what is out here."

Suddenly he stopped and listened. He had gone about a mile. He was expecting the sound. He looked every which way—just tall green grass being whipped by the wind, but it seemed like more than that. He heard a faint barking caught in the gusts. He moved on. He noted the red and yellow flowers. "Probably paintbrush and giant coreopsis," he thought. He squinted at a white gleam off to the side and then walked over to it. "Looks like part of a skeleton." He knew that the Chumash had inhabited this island and others nearby. The barking sound was louder. "Oh, the smell! I must be almost there, probably another half mile to go."

Bill moved on. Suddenly right before him was the Research Station. He stopped not because he had reached his destination, but because he was stunned by a wildlife spectacle like he had never before seen. Below on the shores of Point Bennett, thousands of seals and sea lions were hauled out on the beach! He had arrived above their rookery right in the middle of breeding season. "This will be protected by the National Park Service," he promised himself.

Bill braved San Miguel's unrelenting wind many times, going back and forth to this island by helicopter or plane. By 1976, NPS was seriously investigating the San Miguel resources. By now he knew that there were hundreds, if not thousands, of Chumash middens all over the island.

By November, Bill had worked out an agreement with the Navy for NPS to manage the natural and cultural resources. Now he had responsibility for Anacapa, Santa Barbara, and San Miguel but not the privately owned islands of Santa Cruz and Santa Rosa.

The Park Service had considered the Channel Islands as a park in 1932 and again in the 1950s. Because they were protected mostly by nature, by being far from the mainland, by their rancher-owners, and in the case of San Miguel by the Navy, there was no urgency. But now in the late 1970s, the movement to preserve expanses of the Santa Monica Mountain range and their coastal areas accelerated, and the Channel Islands got swept along in that movement. There was legislation on the table for one park together: the Santa Monica Mountains National Recreation Area and Channel Islands National Seashore. Jill Swift, Sue Nelson, Margot Feuer, Dave Brown, and others had been lobbying in Washington to save the Santa Monica Mountains and their adjacent seacoast. They were starting to make some positive headway.

Bill Ehorn knew that the coastal areas and the nearby islands had been Chumash territory at one time. Bill put together an advisory committee for San Miguel, which concurred on that island's protection, setting the precedent for the others. It included representatives from the Santa Barbara Museum, the Santa Barbara Botanical Gardens, U.S. Fish and Wild Life Services, National Marine Fisheries Service, the United States Navy, California Fish and Game, Dr. Starker Leopold (a UC Berkley professor), and Dr. Carey Stanton, who owned most of Santa Cruz Island. The committee did not have any Native Americans on it, which Bill later noted as a mistake. The Park Service was still learning. Charlie would be one of their teachers.

<u>Speaking up for the islands</u>: As soon as they had learned a new superintendent had arrived, Charlie and Kote showed up at his Ventura office and introduced themselves.

"We wanted to meet you, Mr. Ehorn."

"Bill. I'm informal as you can see." Bill was dressed for a trek out to the islands.

"This is Charlie Cooke, our Chumash chief," Kote started.

Charlie smiled as he offered his hand and turned to Kote. "Dr. Lotah here is our medicine man. He has been trained by the elders."

"Just Kote," and the medicine man offered his hand.

"Well, Charlie and Kote, the islands are full of Chumash remains and some artifacts."

"Yes, our people lived on the Chumash Islands before the ranchers took over there," a tinge of bitterness came through Kote's voice.

Superintendent Ehorn said to himself, "Did I hear *Channel* Islands or *Chumash* Islands?"

The three spent a few more minutes skimming the natural and cultural resources on those islands. In no time, Charlie was on board with Bill, figuratively and actually. Charlie often brought Kote along.

<u>On board to Anacapa</u>: Bill skippered the Sea Ranger, a 42-foot Park Service boat, with Charlie, Kote, and some NPS staff on deck out to Anacapa, the tiniest and closest of the islands. They all climbed up a long set of iron steps along a black lava cliff to the top of the island, the only way to get there at this landing. They were on top of East Anacapa, a high plateau of about 150 acres and one of the three islets that make up Anacapa.

They noted nonnative ice plant taking over in some areas, but could see the Giant Yellow Coreopsis, which grows on these islands, everywhere. Bill showed them a midden. Kote and Charlie touched it—a shell midden, basically a garbage heap. They talked about how the Chumash visited these islets, but did not settle on them. There is no fresh water or firewood on the island. The shell middens suggest they came for the seafood.

They could see an old Coast Guard lighthouse and living quarters, but most of the islet was pristine, a rookery for seagulls.

"Do you know these seagulls were the stars in Alfred Hitchcock's movie, *The Birds*?" one ranger said.

"No, that's not true, but you can see why people would say that," another ranger explained. "You have to tell visitors at some times of the year to be careful not to step on nests or on the hundreds of chicks marching around, but we're okay today."

Standing on top of this tiniest of the islands, the group could see the ocean no matter which way they looked. The water was a clear green. They walked around at the edge of the cliff that surrounded this whole islet. They could see to the next islet, but too far to jump over there. They could see into sea caves below. They could see pinnipeds basking on the shore, nothing like on San Miguel, but they were here too.

They talked under the bright sunshine about protection of all the islands. There were no oak trees here for shade, so no acorns. Acorns had been a Chumash staple, the lack thereof was another sign that the Chumash had not taken up permanent residency here. They talked about eradicating nonnative species and returning the island to its natural state. "We need to allow people out here," they agreed, "but under guidelines that preserve habitats, history, and the gorgeous landscapes and vistas."

They continued along the edge until they got to the lighthouse. There Kote reached for a conch shell and blew it in the direction of the four winds. Charlie took out bundled white sage and the abalone shell they had brought with them and conducted a Chumash blessing, perhaps much as those who had left the middens behind had done. He burned the sage in the abalone shell wafting it across each individual. They left feeling they had all, including the NPS staff, reconnected with seafaring Indians who long ago had come to work here on these islets.

Figure 15: Superintendent Bill Ehorn leaving the Ventura Coast for the closest of the islands, Anacapa, (Courtesy of Bill Ehorn, 1979)

Figure 16: Lighthouse, Anacapa, (CINP Archives, nd)

<u>Cementing the relationship on San Miguel</u>: By the late 1970s, rangers had found Chumash remains on San Miguel and the other islands. By that point, Charlie and Kote were involved. Off they went, Charlie, Kote, and Bill, by helicopter to San Miguel. As they walked, they looked down. When they looked back they could see their footprints being swept away by the constant 40-mile-an-hour winds. A skull emerged in the sands before them. They stopped and stooped down. The three reburied it using the tools they had, their hands. Kote and Charlie stayed down to create a small ground-based huddle. Kote handed Charlie the sage and abalone shell he had with him. Charlie pulled out matches. Still low to the ground, their huddle had foiled the wind; burning sage wafted up from the abalone shell as part of the traditional Chumash burial ceremony.

They walked on and found a spot protected from the wind in a small ravine. There Charlie and Kote talked with Bill about how the currents on the east end of this island came together to capture drifting redwood from up north. They talked about how redwood does not sink, just floats down the coast. They marveled at how the Chumash cut it into planks on the islands and then towed the planks to the mainland. There they crafted sturdy, plank, ocean-going boats called tomols, sealing them with higher-grade asphaltum than they could find on the islands. Bill Ehorn knew some of this history but not all. He had found the Native American consultants he needed, alive and well, standing with him in the same ferocious winds felt by their ancestors.

Figure 17: Charlie, Bill and Cheri Elson on a later helicopter trip to San Miguel, (Courtesy of Fran and Ed Elson, 1984)

<u>To the islands in the old way</u>: Back on land, Kote Lotah was planning an historic and arduous trek. "We are headed out to sea, but not in one of your noisy airplanes. In the tomol!" Kote Lotah was excited as he told Bill Ehorn about his upcoming adventure.

A group of Native Americans decided to revitalize the ancestral Chumash and Tongva Brotherhood of the Tomol in order to recreate the crossing of their ancestral ocean-going boat. Kote Lotah was among them and helped build a replica of the sturdy tomol, a large cargo vessel, to ancestral specifications, from redwood that had drifted down the coast. The Brotherhood then waterproofed the wood as their ancestors had done with a mixture of tar and pine pitch. On July 4, 1976, the U.S. Bicentennial, Kote and several others paddled the Helek, the first tomol built in 142 years, following centuries old trade routes from San Miguel Island to Santa Rosa Island, and finally to Santa Cruz Island several miles off the coast of Ventura and Santa Barbara. Charlie had been invited to be part of the crew paddling out to sea but could not take two weeks off from his job. The event got a lot of media coverage, contributing to newly found interest in Native California peoples, especially the Chumash.

Figure 18: Tomol crossing, landing at Santa Cruz Island in summer of 1976 (CINP Archives, nd)

<u>Mountain ancestors</u>

While the Brotherhood of the Tomol was planning to recreate Chumash life at sea, the Conejo Valley's Bicentennial Committee was developing an exhibit of historic buildings at an old Butterfield Stagecoach site in Newbury Park. The exhibit covered pre-contact to pioneer times. Rad Sutnar, a local developer, was a key member and intimately involved in all aspects including the Chumash Village replica on the Stagecoach Inn Museum property. The Village gave some realism to Rad's interest in Native American history and would soon lead him to Charlie.

That same year, in 1976, the State of California, as a reaction to the growing concerns of California Indians in the aftermath of Alcatraz, created the Native American Heritage Commission (NAHC). In addition to its functions in regard to native lands and plants, the Commission would oversee the adherence to the California Native American Historical, Cultural, and Sacred Sites Act passed also in 1976. In effect, this act makes Native American burial sites cemeteries, requiring the same treatment as a place like Forest Lawn. In addition, it requires the coroner to notify the Native American Heritage Commission when native remains are found. The Commission then must notify most-likely-descendants, who have the right to inspect the remains and any artifacts found. The descendants

87

also have the right to make recommendations regarding treatment of the remains, associated grave items, and reburial. In 1982, Senate Bill 297 empowered NAHC to catalog burials and to resolve disputes regarding their treatment and that of associated artifacts.

In his roles on various boards, as a concerned citizen and as a chief, Charlie became increasingly involved in issues around Native American sites, especially if they were slated for development.

Starting a long relationship with state parks: Malibu Creek State Park is in the Santa Monica Mountains with access from Las Virgenes Road, a road that will take you through Malibu Canyon all the way to the ocean. The Malibu Creek area had been owned by the movie industry for a while. The man-made lake on the property had been used for battles with model warships. Hollywood studios shot Cary Grant movies, *Plant of the Apes*, and the TV series, *MASH* there. *MASH* was still on site as the California State Park System took over the property and was getting ready to lay the foundation for a parking lot in anticipation of many park visitors.

The Malibu Creek area had been a prime area for the ancestral Chumash. Dr. Thomas Blackburn, a well-respected anthropologist, had initiated archaeological studies in the area in 1960. By the end of the 60s, archaeologists knew that the Chumash village of Talepop had been somewhere in the general area, so it was not surprising when workers struck burials in 1977 as they started enlarging the State Park's parking lot. Charlie came to the site as a representative of the California Indian Legal Services Board. He worked with Dennis Dobernick, the State Park Manager for the area, and then with the State Park archaeologist on a re-internment plan to move the burials close by. Kote came to conduct the re-internment ceremony. Charlie offered the ancestral prayers. Then work went on as planned.

Three years later, in 1980, Dennis Dobernick remembered Charlie's work with the parking lot issue and recommended him as a board member for the State Park's Native American Advisory Council that started Charlie's 15-year service to that group.

Figure 19: Malibu Creek State Park (Author's photo, 2010)

<u>Close to home</u>: Because Charlie was out in the field since the days of working with Vince Ibanez, he knew artifacts—what they looked like and how they should be handled. Vicki Goldschlager was hiking in the unspoiled mountains near her Newbury Park home with her husband one 1976 weekend when they both saw the rim of a large bowl barely breaking though the ground and dug it out. Vicki knew enough to identify it as a Native American artifact. She had already heard of Charlie and decided to call him. She was thrilled when she discovered that the Chumash chief lived on her street. She drove to see him with the bowl in her car. It was bulky, about 14 inches in diameter and about 10 inches deep. Charlie helped get it out of her car. It was still heavy with dirt in it as Charlie put it down gently on his front lawn. At first, the meeting was a bit strained.

"Charlie, my husband and I found this bowl in the mountains. We think it's Native American, maybe Chumash."

"Chumash bowls, baskets, and other cultural items need to stay right where they are, especially if they are part of a burial."

"Oh," Vicki saw some sternness. She understood where Charlie was going and raced through her explanation. "No, no, we are not taking the bowl, we are trying to protect it before anyone else finds it and it disappears for good. It could have been destroyed on that trail we were on. It's a horse trail. I don't think this was near a burial. Would you take it and give it to

89

the Stagecoach Inn Museum near here? They have a Chumash room, don't they?"

"Yes, they do." He crouched down and turned the bowl around, looking at its every surface, noting its reddish brown color. "Thanks for bringing this to me. This is the largest bowl I have ever seen outside of the Channel Islands. Then he ran his hands and eyes over the outside surfaces. "It's gritty and weathered and worn, but no cracks."

"What was it used for?"

"It's heavy, even without the dirt in it. The Chumash would have used it close to where you found it. It might have held food—but not hot. It's sandstone. Anything hot would have cracked it. "

Charlie ran his fingers slowly over the rim feeling the inscribed ring. "This rim here, it probably held beads or shell."

Vicki turned the bowl over to Charlie and left. He dug though the dirt and found arrowheads inside. "This could have been a ceremonial bowl," he thought.

Charlie told the Candelaria Indian Council about the bowl. They wanted it, but he told them he was going to place it near where it was found. Sometime later, he took it to the Stagecoach Inn Museum, the old horse-drawn Butterfield stage stop. There, he and Harriet Baker, the museum director, signed an agreement that would allow the museum and any Indian Cultural Center ever established in the area to alternate years displaying it. Harriet put the bowl on display in the Chumash Room and there it stayed for many years.

Land developments

Charlie would run into Vicki at meetings throughout the area. He attended Thousand Oaks City Council meetings to make sure the council was aware of Native American and Chumash interests. He met one-on-one with then Mayor Frances Prince and individual city council members.

He also would run into Rad Sutnar who was a vice president for Shapell Industries, Ventura Division. Shapell was in the process of developing the MGM Ranch property in Newbury Park into a light industrial center. Since there were archaeological sites there, Charlie showed up at hearings on the project. He brought city officials out to look at the sites and for a while, the city put the project on hold. More hearings. Rad saw Charlie as quiet but speaking up at the right time and started to engage with him. In time, Charlie and other Native Americans proposed a solution: avoid the sites altogether or fill them over after doing enough exploration to record what was there for the sake of history. Eventually, Rad oversaw the development, filling in and avoiding archaeological sites.

Danielson Ranch: Building was mushrooming across the valley floor and encroaching on the mountains. Besides the MGM development, there were several other proposed developments in the Newbury Park area. One of them would result in high-density housing near Point Mugu State Park on adjacent property that still belonged to Mr. Danielson. He wanted to sell. The nearby residents started meeting. About 1978, Bob Lewis hosted a meeting in his living room. It was packed. Neighbor after neighbor rang the doorbell. Mayor Francis Prince and Council Member Madge Schaeffer came. Bob had heard about and invited Charlie. His two young boys waited eagerly for the chief to appear, but when he did, he was in his usual garb, jeans and a work shirt.

"A chief comes in any clothes," was his unstated message. They warmed to him and then disappeared to play.

"So what's the situation?" Bob asked at the start of the meeting.

The city officials spoke up.

"Shapell is planning thousands of homes in the back country."

"You mean in addition to the industrial park?" one resident worried out loud.

"You mean where that beautiful canyon is?" a hiker asked.

"Yes, and that Shapell project will bring a sea of cars."

"And people. We need to think about how that will affect our road systems, yes, but also our school systems, our water and sewer systems, police, fire . . . ," one of the city council representatives quickly summarized some of the infrastructure challenges they would be facing.

"And the Dos Vientos project is also slated to add about 3000 homes."

Charlie listened.

"Warmington is planning to build about 600 to 700 homes on the Danielson property near Mugu State Park."

"That's across the street from me!"

"Me too!"

Charlie leaned forward.

"That will affect our hiking trails," one of the residents pined.

"The traffic will be horrendous around here."

Then Charlie spoke, "There are Indian cultural resources in the area. However, if the area gets built—better if not—but if it does, we need to protect our ancestral resources. That means builders need to avoid them, go around them—or other mitigation measures we can discuss."

Bob asked, "Who lived here? Were there Indians in this area? What are we talking about? Pueblos?"

Charlie answered, "The Chumash, the Tongva. Artifacts, rock art, burial grounds, whole villages, trails." And then he elaborated on each topic for a few minutes and answered questions.

The mayor and councilwoman started talking about metering. Metering involved restricting housing in certain areas such as on slopes of 25 percent or more—a ridgeline protection measure.

Charlie listened and learned the city terminology. "Good plans. But still development anywhere needs to respect Indian resources."

"And the scenery," a neighbor added. "Will we still see the bluffs?"

"The streams, will they reroute them?"

The meeting went on with Charlie interjecting now and then with more information on cultural resources and the environment of the area. He let them know, as Kote would say, that they were the New American Tribe; but Charlie said that in his own way.

"You are protectors of the land now too. Our heritage and the land, they go together."

Charlie attended subsequent meetings and hearings on the proposed developments. Lee Laxdahl, a citizen deeply concerned about overbuilding, called Vicki about the situation and soon joined Bob Lewis in authoring a city measure to slow development to five hundred housing units a year and to keep building off ridgelines.

Now and then, a few activists would suggest archaeological sites where there really were none. When they tried to enlist Charlie's help, he ignored them and did nothing to support their claims.

By 1977, Charlie was talking about the benefits of the slow growth measure every chance he got, at meetings and one-on-one. Bob Lewis and Vicki Goldschlager were at many of these meetings. So was Rad Sutnar, at times

TIQ SLO'W, The Making of a Modern Day Chief

on the opposing side, but they would hear the same consistent message from the chief:

"We need to protect native burials and artifacts."

"Respect our Mother Earth."

"The ancient trade route to the ocean is right here in the Thousand Oaks area. Hikers take that trail now down Sycamore Canyon."

"Let's save the legacy for our children."

"Native interests and environmental interests are linked."

Voters passed Measure A, the Slow Growth Measure, in 1980. Late nights around kitchen tables, flyers, door-to-door campaigns, and much more effort contributed to the success. Certainly, Charlie had been only one voice, but one that spoke with no animosity, just conviction; and he added the overlooked Native American perspective that instantly connected with people. Lee Laxdahl went on to become mayor. Bob Lewis spent many years as a city planning commissioner before he himself became mayor. Charlie met with them often and spoke at numerous hearings on behalf of responsible land development. They were among the local politicians and developers like Rad who called on him and respected him for the calm, sincere, but determined way he addressed growth and related issues.

The college at Ferndale Ranch: By the late 70s, Charlie was also attending many evening meetings as part of his role on the California Indian Legal Services Board. He had become so interested in archaeology that he was now a member of the Ventura Archaeological Society. Dr. Alex Kirkish, the society president and a Ventura County Public Works archaeologist, led these meetings at the Ventura County Museum. One evening, he noticed a very regular guy sitting across from him. He also noticed his long, straight, black hair combed to either side, his round face, and pronounced cheekbones.

"Hmm," Alex, thought to himself, "this might be a rough meeting. Archaeologists aren't always popular with Native Americans." And then the man smiled at him. "I'd like to meet this man," thought Alex.

They started talking after the meeting and kept talking all the way out to the parking lot.

"Neat truck, Charlie!"

"Yeah, I like trucks. I drive a cement mixer for a living, but I don't think that counts. Ever since I was a kid watching an old German fellow drive his up and down the road near our home, I wanted one of my own, so I got this one." Charlie punctuated his statement by giving his red and white Ford truck a pat.

Several more meetings and Alex noted that this big guy—who was actually a teamster—had a way with his tone of voice and his very persona that calmed people down. His statements were always reasonable. People could see that his intent was simply to find a good solution.

"Charlie, I'm doing some surveys and projects for the county. I could use your help."

"I don't know much about archaeology."

"Well, you'll learn about archaeology, and I'll learn about Native Americans."

So almost immediately Alex and Charlie started a long association. In late 1977, the Catholic Church started preparing a site for a new college, St. Thomas Aquinas, on what had been the Ferndale Ranch in Santa Paula. Alex attended many meetings at the Ventura County Government Center for environmental reviews in regard to the Aquinas development. To prepare and follow up he consulted both Charlie and Kote.

While excavating, the construction workers exhumed five bodies and brought an Indian cemetery to light. "Ah," Charlie thought, "that's why I had those odd feelings during high school when I was working here to buy that calf for my Future Farmers project!"

Charlie played a major role in resolving the conflict between finishing the construction and respecting the burials. He engaged in conversations like this one:

"We need to get on with this project," said the developer, who was losing money as his equipment sat idle.

Charlie happened to be on site that day, "I understand, but we cannot disturb our ancestors."

"What do you mean you understand? You are just interested in a long gone and dead heritage."

Charlie resisted an angry comeback. "I work in construction myself. I drive a cement mixer."

The developer's eyes widened.

"What if we re-inter the burials on the site but outside the construction zone?"

The developer was taken aback. He hesitated.

"I can work with everyone to make the reburial happen soon."

The developer scratched his head.

Calmly and with a slight smile, Charlie said, "I know you can understand how we feel about our ancestors." He spoke softly and shook his head slowly as he continued. "Certainly you would not allow someone to dig up your relatives from a few generations back and put them just anywhere."

Some more conversations on the side and in meetings, and Charlie managed to get most people involved to understand the Native American point of view regarding burials and artifacts. "Leave them in the ground where found. If that is impossible, move them close to where they were."

He helped get people together including Native American splinter groups. He calmed them down by focusing on common values—in this case respect for Indian burials. Then he called on Kote Lotah to conduct the reburial ceremony that the Indians from various groups had talked about together. As part of the ceremony, Kote rubbed his hands on a special rock as his ancestors had done to call for rain. The area had been recognized as a power spot by the Chumash with a rain rock and a fertility rock that women sat on when they hoped to become pregnant. Suddenly, rain came down in a much-needed torrent. It was July when it normally did not rain. After the ceremony, Kote warned the site supervisor, "Now, do not disturb these burials."

Calleguas Creek: Not all of Charlie's negotiations ended as he would have liked. In 1978, somewhat in parallel with the Aquinas development, workers for the Army Corps of Engineers started rechanneling Calleguas Creek for the Ventura County Water District. The creek funneled water into the ocean along the coast in Ventura County. Again, workers struck an Indian cemetery. As work progressed, the burials became exposed, started washing away, and sat right in the path of bulldozers. Alex had monitored this site some years prior and had stopped the bulldozers then, but this time the situation looked dire.

Charlie and Kote got involved. Kote was particularly adamant about burials staying right where they were found. Charlie often was okay with elsewhere but nearby. However, in this situation, Charlie concurred with Kote. The two led a group that filed a lawsuit to stop the rechanneling. In the end, the court found that the Army Corps of Engineers had followed the environmental review process established by the California Environmental Quality Act of 1970.

Work resumed. In the process, the developers hired Charlie's Indian relatives as project monitors. Eventually, the monitors agreed to have the burials re-interred some miles away at Oakbrook Park. Charlie and others believed that the burials should be kept near their original site, but he also believed it was better to re-inter than lose a battle that might result in destruction of ancestral bones and artifacts. The Calleguas controversy over the burials started an undercurrent among the local Chumash. Charlie just kept on learning about Native American customs and archaeology. He kept navigating controversies—sometimes helping settle them the way he saw fit, sometimes having to accept the outcome and move on.

The college again: Back at Aquinas in November, the developer agreed to an orange chain link fence to protect the burials from the construction work, but the site supervisor took down the fence and as a result the burials were unearthed again.

Again, Kote conducted a reburial ceremony. Again he rubbed the rain rock. Again it rained. This time Charlie told the developer that there would be serious repercussions for the disrespect that had been paid to Indian ancestors. In the back of his mind, he had an eerie feeling about the future of the site, but he couldn't put his finger on it. Six weeks later the supervisor died from a heart attack. The backhoe operator was accidentally electrocuted on site. Some believed that the ancestors, in their own way, had spoken.

Teachings of elders

Charlie was learning a lot about Chumash ceremony from Kote at Aquinas and elsewhere, who in turn had learned from a highly respected man Southern California Indians called Grandfather Victor. Victor Lopez lived as an ordinary youth and then went to work for the forest service. One day on his rounds, he encountered a Chumash elder named Justo camping next to a rock shelter in the Santa Susana Mountains in Simi. Justo lived simply with a wooden bucket for water, a fire hearth, and a table he made from mountain wood. Deerskins lined the wooden bed he had made from willow. The elder scolded young Victor for his ordinary ways, admonished him to start acting like a Chumash, and strongly suggested he learn Chumash spiritual teachings.

Time after time, Victor sat on the ground next to Justo and his coyote. He listened, asked questions, and listened some more. Victor stayed dedicated to his forest service job protecting lands and resources, but Justo helped him understand who he really was. The elder performed a naming ceremony.

Victor became Sky Eagle. Justo taught Sky Eagle Chumash spirituality and medicine which started the handoffs to Kote, Charlie, and others.

Kote spent long days and nights with Grandfather Sky Eagle. He listened to Grandfather's old stories, his instructions on the ways of ceremonies and medicine, and to his accounts of Chumash history. He also saw the pride Grandfather Victor had in wearing the forest service uniform. He took seriously protecting the land of his ancestors for all then and now. In the process of teaching Kote, Grandfather said to the young man, "You have to know who you are and where you come from. Anything and everything is about our cultural and genealogical line. It was there for us from the beginning, if you know how to retrieve it. Nothing is lost, just people forgot how to retrieve it."

Kote conveyed by example and words to the local Chumash that they needed to honor Grandfather Victor, Sky Eagle, whom he saw as a master of the art of retrieving Chumash history. Charlie continued to learn from Kote. The two agreed that their quest to bring their Chumash history and heritage alive was central to honoring Grandfather Victor.

Charlie's wild days were far behind him now, no time for anything but his family, his job, and Native American causes.

As a new decade was dawning, Charlie had made a mark among Native American leaders, anthropologists, archaeologists, park leadership, politicians, and the people at large. Some were yet to find out about him as they conducted their own marches toward preservation, but those who knew him were starting to call on him more and more.

Man, I am talking to a chief! Here I was suddenly on the islands, the birthplace of the Chumash. I was so happy Charlie came into my life. I needed someone like him. I could ask him anything about the Chumash on the islands. I really wanted to get to know him and get his advice. Charlie is knowledgeable and confident about cultural resources. He is a man of few words but when he speaks it is well thought out. He makes a huge presence. (Bill Ehorn, first Superintendent, Channel Islands National Park, June 9, 2011)

Wow, the chief of the Southern Chumash lived on my street! There was a profound sense about him, a communication skill that reached long range, like that of the whale. Both he and I believed in walking gently on the land. (Vicki Goldschlager)

Charlie played a major role in resolving the native burials issue while building St. Thomas Aquinas College. People were up in arms: some incensed about irreparable damage done to native burials, others focused on the building project. Charlie helped calm people by getting them together. He'd say things like, "We can work this out." and proceeded with that mantra. He has the ability to calm people down. He does not get excited easily. The words he uses, his tone of voice, what he projects, his persona, all play a part in how he moves people to a good solution. (Dr. Alex Kirkish).

I saw him dealing with developers. I was at thousands of hearings and he was at many. Others came to City Council and claimed to be chief. However, Charlie spoke most credibly—never a hidden agenda. I never saw anyone try to attack Charlie—to say that what he was speaking was not accurate. Instead of trying to discredit him, they tried to come up with a solution. I saw respect for Charlie from developers. (Bob Lewis, Former Planning Commissioner and Mayor of Thousand Oaks, CA. March 31, 2012)

How Charlie worked with developers: It's a chemistry—a mirror. If they were reasonable, honest, and forward so was Charlie. He helped to find a solution. If not, Charlie stuck to what he was asking for. The community would back him up. There was politics on all sides: non-Indians using native heritage and sites to further their agendas even when not real, and some people becoming professional Indians, not Charlie. He was an Indian but did not use that for commercial purpose or to market himself. That's what makes him so different. (Rad Sutnar, CEO of Sutnar Consulting Plus, former executive for Shapell Industries and Prudential Insurance Company of America, Real Estate Division, April 21, 2012)

While we could not keep the land as it was forever, we could save the history through artifacts and burials. In 1852, the San Francisco Land Grant for Newhall and Saugus gave 350 acres an individual but the Spanish Land Grab took it all. We all need to live in harmony and understand that some things are in the past. Fight the wars we lost in a different way. Different way—get recognition that we exist and are here. (Alvin Cooke)

He was always sticking up for ancestors at cultural sites; he was one of the ones who slowed down the bulldozers. He was able to mediate many communities, many professions at the same time. He was out there before CEQA, before it was cool, with no money, no resources, but ingenuity and stubbornness. (Dr. Wendy Teeter, Curator of Archaeology, Fowler Museum, UCLA, February 9, 2009)

TIQ SLO'W, The Making of a Modern Day Chief

Chapter 6: More causes, friends, and allies, 1974-79

"Yeah, he takes off work to . . ." and the sentence drowns in the rumbling of trucks.

At the weigh station in Santa Paula, Patty Garcia had heard from other truck drivers even before she came to work for Livingston Graham that Charlie took time off to make sure native sites and burials were respected by developers. As she got to know Charlie, she told him she was Chumash, that she and her husband, Richard, also a cement mixer driver, had found artifacts on a Ventura beach, and that she was fighting an Ojai development as a concerned California Indian. Patty was getting around. Ojai was about 15 miles inland from the Ventura Beach.

<u>Respect for burials</u>

Charlie told Patty, "There in Ojai, tell them who you are and ask what they plan to do if they hit a burial."

Then Charlie asked her to meet him at Reyes Adobe, a historic ranch house owned by the Los Angeles County Park and Recreation Department on a site close to the Ventura and Los Angeles County line. Archaeologists had found evidence of Chumash life at the Reyes Adobe site. Charlie was monitoring to make sure any burials that were excavated were treated with respect.

Charlie called Kote out to Reyes Adobe because Kote was working on burial issues at Hammond Meadows in Santa Barbara. Eventually, all three, Charlie, Kote, and Patty, got involved in strengthening laws to keep burials in the ground. The California Native American Historical, Cultural, and Sacred Sites Act, passed in 1976, made it possible to stop development projects under certain conditions. As a result, the three were continually making recommendations regarding burial sites on development projects, be they federal, state, county, city, or private lands. Charlie was particularly creative in solving problems so that developers could move forward yet respect Indian heritage. For example, when burials were found on a highway project, Charlie recommended that a 12-foot trench be dug at the median and the burials be re-interred there. They were, and the highway project finished allowing more reasonable commutes for a growing population.

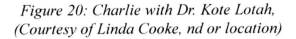

*Figure 20: Charlie with Dr. Kote Lotah,
(Courtesy of Linda Cooke, nd or location)*

Clay Singer had returned to the LA area in 1975 and started doing work that involved California Indian sites. He quickly became concerned about desecration of burial sites in the Conejo Valley. This valley, north of Los Angeles, was within commuting distance and growing fast. When Clay needed Indian input to a project, he did not know how to arrange for it. His professors, after all, had not believed in the value of contacting modern Indians, believing that any cultural knowledge they had would be book learned. Clay tried the Indian Center in Culver City. They told him to go to bars downtown to find Indians. He did, but did not find any.

When Clay uncovered an Indian burial site at a proposed development, he contacted another anthropologist-archaeologist he knew, Dr. Alex Kirkish. Alex introduced him to Chief Charlie Cooke at a burial site in Northridge, 20 miles east of the Conejo Valley. He noted his cordial but focused demeanor, already part of his identity. Not too long after, he needed the permission of California Indians for another dig. Finally, he knew who he needed to contact. He went to a construction site where Charlie was working. There was Charlie expecting him. No tattoos, no long hair, no native dress, just a strong physique dressed as an everyday truck driver. "So," thought Clay, "the professors don't know everything! California Indians are alive, not extinct, and they look like the rest of us! "

"Charlie, there are burials at the site I am working on. I need to tell you, I am working there for the developer."

"Can you move them to a place close by?"

Dust swirled among all the rock and gravel at the site, and it was noisy. The grinding roll of other trucks reverberated all around them as Charlie asked, "Clay, what's your heritage?"

"I'm not Native American, if that's what you mean. I'm of Eastern European and Polish extraction."

"Well, then, why aren't you investigating your own heritage?"

"Right now, I'm interested in yours."

Before they knew it, they were bantering back and forth, joking with each other and saying almost the same thing at the same time:

"You can't transmit heritage by blood."

"Culture is transmitted in the mind."

"DNA might cause you to catch a disease not culture."

"Some Native Americans don't know much about their own culture."

Charlie told Clay to call him, finished with the job, and drove back to the scale house next to the Livingston Graham site in Santa Paula. His mixer was getting weighed off to the side as he chatted with other drivers while he waited. Once in a while he would hear rumors of Indian sites being buried under concrete throughout the area.

"Hey, Charlie, your truck is good to go," the young weigh master shouted.

He was still chatting with his fellow truck drivers. Patty could hear some of the conversation and noted that Charlie stayed calm no matter how heated the discussion became. Now they were laughing. Patty recognized Charlie's hearty laugh. It cheered her up.

"Charlie . . ."

"Okay, Patty, I'm coming. Sorry to keep you waiting"

Clay got the permission he needed as long as he proceeded with respect. Clay worked with the developer to make sure that the burials were moved and reburied with respect. The Porter Ranch development in the northwest San Fernando Valley went up after some controversy. The controversy focused on traffic and the environment, not burials since that issue had been handled. Charlie opened doors for Clay. But the chief would call on him to return the favors.

Prankster and problem solver

Charlie was still a member of the Indian Legal Services Board, and now so was Vince Ibanez. The meetings, held in Sacramento, were serious, dealing with helping Indians with property, civil accusations, and family law issues, but that did not keep Charlie from having a little fun. After these meetings a number of the board members would go to a restaurant nearby. One night, a rather pompous board member slipped his jacket over the back of his chair, sat down, and started talking, and talking, and talking. Charlie slipped a spoon into the fellow's jacket pocket. Vince saw this and slipped a fork into another pocket. Charlie and Vince kept slipping silverware into the jacket as the man continued on with his braggadocio. Finally, they were done with dinner. The man stood up, still talking, and reached for his jacket. Metal hit the floor, piece after piece. At first he was angry, but then he had to laugh along with everyone else.

Charlie worked seriously with Vince as an advisor on some of his projects, no joking matters. Vince by now was also a NAHC commissioner and called on Charlie in that capacity. Charlie found himself in Sacramento helping to resolve a situation with burials under a proposed shopping center parking lot. A collaborative solution: cap the burials. He gathered people to help the Synkyone Tribe in the Bay Area who were protesting clear cutting on their ancestral land. The Synkyones won that fight and got a wilderness area and state park out of it. Sometimes, Charlie's input was so simple and obvious, but for some reason not so to others. Vince was monitoring at Leo Cabrillo State Park. He stopped by San Juan Capistrano where Charlie was working on an archaeological site. People were looking at bones thinking they were human but were confused because the bones were very big. "Look at the ends," Charlie said. "They are cut. What we have here are butchered cattle bones."

At home, it was another late evening at another meeting and then another. Charlie drove his truck by day and visited sites in the late afternoon and attended meetings by night. Some weeks he'd attend three or four meetings. Some would not adjourn until 1 a.m. and then he'd be in his truck on his way to work by 6:30 a.m. While the boys were growing up, Linda was a stay-at-home-mom. Sometimes it seemed to Linda that she was raising the boys alone.

Point Conception: arguing for the environment and a sacred site

"We do not all agree on this project . . ."

Charlie was at a hearing held by the California Coastal Commission, listening to arguments about building a $1.6 billion Western Liquid Natural Gas (WLNG) terminal site and pipeline at Point Conception. He knew the

Coastal Commission had been established in 1972 to identify and prevent ecological and environmental damage to the California Coast and to protect it for posterity, which was aligned with his concerns.

He had been listening for a while now about where a gas line was to be laid. Charlie knew he would not make it home tonight to watch Damon and Jason playing a pick-up soccer game with friends. They were in junior high now. He pictured coaching their Mighty Mights team when they were six and seven and going fishing with them on occasion.

The discussion playing out in front of him brought him back to where he was this evening, the Lohero Theater in Santa Barbara. He was there to watch, not give testimony. Other Indian people were there too. It was already late in the process. Construction was about to start on a piece of land that jets out where the Santa Barbara Channel meets the Pacific Ocean. It is a breathtakingly beautiful spot, with waves crashing on rocks and birds soaring overhead.

"Point Conception is where the Chumash enter the spirit world. A gas line would disturb the area." Charlie heard a Chumash elder speak and his ears perked up.

"All Chumash do not believe that souls pass from this mortal world to paradise at the Point." Charlie heard an emphatic, opposing point of view.

And then another speaker stood up. "I have a few last statements . . ." Dr. Chester King had come down from San Jose where he worked for the archeological firm that had prepared the report. He was summarizing. Charlie had listened to every word Dr. King said. "The land, the sea, and my heritage are all at stake here," he thought. The meeting was over and people were dispersing.

"I'm glad to meet you, Charlie. I understand you are a member of the California Indian Legal Services Board. Do you know Dennis Hoptowit?"

"Oh, of course, he's an Indian lawyer working with the board."

"I've worked with him too."

"Good, then you understand our issues out at Point Conception—about protecting the environment you talked about and our native beliefs." Charlie made sure he and Chester were on the same page.

Charlie went home and settled back into driving his cement truck and to weekend activities, sometimes with his family, sometimes on the behalf of Native Americans. Sometimes, his weekends were about riding and roping.

Rodeo: cowboys and neighbors

A calf was charging across the dirt at the Lang Ranch in Agoura, inland and not too far from Charlie's Newbury Park home. Charlie roped him quickly and wrestled him to the ground, similar as he might do at a rodeo, but this was as a cowboy. He was there helping on the weekend with the branding. Afterwards he enjoyed the camaraderie of friends at a barbecue with Linda and their two boys in tow. These weekend volunteer cowboy stints were akin to barn raisings. It was important to help out friends and neighbors. He also participated in roping club events. It was fun on the ranches and in the rodeo arenas, but the coast was calling.

Figure 21: Charlie (on white horse) and Smokey Lang winning a Camarillo Roping Club event (Courtesy of Linda Cooke, 1978)

Figure 22: Charlie on Blue with rope (Courtesy of Linda Cooke, 1970s)

The Point Conception occupation

The waves were crashing and the sea gulls, brown pelicans, and terns were soaring and diving into the water as a group of men built Indian shelters and moved supplies around. Like at Alcatraz, a group of Indians was occupying the point. They were protesting the proposed gas line. And like at Alcatraz, Charlie felt he needed to be there.

"Clay, I need for you to join me at Point Conception. Can you make it?" Charlie was on the phone to his friend.

"I'll be there."

When Charlie arrived, he saw a native medicine man burning sage in an abalone shell and turning to raise it to the four winds. It was Dr. Kote Lotah, who by now was recognized by some conventional MDs as a healer. He noticed a traditional native sweat lodge not too far from the shore. Clay Singer arrived around the same time, now fully invested in learning from Indians. Clay and Charlie were only there a few days, but they helped to move supplies and build aps.

"Hey, Kote, how many of these aps should we build?"

"Just keep building. There's more tule over there."

The aps were dome-shaped huts with a skeleton of willow branches thatched over with tule, also known as bulrush.

"We're about done with the first row."

"Make sure the second row overlaps, like shingles to keep the rain out"

Charlie, Clay, and others were recreating an ancient village along the seacoast.

"Kote, how long do you expect to be here?" Charlie asked as he started another row of tule.

"As long as it takes to make sure the Western Liquid Natural Gas Processing Plant is not built here—and no pipeline here." Kote's eyes were intense as they had been when he declared that Charlie was their chief.

"Chester is still working on the environmental impact report. Maybe that will help."

The evenings were full of stars in a clear dark sky. Clay, Kote, and some others sat around a fire inside the ap they had finished that day. They could hear the waves as they ate fish from the sea right outside their door. They told stories as the smoke rose through the hole they had left at the top, just as did their ancestors until they moved to the missions.

Clay asked, "How are you and Linda doing with your horses, Charlie?"

Charlie told stories about Idaho Mail Man, Old Jim, and other horses he had ridden over the years. "I still have old Blue. But I am the only one who can stand to ride him. Linda and a friend of hers took him and her horse on a trail the other day. Neither girl could stand Blue for long, so they took turns riding him. They came home complaining. They really couldn't control him like they wanted."

"But Linda's an expert rider."

"Yes, but Blue charges. He's not a smooth ride. Now that horse of Linda's, that's a smooth ride. But what a grouch—just like his name! He's mean to the horses in the coral. Give me old Blue anytime. They can have Grouch!"

And then Charlie left the point and went back to work driving the cement mixer truck by day and attending meetings at night and on weekends. Again he had learned more about Native American ceremonies and traditions from Kote. He also was learning more and more from anthropologists and archaeologists. He would work with practitioners like Dr. Chester King and talk with professors like Dr. Lowell Bean. At the same time he was starting to engage on the civic front.

Coordinated advocacies, Santa Monica Mountains Conservancy established

The four preservation advocates who spanned the mountains and coast from the San Fernando Valley to Ventura—Jill Swift, Sue Nelson, Margot Feuer, and Dave Brown—with many others amassed along the way had continued the push to protect the area. Several U.S. congressmen had authored bills to put the mountains into the National Park System, but the bills had not yet made it all the way through the political system.

In the spring of 1976, the California State Legislature established the Santa Monica Mountains Comprehensive Planning Commission. In February 1977, Governor Jerry Brown appointed Joseph T. Edmiston as Executive Director of the Commission. The Legislature adopted the Santa Monica Mountains Comprehensive Plan in February 1979 and enacted the legislation creating the Santa Monica Mountains Conservancy (SMM Conservancy), effective January 1, 1980, with Joe Edmiston as its executive director. Part of the conservancy's original mission was to acquire open spaces in the Santa Monica Mountains and turn them over to permanent caretaker agencies such as the National Park Service and the California

State Parks, and then sunset, in other words dissolve and go off the books, in 1981. State and federal issues in the early 1980s stalled any such land transfers, leaving the conservancy as the caretaker agency. The Legislature thus extended the conservancy's sunset date several times and eventually made it a permanent state agency. Many of the open spaces acquired by the conservancy since its inception, were originally inhabited by the Chumash and Tongva peoples.

The Chumash, in particular, were becoming very active in the Conejo Valley area. Several seemed to be vying to be the legitimate spokesman for the Chumash people. In fact, local media were reporting that several Native Americans were claiming to be chiefs or at least leaders of various groups. Ed Heidig, who was working with Joe, suggested that Joe meet with these people individually. Some of these individuals told Joe not to talk to anyone else if he wanted their cooperation. When he met with Charlie, he saw a big, jolly, roly-poly bear of a guy. He seemed very easy to deal with. He made no demands. He saw that Charlie was living a real workingman's life and did not define himself solely as an advocate. Charlie's sphere of influence kept growing by his being committed to preserving, but also by sharing his knowledge of the natural and cultural resources that the Chumash, Tongva, and other Native Americans in this and nearby areas had stewarded for thousands of years.

The occupation ends

A little over 14 months after Charlie left Point Conception, the occupation ended. Kote and another Native American, WAN-SAK, were the last ones to leave the site, but not before two encampments and one takeover. In the end, Kote was arrested, as he understood the charges, for taking over the guards, retaking the point, illegal praying, and vandalism. He was offered five days in jail or community service at a hospital. Since the hospital would only let him sweep floors rather than come in as a Chumash doctor; he chose jail. He believed that the California Indian Legal Services fund was involved in bailing him out. It was over, but not really.

I couldn't have done what I did as well without knowing Charlie. It would have been less rewarding. I was peripheral to the Chumash culture when I met him. Native families were an influence on me. Charlie's was one of those families. Charlie listened to what I had to say and I to him. (Clay Singer, anthropologist, July 9, 2009)

Charlie advanced the recognition of Chumash culture while being fully functional in the modern world. Others have their place. For example one of Charlie's protégés, Mati Waiya, draws attention to the native story with wonderful drama. In contrast, Charlie is a gentle giant. Their core values are the same. They exemplify them differently.

Some of Charlie's native brethren can be contentious. Charlie was to give an invocation at an event at Temescal Canyon some years ago, a place that was a borderline between Tongva and Chumash areas. After the event, a certain Tongva called me to complain that Charlie gave a blessing in a Tongva area, but was not Tongva. [Charlie actually is part Tongva.] Charlie would not make a call like that. Charlie does not put lines in the sand. That is probably why we are talking about Charlie and not some others. (Joe Edmiston, Executive Director, Santa Monica Mountains Conservancy, July 7, 2011)

Charlie is a guy who does not take no for an answer. He is going to work with you until you see the light. In the day, Charlie was there . . . Where we were, he was there. Whatever we were doing, he was helping us. (Vincent Ibanez, former NAHC Commissioner and CILS Board member, Pechanga Elder, quoted from recorded interview of March 6, 2012)

Chapter 7: Seeing what the ancestors saw, 1979-83

From one contact after another Charlie became involved with the Northridge Archeological Research Center (NARC) at California State University at Northridge (CSUN). NARC hosted talks and was also involved in archaeological digs. Clay Singer was the director of NARC and was also teaching at CSUN.

"Listen to what Native Americans have to say and involve them as monitors on archaeological digs," he told his students almost chuckling to himself, remembering quite different advice he had heard as a student.

Interest in rock art sites

Charlie came to NARC meetings and got involved with some of the digs. Through NARC he met some more archaeologists, Gwen and John Romani, Dan Larson, and a student who was taking Professor Singer very seriously, Bryn Barabas Potter. *Crystals in the Sky*, by Travis Hudson and Ernest Underhay, published in 1978, sparked an interest among California anthropologists about the possible astronomical purposes of rock art. John Romani speculated that a rock art site in the Santa Susana Mountains involved astronomy. Soon Charlie found himself hiking into the mountains to study ancient painted and carved rock, pictographs and petroglyphs, with John, Gwen, Dan, Bryn, and others.

Figure 23: Pictograph, undisclosed site, (SMMNRA Archives, c 1982)

The group arrived at a parking lot in the Santa Susana Mountains. It was about 4 a.m. on the summer solstice in 1983. On this hike, Dr. Edwin Krupp, editor of *In Search of Ancient Astronomies*, published in 1977, joined the group. They took off into the hills, through brush and under trees until they reached an open area with large flat rocks in a bear paw configuration—a center stone with three other stones lining it on one side.

Dr. Krupp talked for a short while, explaining what they would see. He pointed to a notch in the hills where the sun would rise and then create a shadow across the palm of the bear paw which was the slab of stone with mortar holes in it on the ground in front of them. The sky started to lighten. John Romani talked about how the petroglyphs at this site were some of the finest rock art in Southern California. Chester King was along and he added that the site was on the National Register of Historic Places. Charlie and Bryn asked a few questions. The sun started to rise behind one of the hills. Everyone fixed their eyes on the center rock, and then they saw it.

A shadow struck the center pad of the bear paw right where Dr. Krupp said it would. Charlie watched the same solstice phenomenon that his ancestors had seen. He added rock art and solstice sites to his fights for Native American preservation. This hike and the professionals on it added to the circle that was deepening his knowledge of archaeology and related science, but a subtle trade was going on. Like Clay Singer and others that Charlie had befriended, Dr. Krupp initially had little direct familiarity with Chumash or California Indians. Charlie influenced others by his very being.

Before I met Charlie Cooke, California Indians were something I only knew from books. They were, for me, an ancient presence in California and part of California history. Charlie, on the other hand, was an unexpected experience. He was a first-hand encounter with Chumash today. Not only are the Chumash still around, they live and work in Southern California like the rest of us. So, getting to know Charlie was a revelation and a pleasure. That contact with Charlie always enriched my understanding and altered my perspective. Whenever we met to examine a rock art site, he was collaborative, cooperative, enthusiastic, and engaged. Working with him was always a conversation, from which, I think, we both felt better informed. Charlie excels at one-on-one relationships. I count myself lucky to be one of those ones. (Dr. Edwin C. Krupp, Director, Griffith Observatory, quoted from email of May 4, 2012)

Figure 24: Undisclosed Summer Solstice site, Dr. Ed Krupp on ladder,
Charlie Cooke below (SMMNRA Archives, nd)

Concern for open spaces

In the same time frame, Charlie was involved with some land preservation campaigns in Topanga Canyon, an area of beautiful ridgelines, steep canyon walls, flowing streams, and with both Chumash and Tongva history, a wide-open expanse that his ancestors also saw. Charlie worked with TASC (Topanga Association for a Scenic Community), with Sue Nelson, and with others on fundraisers to buy some land and stop its development. He brought together Native American leaders in support of making the area a protected area and parkland. In the end, Joe Edmiston was instrumental in purchasing some of the land for the Santa Monica Mountains National Recreation Area (SMMNRA). Eventually, it became part of Topanga State Park and part of SMMNRA.

Dr. Krupp also visited Topanga Canyon for one reason or another. One day he saw a truck parked in a canyon shopping center by a canyon store. Its bumper sticker read, "Chumash and proud of it." At the time, he had no idea who it belonged to.

Charlie gives his time and energy to the Native American movement and at the same time is a constant learner and quiet teacher. He is extremely knowledgeable about the area, about Native Americans, about history, about the Chumash from working with archaeologists like me but also from the oral tradition of his family. His family has been here for over 1000 years. Regarding rocks, plants, and animals of the area, he is encyclopedic. I gained a better appreciation of Chumash through Charlie, not only their history but also that the Chumash are not static, but changing. (Dr. Alex Kirkish)

Charlie's narrative encompasses other California Indian families. He makes the point, "We are still here and proud of our identities." He is a compelling leader and was a key at an important cross road in Southern California native history. He led or participated in the formation of the San Fernando Mission Band and California Indian Legal Services. He was active in protecting burials and sacred sites. (Dr. John Johnson)

Charlie does not describe himself as a traditionalist and yet he embodies traditional values. You will see him talking shoulder-to-shoulder with a Native American man rather than face-to-face. His connection to anthropologists and archaeologists has to do with learning and teaching about the land and influencing its future. (Phil Holmes, April 4, 2011)

Charlie understands that some change will happen. He deals in the real world and accepts it. He is not an extreme activist, but his values are Native American values. He likes the land and is proud of his heritage. He strongly values social ties and maintaining them. He has a sense of etiquette. He is conscious of place in relation to other people. (Dr. Chester King)

PART THREE, PLANNING THE FUTURE: Joining forces with parks and archaeologists

How does this supposedly unsophisticated person have this very broad view of what a park should be, how it can be useful to people, and how it can relate to Indian culture specifically? How does a person who does not appear to be directive become a leader of how things happen for the future of a place? How does an American Indian, whose culture was looked at by some as less than equal at the time, turn out to be such an effective proponent?

He drove up in his cement truck and clamored out of the cab. He was in work clothes—shirt, jeans, and baseball cap. He came across as totally genuine and very honest. What nice eyes he had! You couldn't help but trust him because of the way he looked at us. He was sure of what he believed—always willing to communicate that, but not in a directive manner. Every time you'd see him, you'd light up inside. (John Reynolds, first Assistant Superintendent, SMMNRA, May 5, 2011)

Map 5: Santa Monica Mountain Recreation Area and Related Locations
(Courtesy of James Mansfield)

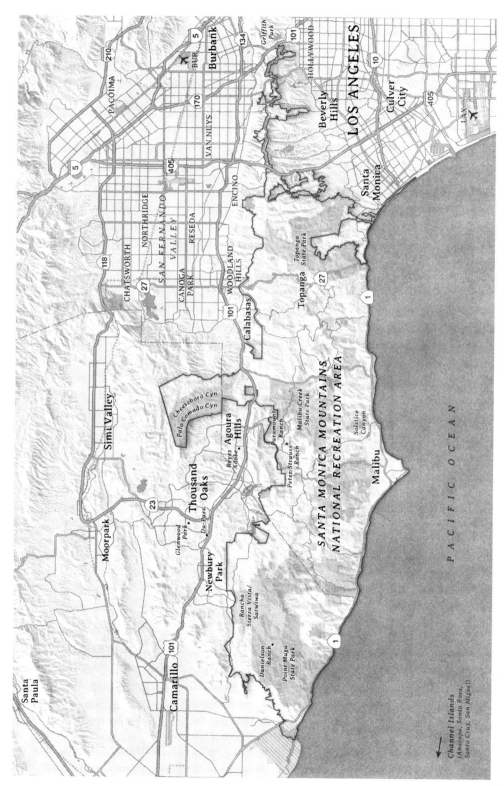

115

Chapter 8: New In Town, 1979-80

Rolling hills and mountains with magnificent rock outcroppings, dotted with yucca, prickly pear, scrub oaks, and other native Southern California plants, and then more rolling hills and mountains. And now this view would be preserved.

Bob Chandler winds off the 101 Freeway, at the Borchard Road exit in Newbury Park, just west of Thousand Oaks and about halfway between Los Angeles and Santa Barbara. As he makes his way through the small town he can see a large rocky bluff in the distance. These are the same hills and rocky bluff that has had the 98-year-old woman wondering for over 30 years about what happened to the native peoples who had inhabited the area.

Bob was making his way into the western Santa Monica Mountains from his new office on Ventura Boulevard in the Woodland Hills area of the San Fernando Valley. There was one piece of land out there he wanted to visit right under the bluffs, the Danielson Ranch. The California State Park System had acquired part of it already and renamed it Point Mugu State Park, a park that sloped from mountaintop to ocean. NPS was trying to acquire the rest. Bob had just left his post as a superintendent at the Jefferson National Expansion Memorial, an urban National Park with the Gateway Arch in St. Louis as its centerpiece. What a change! Some thought it was the end of his career, but not Bob. Rugged landscapes and growing cityscapes coexisting! He was ready for the challenge.

NPS officially in the mountains

The four Santa Monica Mountain advocates had found each other at meetings about the mountains and when lobbying in Washington, D.C. where they interacted with California representatives across party lines, Phil Burton, Anthony Beilenson, and Barry Goldwater, Jr. Finally they had success.

In November 1978, Congress established the Santa Monica Mountains National Recreation Area (SMMNRA) by passing U.S. Congressman Phil Burton's non-partisan Omnibus Park Bill. The bipartisan support was a factor, as well as the lobbying spearheaded by Congressman Beilenson. SMMNRA was only one of the sites established in that bill, but it was one of the biggest.

Bob was here in January 1979 as the first superintendent of the newly formed recreation area that spans an area along the coast and several miles inland from Griffith Park in Los Angeles to Point Mugu in Ventura County. But Bob's job was just beginning. This was a complicated recreation area, out of the usual NPS paradigm—and before he could finalize plans at Danielson or anywhere else, he knew he had to make the rounds of established state, city, and county parks in an effort to get to know and hear from people.

Today his stop was at Glenwood Park in Thousand Oaks in the Conejo Valley. It was a typical city park, with a small building, a playing field, barbecue grills, and picnic tables. A number of people there had come to hear what the new guy in town had to say.

He talked about the opportunity they had together to create a new and needed approach for a national park across these stunning mountains interlaced with existing city, county, state, federal, and private holdings spanning rural and urban environments.

Figure 25: Superintendent Bob Chandler speaking to a crowd in the Santa Monica Mountains, Charlie at left in sunglasses, holding staff (SMMNRA Archives, nd)

Native heritage introduced to first SMMNRA leadership

By now Charlie was well associated with Native American causes in the area. He was doing less and less roping and instead was deftly moving in all the circles that mattered to preserving native heritage. He was at park meetings, city council meetings, Heritage Commission meetings, Legal Service Council meetings, and land development hearings. He was walking and riding in the hills and valleys where his ancestors had trod, and as he was finding, were buried. All along he was learning more and more about anthropology and archaeology.

Charlie also attended gatherings he knew were important to preserving native heritage. He had been at Glenwood and heard Bob speak. He was not going to lose his chance with the visionary new superintendent. So very shortly afterwards, Charlie stopped on his way home from work at Bob's office on Ventura Boulevard in the San Fernando Valley. With no hesitation, he walked right in. It was about 5 p.m.

"Hello, Mr. Chandler, I'd like to be one of the first to welcome you. I hope I am not interrupting. I'm sure you have your hands full with just arriving in town and all."

"Please sit down. What can I do for you?"

Charlie smiled warmly. "I was there at Glenwood. I am Chumash, one of the original peoples of this area . . ."

"Oh, glad you came by! I intend to learn all about this area."

"We inhabited this area up and down the coast and on the islands for thousands of years. We lost our heritage for a while when we were in the missions, but we're still here. Some of us are still on ranches as cowboys, but you'll find us in all walks of life."

"Do you ride, Charlie?"

"In my spare time. I ride and rope as a hobby, less and less now though. I drive a cement mixer for a living. Got to support the family, you know."

"Yes, I understand."

"Do you have a family?"

"My wife, two sons, and daughter. They aren't here yet."

"It's a great place for a family,"

And Charlie drifted into the Chumash respect for family—children and elders, ability to live off the lush land and bountiful sea, their ability to hunt and fish, their long tradition of gathering plants for food and medicine. Bob, always a learner, asked some questions along the way. Charlie thought about all the other things he wanted to talk about: powwows, native dancers, the shell monetary system, waterproof baskets, and the magnificent trading vessel, the tomol. He wanted to talk about how their traditions and heritage were almost lost, but he sensed he'd have more chances. As he was starting to say good-bye, he saw a spark and asked, "What do you think about creating a site in the new recreation area that celebrates Native American people?"

"I want to know more so I can seriously think about it."

The two talked a while longer and then Charlie left. He wanted to check on his horses. He needed to get home to Newbury Park about forty miles north before too late. Besides, he appreciated that Bob had graciously fit him in on one of his first days in the new job.

Bob started to go through some items on his desk. He thought to himself, "Who is this man? Was he representing himself or the Chumash? It's clear he wants to make sure that the new national park will promote Native American recognition. I see that right off. He could have been aggressive and pushy, but instead he was soft spoken. He was very nice."

Charlie became a constant reminder to Bob of Native American representation at the park. He stopped in several times a week on his way home from work no matter where the office was. Bob moved it a few times over the next few years—at first to a few locations in the San Fernando Valley. Charlie was working in the Valley at Chatsworth nearby at the time. He'd park his huge, grey, crusty mixer truck right outside and pop in about 4:30 in the afternoon. His message was consistent.

"Good afternoon, Bob. How are we coming along with the plans for a native cultural center?"

And the next week, "Good afternoon, Bob. How are we coming along with the plans for a native cultural center? I attended a homeowners meeting over there near Danielson Ranch. A developer is planning on building on that property. The bluffs there are a sacred area."

Figure 26: Danielson Ranch (SMMNRA Archives, 1975)

Like Joe Edmiston, Bob learned that no one in the area officially spoke for the Chumash—but over time learned that Charlie's voice was trusted in the broader Native American and nonnative communities. He saw a well-spoken man with a friendly demeanor.

As more time went on, Bob noticed people got a good feeling from Charlie. He conveyed that he was there to show his interest for what he cared about most. Bob never saw him contribute to conflict. He was calm in his expression, but did not hesitate to speak out for the future of the area.

New SMMNRA staff gets unsolicited local input

Bob started asking people about the Chumash. At first he got blank stares, but he remained determined to learn about the land and its people. He started hiring staff with specific expertise needed for this new kind of park. Just as important, they had to be enthusiastic and open to learning.

He hired Bill Anderson as his management assistant. Bill had been at Golden Gate National Recreation Area. Golden Gate was an urban park with many of the same challenges that SMMNRA would be facing.

Bob hired John Reynolds, from the NPS Denver Service Center, as his assistant superintendent with responsibilities for long-range planning for SMMNRA. The Denver Center handled all planning, design, and construction for the Park Service so John had that experience. But perhaps, just as important, John had experience with Native Americans not only with the Alaska Land Bridge but from way back as a youngster. He grew up on national park sites. He went to school and played with Indians at the Pipestone National Monument in Minnesota where his father was superintendent. He and his family participated in their yearly pageants, including traditional dancing with friends and classmates.

Bill Anderson hired Marti Leicester to oversee educational programs. Bill and Marti hired Bill Redmond as a ranger in charge of large events. Bill Redmond had been organizing folk festivals and the Renaissance Fair in Agoura for years, an event that could draw 20,000 people over its run. Nancy Fries came to SMMNRA as a planner from the NPS Denver Service Center. Bill Ehorn started attending SMMNRA meetings since the Channel Islands had been discussed as a part of the same park.

Charlie started dropping by after work more and more often, but so did others. By summer of 1979 people showed up at headquarters and at public forums with two different attitudes: those who liked the idea of NPS saving the mountains, people like Dave Brown who knew a lot about natural resources in the mountains; and a large group concerned about the government taking their land. In addition, there was a large majority with no feelings at all about the new recreation area.

Those in support and those with concerns came by to talk to Bob and some of his staff on a constant basis.

"So Mr. Chandler, if the Park Service wants my prime land, I will sell for . . ."

Bob and his staff would take offers under consideration. But first they needed to understand the natural and cultural assets of all the land in the recreation area.

"When are you going to make up your mind about that land next to where we're developing?"

Bob and his staff knew that developers worried that NPS acquisitions might affect or stop their developments.

"We have a private and very successful recreational facility."

Bob and his staff believed that private recreational facilities such as camps and vacation ranches could continue to operate. After all the mountains had always been here, and they had enjoyed a synergy with these private concerns so far.

And in the middle of all these comments,

"You know the Chumash built their homes and fed themselves with what they found in these mountains. They were a peaceful people blessed by nature's bounty." It was Charlie on one of his almost daily visits.

The enthusiastic response from the staff, "How about if you come along next time we go exploring and show us what you mean?"

Advocacy groups for hiking, biking, riding, and other interests came to the office. They also came to public hearings. The hearings were a vehicle to gain input to both the Land Protection and General Management Plans. Charlie attended many of these hearings.

In addition, Native American groups started to become involved with the newly arrived National Park Service staff, groups such as Candelaria, and Indian Center West in Culver City.

Figure 27: Bob Chandler at a SMMNRA meeting, Sue Nelson and Carey Peck at the table. (SMMNRA Archives, c. 1980)

SMMNRA solicits input to its management plan

By the spring of 1980, NPS formed an advisory commission for the recreation area. Charlie attended the monthly meetings and continued to appear at the office after driving his cement truck all day to talk about whatever the staff was working on.

"Hi, Ruth, how's it going out there?"

Ruth Kilday had returned home to the Santa Monica Mountains after being on staff at Golden Gate National Recreation Area. She was the new public information officer for SMMNRA and liaison to the Advisory Commission. Her family had been ranchers in the area so she knew the beaches and canyons nearby well. She saw right off that Charlie had a deep knowledge of the local geography. He appreciated her knowledge as well and said so.

"It's good that a rancher's daughter from around here is working on park issues."

Ruth showed Charlie a draft of the new park brochure she was putting together and then took off to make some end-of-the-day calls.

"Hey, Lady, how are you? What's going on?" he said to Nancy Fries.

"I'm working on the management plan for the mountains as usual."

"Anything else? How are we including the Channel Islands?" Charlie had no idea that this question had more than one aspect to it.

"I'm not ready to talk about that," Nancy had an inkling that Charlie sensed something she was not ready to share. "Here, look at this map, Charlie. Do you know anything about this location?" And of course he did. The staff had learned by now that talking to Charlie was a good way to accumulate knowledge about the mountains. They saw him as friendly, never adversarial, and always helpful.

Soon Bob and his staff realized that the new Santa Monica Mountains National Recreation Area needed an anthropologist. John interviewed several candidates and selected Phil Holmes. From the interactions in his interview, Phil saw right off that he would be working with visionary people that he could respect. He rejected a higher offer and so started his over 30-year career with the National Park Service, all at SMMNRA.

Phil immediately set to work on a survey to learn how people in the area envisioned use of the new recreation area.

Charlie came to the NPS office after work several times a week for two to three years. We were glad to see him come. We'd all stop what we were doing and sit and talk with him about topics from concepts for the many places in the recreation area to how Indians fit it. He had a commanding presence so we would stop to give him the time he was taking from his family. He was big enough and powerful enough that he seemed a part of his truck and he looked like he could control that big heavy truck full of cement. It was like we were a part of his family—dropping in was okay—we were all doing the same things together. (John Reynolds)

There was a quiet confidence. He knew what he was talking about. He spoke quietly and carefully chose words. You would find yourself listening carefully. Some tried to get you to think they knew what they talked about by talking louder. Charlie was breath of fresh air. You found yourself introspectively analyzing what he said, the way he did it—calm but confident; forceful, but not overbearing. You knew that he had listened to a variety of divergent positions among the Chumash and spent time to resolve conflicts. He brought the consensus or a couple of options. (Bill Anderson, first Management Assistant to the Superintendent in 1979, SMMNRA, June 3, 2011)

Chapter 9: Four Wheeling It, 1979-1980

Ever since he had arrived in 1979, Bob Chandler moved around the community among established county, city, and state park sites meeting and talking with people about plans for the recreation area. But he also wanted to hike, touch, see, and feel the raw mountains, valleys, canyons, and coast.

"I can just imagine the speculations when people see or hear me off-roading in a truck or car with our insignia on it," he thought to himself once or twice. Then he leased three yellow Broncos with four-wheel drive. By the time John Reynolds was on staff, the Broncos had been out and about several times. Today one of the Broncos was bouncing off-road in Cheeseboro Canyon. John was driving with Bob in the passenger seat. Bill Anderson and Nancy Fries were in the backseat talking to each other.

Cheeseboro Canyon: Charlie's invisible influence

"Stop here," Bob said looking out the window.

John turned off the motor. Bob swung open the front door, a little difficult since they were on a slight incline. Bill Anderson jumped out from the back seat. Nancy Fries followed, and lastly John set the brake and stepped out.

"There, there, John," Bob pointed as he continued, "Do you see? Look, some trees growing over there. That means water!"

Bill Anderson added, "Scraggly looking things! You know, one of those late afternoons when Charlie stopped by he said something about where there is vegetation—even like this, there would almost certainly be a stream. Something is keeping those gnarled trees going."

"I showed him this spot on a map," Nancy interjected. "He was in a personal storytelling mood. He told me he worked as a ranch hand in this area."

They started walking, climbing over a few large rocks, and then they saw it. It was only a trickle, but it was a stream.

Bob leaned over and touched the water. It was clean and clear. He ran some wet soil through his fingers and then swished them in the water to wash them off. He stood up.

"And if there is water, native people probably lived here. Charlie said that too. In fact, we know there were Chumash settlements in this canyon."

They walked for a while on a trail left by ranchers, probably a trail originally made by the Chumash. They looked up to see some type of raptor soaring overhead, too high to tell whether it was a hawk or another bird of prey that nested in the wide-armed oaks they could see all around.

124

It was getting late as they started back to the yellow Bronco.

"Can't miss this car! And to think we have three of them roaming these mountains. Where are Bill Redmond and Marti Leicester today?" John laughed as they approached the bright yellow four-wheeler. "What were you thinking, Bob? Yellow. . . and we wouldn't be conspicuous?"

"That's all they had. Anyway, so far so good!" He looked at his watch, "Bill and Marti—probably talking to Charlie about the education programs they are planning."

They looked around quietly for a few minutes taking in the scenery. It wasn't all pretty. They could see scars. For more than 150 years, ranchers had run cattle in these canyons. Heavy grazing killed off some native plants. They could see European annuals that took their places: wild oats, mustard, and thistles. They also knew that some of the native animals were gone. Ranchers killed off the grizzly bears. But coyotes, bobcats, and deer still ran wild. And best of all, the entire canyon created a respite from the cityscapes just over the hills.

Bob broke the silence, "Let's get Charlie out here. I'll bet he knows this canyon well, especially if he worked here as a ranch hand. Maybe this is an area we should preserve not only for its natural, but maybe for its cultural resources." Bob punctuated his comment by sliding back into the passenger seat and letting the heavy door slam. Another slam behind him and all four were in, bouncing back to civilization as a reddish hue overtook the mountain sky around them.

"Do you think Charlie stopped at our office today? How can he give us so much time?"

Bill answered from the back seat. "Probably did. With all the people coming in wanting us to buy their land, not buy their land, make a trail, not make a trail, allow riding, not allow riding . . ."

"Charlie is different. He just wants us to know why the land matters," Nancy interjected.

"Of course, it's common sense, but you get what he means about vegetation and water supporting life when you see it, when you feel the soil and the water. We need to get out in the mountains more—and yes, John, in the yellow Broncos."

"Where are we going next?"

"I think we'd better get out to the Danielson Ranch. Charlie too! He brought that place to our attention. The developers have their earthmoving equipment poised to build over six hundred homes there. But we're buying it." Bob sounded definite.

"Did you hear, the Channel Islands National Monument is finally a national park? President Carter signed it into law a few weeks ago, March 5, 1980."

"Ehorn worked hard on that. He still has the two big islands to fold in. Charlie and Kote are helping him out when they can with information about the Chumash. Don't know how Charlie fits that in. He seems so tied up with us."

By the end of 1980, Bob Chandler closed the deal on the Danielson Ranch with some ideas in mind on how to develop it. It was the first SMMNRA acquisition, somewhat to the dismay of the three women proponents who had lobbied for acquisitions closer to the center of the mountains. Those acquisitions came in time.

After NPS bought Danielson, the staff began creating a Development Concept Plan (DCP), part of their usual process when acquiring land that could accommodate intensive public uses such as a visitor activity site. A DCP depicts in narrative and graphics how NPS will make use of and manage the site. In the spring of 1980, SMMNRA leadership formed an advisory committee that held monthly meetings. The leadership also held community meetings to gather input from citizens living in the mountain range areas. Charlie got involved with the Danielson property in a very hands-on way, attending advisory and community meetings. The National Park Service soon began to refer to the area with the name a previous owner had used, Rancho Sierra Vista.

Figure 28: John Reynolds, Bob Chandler, Bill Anderson, reunion Circle X Ranch (Photo courtesy of Bill Anderson, c 1984)

The Danielson Property: Charlie's onsite influence

They were headed to a natural bowl at Rancho Sierra Vista. The NPS staff and Charlie were totally removed from civilization even though it was within walking distance: no lights, no cars honking, and no people bustling about. To get there, they had turned off a main road onto a narrow one-way, roughly-paved ranch road. They immediately passed rusted ranching equipment, then a cluster of bunkhouses on their left, and then equestrian facilities quickly on their right. They continued, hoping no one would come the other way. About a mile in, they parked under a lone small house shaded by a mulberry in the front and a mimosa tree in the back. They walked a short distance, out of the shade, up a dirt trail, past a cattle pond, into the sun.

"Here," Charlie said, "Let's sit here."

They sat right on the ground in a natural bowl this late afternoon, to talk—really more to dream about what could be. Somehow, just being there, they could sense what would harmonize and what would just harm.

They talked about NPS ideas.

"What a recreation area! Look around! So many things to do here! You can hike up hill from here all the way to that windmill. Do you see it? We'll need to spruce up the original or make some new trails."

"There's a gorgeous waterfall that you can't see from here, way back there."

"You can hike to the ocean though the canyon over there, but we need a parking lot. This flat area where we're sitting might be a good place for that."

Charlie looked down at the ground in the bowl and tried to see a parking lot. Instead he saw rivulets. He got up and walked around. He saw white sage that his ancestors had used in ceremonies. He rubbed some between his fingers. He was now, himself, using it in Chumash blessings.

He raised his eyes to what the locals called Boney Mountain. It seemed the bluffs up at the top were staring at him, white, straight up and somewhat stern today. He nodded to the massive stone faces as he turned to the others and sat down again. In his usual quiet voice he started to explain.

"The Chumash celebrated winter solstices up there, one of their most important celebrations. Boney is sacred. Where we are right now—well, do you hear any street noise? Do you see any modern buildings? We're in a place protected from all that urban sprawl and commotion. The peace here lets this natural bowl stay connected with Boney. It completes Boney. Nothing stops you from feeling the sacred power. You do not have to be on the mountain. You can be of the mountain."

They felt the soothing ocean breeze come in through the passes as it often did here in the late afternoon. They noticed birds flitting among the trees nearby. Sitting there on the ground in the bowl, they sensed Boney's eons. Generations had almost certainly looked up to those bluffs from the bowl. A parking lot did not feel right.

Charlie continued to talk with the staff on site, in the office, at meetings, everywhere about creating an interaction with the whole landscape—Boney to bowl. He listened to NPS ideas such as creating a Chumash Village and helped evolve that to include a building to introduce Chumash culture spanning the urban to the ancient—not a museum, but a place where today's Native Americans would give programs. Charlie talked about the raptors, mountain lions, coyotes, and about a Chumash Center sharing their space, but not where the developed ranch was. The ranch could tell its own story. Leave the bowl as a natural native area. He talked, they listened. They talked, he listened.

Figure 29: Natural area at Danielson Ranch site (Author's photo, 2013)

<u>Connecting the Park Service with Native Americans</u>

After work one day, Charlie talked with John Reynolds about Native

Americans in general.

"Did you know that Los Angeles has the greatest concentration of Native Americans in the United States?"

"Yes." John was somewhat familiar with Native American history and knew that they had moved to the Greater Los Angeles area from all across the country, including Alaska, Hawaii, and some of the territories.

"They are from almost every tribe you can think of. Indian Center West is a gathering place for them. John Dawson is the director for the place."

"What tribe?"

"He's San Carlos Apache. Sallie Cuaresma is another person active there. She's Cherokee and Creek. Do you want to meet them? A lot of the new recreation area is in LA County."

And so John Reynolds found himself attending meetings at Indian Center West in Culver City.

Charlie also invited Phil to these meetings. Charlie was building acceptance both ways.

At one of these meetings, a young Indian woman argued resolutely about an agenda item. She peppered her stance with references to an old man's words on the matter. The old man sat quietly in the back and then suddenly stood up. He explained what he had really meant and then sat down quietly. The agenda item was settled with his very short speech. From his studies at California State Northridge and just plain experience, Phil understood that different cultures exhibit different behaviors. He was seeing this in action at the Culver City meetings.

John and Phil talked about what they had noticed at the meeting,

"The elder's word was key to the argument. Non-talkers can be very important," John said thinking out loud.

"Did you get native input when you worked on the management plan at Yosemite?" Phil knew that John had some previous experience working with Native Americans.

"You bet."

"I'm learning. We need to listen to who the Native Americans listen to, even if they seem quiet to us. Charlie is one of those people."

"Good advice. But Charlie—I wouldn't consider him quiet." John usually saw Charlie in a leadership stance even if not talking.

Phil countered, "He might be in the presence of his elders. I have noticed when he is with other native peoples he talks with men shoulder to shoulder, which is their way, but not when he is with us. He adapts almost subconsciously. I've seen him with developers. He looks them in the eye and speaks in a business to business way."

They agreed they would attend the next meeting and as many as they could after that.

Charlie brought the land to life which made it matter to a lot of people as they were trying to make the case for the new recreation area. It can look like just scraggly hillsides. How can you call this a creek? There is no water in it. We'd ask, why are we buying this? Then you'd hear the stories that went with it—not just a scraggly hillside. People made homes here. They lived off of this land. This is how they dealt with no water in August. These are the animals they hunted. You got it after listening to him. You can respect the lush redwood forests and these scraggly hillsides too. (Bill Redmond, original SMMNRA Ranger, June 28, 2011)

His greatest achievement: Bringing to the early NPS staff the consensus regarding the historical and archaeological sites to be preserved. This was a massive achievement. We knew very little at the time about this. Why would NPS listen to him, a truck driver? Because of believability. We knew he had seen the sites or members of his Chumash community had been there. He was communicating their value. He would say, "Here is what is here. Here is the significance to our people and this is why you should be preserving it." (Bill Anderson)

Charlie saw American Indians as here and alive. NPS expected Charlie to be a representative of them. He probably represented some, but probably not all Native Americans in the area. One person can't represent an entire cultural community and there isn't necessarily agreement within a group just because of their cultural heritage. But Charlie bridges contemporary times to the past. He exemplifies care for people that extends from the past to today. (Nancy Fries, Chief of Planning and second Assistant Superintendent, Land Use and Planning SMMNRA, June 8, 2011, email of July 27, 2011)

Chapter 10: Not Just a Museum, 1980

The small Santa Monica Mountains NPS staff was assembled around a table at headquarters, still in the San Fernando Valley. They were talking about a potential visitor use survey the Denver Service Center was helping them plan for the newly launched recreation area—the survey Phil was working on.

One person asked, "Are you planning for minorities?"

"Sure, we will interview Blacks, Asians, and Hispanics," Phil answered.

"What about Native Americans?" another asked.

"Native Americans? I thought there weren't any in California," quipped someone else.

Phil did not miss a beat. He knew better and said so.

"Okay, smart aleck, you find and interview them," John Reynolds challenged knowing full well that there were Native Americans in the area.

Shortly afterwards, John asked Phil to attend a meeting with him. Conejo Future Foundation (CFF) wanted to talk about promoting a Native American culture center in the area.

The NPS anthropologist, the chief, the Future Foundation

A few days later, in the evening, Phil parked his 1965 white Jeep pick-up truck at a building in central Thousand Oaks, the main town in the Conejo Valley. The truck was leftover from his handyman days. He climbed down from the wooden toolbox seat he had made when the original seat started popping springs. He noticed a red and white truck parked next to him.

Phil walked into the meeting looking official and trim in the NPS field uniform of the day: dark green jeans with a grey short-sleeved shirt and dark green tie. Of course, the NPS arrowhead insignia was on his left sleeve. His badge and nametag identified him. Charlie, in his work jeans and plaid work shirt, was already there, sitting next to Jessie Roybal, still president of Candelaria.

Rad Sutnar was off to the side talking with Doris Granholm, the president of CFF. He had urged her to involve CFF with a possible Native American center. Rad moved over to talk with Clay Singer for a few moments about preserving archaeological sites in the area.

Doris, a tall, slim woman, gave a seasoned professional air. She walked to the head of the conference table and sat down. Clay and Rad took her cue and sat down too. As president of Conejo Future Foundation, she welcomed everyone and then gave some background.

"The Future Foundation was formed by community leaders. We're here to foster planning of the next few decades for our Conejo Valley. We know it is important to involve the diverse groups and public and private interests," she nodded at everyone and continued with satisfaction, "which we have at this table."

She opened discussion on the main topic of this meeting by saying, "We are interested in supporting a Chumash Cultural Center out at the Danielson Ranch. Some call it Rancho Sierra Vista."

"Yes," said Phil, "The National Park Service now owns that land. One of the earlier owners called it Rancho Sierra Vista, and that's what we're calling it."

Charlie added, "Ranching was part of the history, but before that, it was a Chumash area, right there under Boney Mountain."

"You mean those large white rock outcroppings? They are magnificent." Someone commented.

Clay weighed in saying he found evidence of the lost Chumash Village of Satwiwa nearby.

Phil added that Dr. Chester King thought the Village of Satwiwa was at Round Mountain in Camarillo, not in the shadow of the bluffs.

Rad commented that this new center would be a natural outgrowth of the bicentennial project at the Stagecoach Inn Museum.

Jessie hinted at the need to create something that would pay for itself. She was thinking about ways to fund the project.

Charlie could get serious when he felt the situation warranted it. This was such a time.

"Boney is a sacred Chumash site. We need to work together to preserve it and make it a learning center. I will do everything I can."

Everyone paid attention. By now the community recognized Charlie as Chief of the Southern Chumash, and he was a well-liked member of the community. As a result more and more native and nonnative people in the area respected his ideas and input.

Doris reiterated Conejo Future Foundation's strong interest in moving along the cultural center idea. The meeting ended. The center at the Danielson site was launched as an idea, but details were yet to be developed.

"I'm hungry. Worked all day delivering cement . . ." Phil heard Charlie say.

At Du-par's: the start of informal meetings that shaped the center

Phil liked Du-par's, a mainstay rustic restaurant tucked in an intersection corner in Thousand Oaks. He suggested to Charlie that he join him there. Charlie got into his Ford truck and followed him to Du-par's. They slid into seats at a table sometime around 10:30 p.m.

"Phil, different people look at this in different ways."

"What do you mean?" Phil pulled out a notepad from his front shirt pocket.

"Not sure, but I sensed different unspoken ideas. Oh, we've been here a while. It's after midnight. I gotta get to work in the morning."

"Me too." Phil looked at his notepad. "I've got to start interviewing Native Americans tomorrow."

Charlie agreed to be on the interview list. He talked a bit more about the different ideas he sensed. They finished eating quickly and left agreeing to continue this conversation soon.

The next day, Phil dove right into finding Native Americans to interview. Charlie was one of the first. Phil used a snowball approach, asking people he interviewed if there were other Native Americans he should talk to.

Before long, Phil became the NPS liaison to Native Americans. Charlie was in the right place at the right time because he had worked every opportunity, and he kept at it.

Back at the rustic restaurant, after another meeting, Charlie picked up from where he left off with their first Du-par's discussion. "Phil, now I'm sure there are different ideas out there."

By now Phil knew Charlie's intuitive senses were right, and that he did his own type of research.

"You're right, Charlie. Jessie told me that Candelaria thinks a high rise hotel at the Danielson site would help pay for a Chumash museum on the first floor."

"Well, Jessie is concerned about funds. So she comes up with a hotel and office building. I'm not sure about a museum. There are already stones and bones museums about the Chumash in Ventura. Somehow we need to make sure people see the Chumash as alive and well."

Phil leaned forward. "It's not just the museum. I had to explain that a commercial building would not conform to National Park Service policies. But some of the other proposals would. The Tongva have proposed their own center at University High School near their sacred springs."

"Yes, but that's in Sawtelle, near Santa Monica. The Tongva want to make sure they are recognized too. I understand."

"Ah, I see," Phil thought out loud, "so they propose their own site. And a group is proposing an Urban Indian Center at an indefinite location."

"Yes, we need to think about everyone's concerns as we move on this. There was heavy equipment parked on the main road there by Danielson ready to start the development of 640 homes. Candelaria was talking about stopping the bulldozers."

"They're gone. No bulldozers, dump trucks, or anything else like that. The Slow Growth measure passed—you helped some with that."

"I went to meetings and spoke up but a lot of other people did the real work."

"Well, that measure was one thing that made the venture less appealing to any developer but appealing to us. So the bulldozers—gone as soon as the property went into escrow. The Park Service owns that land now!"

"Good. Now we need to move on the cultural center idea." Charlie's tired eyes still twinkled as he looked at his watch. "It's 2 a.m.! I gotta get to work in a few hours."

Figure 30: Du-par's Restaurant, (Photo by Alice Berejikian, Local History Collection, Thousand Oaks Library, nd)

Imagine a wise chieftain of his people who knows that going on the warpath is no longer an option but faithfully representing his people is a necessity. (Joe Edmiston)

Charlie is out there proving Native Americans are still here. He is an ambassador of good will for Native Americans. (Kote Lotah)

Charlie represented his Native American people really well. He'd take a moment to teach you about his culture: sites—what people used to do there and why the site is important rather than saying you don't know anything about our culture. He was educational not confrontational. I learned more about Chumash culture from Charlie than any other way, including reading because he took the time to explain the importance rather than saying it's important, why aren't you guys dealing with it. I remember his saying, "Let me explain why this is important here. Let me explain why this is important to the Chumash people. Let me explain. Let me explain . . ." (Bill Anderson)

Charlie was an important player with Bob Chandler in making sure that Danielson Ranch was one of park's highest priorities for purchase. I don't know if he was thinking of a cultural center at that time. It was an important purchase because as the largest public property in the west end of the new recreation area it could provide a focus for the west end. It was adjacent to Point Mugu State Park so hikers could access the ocean from the top—through Sycamore Canyon. Charlie was critical to the acquisition and the plan for the Danielson Ranch, especially the back bowl where Satwiwa was developed. He brought to us at NPS an understanding of the Chumash relationship to the mountains. (John Reynolds)

Chapter 11: Unwittingly Cupid, 1981

By 1981, Charlie and Linda's boys, Damon and Jason, were in high school. Charlie had spent time over the years telling them about Native American culture so they knew about his involvement and that he was at least part Chumash. At school one of Damon's friends asked,

"How was the rodeo last weekend, Damon? Did you compete?"

"Not yet. Maybe when I'm a senior. I just watched my dad." Charlie was still roping but not as often as he used to. "It's pretty exciting. The steer can't get away from him."

"Wow, he must be a great roper."

"Yeah, he was raised on ranches. And he's Chumash; they're good cowboys!"

"Chumash, what's that?" His teenage friend gave Damon a blank stare.

Damon had seen that reaction many times. He wondered why he continued to bring this up. He never told his dad about these reactions, but his dad knew. Charlie started getting invitations to talk about Native American heritage at schools and at park programs for children. He accepted as many invitations as possible, so now he was going to meetings evenings and fitting in talks with school children on days off as much as possible.

Figure 31: Charlie talking with children, unidentified park site (SMMNRA Archives, 1982)

Mentoring another Native American

At about the same time the National Park Service was starting to make its mark in the Santa Monica Mountains, Charlie was still stopping in at the archeological site at Reyes Adobe in Agoura Hills, a little east of the Conejo Valley on the Los Angeles/Ventura County border. He had learned to monitor archeological sites at first by just showing up and watching archaeologists identify artifacts. These were people he had befriended at archaeological society meetings. For example, he accompanied Clay Singer on over 20 surface studies in the Thousand Oaks and Agoura Hills areas. He did this without being paid, to learn but also to stay aware of what was happening to his ancestral sites. Soon he was doing small paid monitoring jobs on days off at places like the Wood Ranch development in Simi Valley. Eventually he worked for and was paid by private archaeological firms, university organizations, and sometimes the State or National Park Service—and he still did some of the work gratis as part of his chief role and positions he held in native organizations. Linda was more and more on her own with the boys.

On one of Charlie's cement truck stops to be weighed at the Santa Paula site, Patty told him that she and then husband, Richard Garcia, had found artifacts on a beach in Ventura after a rainfall. Patty knew that she was at least a fourth-generation Native American from Santa Cruz Island off the coast of Santa Barbara. She was at least 75 percent Chumash, and she wanted to know more about her heritage.

"She cares, but doesn't really know our culture," he thought. "Hmm, I know a way to help her and me too. Linda wants me home more."

"Patty, how would you like to do some paid monitoring on your days off at the Reyes Adobe site? I can't handle it all. I'll show you what to do."

Charlie knew that Kote's mother had called a series of meetings in Santa Barbara so that the Chumash and the community there could learn about Chumash heritage and issues, including burial traditions. So Charlie called Kote out to Reyes Adobe. This was the start of the three working together on the behalf of native causes.

Giving talks on archaeological issues, unintended matchmaking

"Come on in, Charlie. We're looking forward to your talk tonight." Charlie had come to talk about archaeological sites to a group of Native Americans.

"Something smells good," Charlie complimented Patty as she closed the door to her house in Saticoy.

137

"It's native food, like my mother used to make."

The doorbell rang again. Charlie swung the door open.

"Hi, Kote, glad you could make it. You know Patty."

"We worked at Reyes Adobe, right?" Kote complimented Patty. "You did a good job monitoring there."

"The builder was cooperative," Patty motioned Kote into the living room.

"Well, thanks for hosting this meeting, Patty. Something smells good." Kote looked toward the kitchen.

"I'd better check on the food. Charlie, you are in charge of the door for a while. Kote, make yourself at home." Patty scurried off to the kitchen.

"What do you think, Kote? Smart gal, huh?" Charlie laughed heartily. Patty recognized the laugh as she arranged food in the kitchen. What was Charlie up to?

Patty's husband Richard came in with a bowl for the buffet table. Charlie introduced him to Kote.

Kote looked over at the buffet table. He saw Indian stew, bread, and wild greens.

"Well, the old folks must have raised her," Kote continued using Chumash words sounding like "*Ki-sa-tho, atipo, kelikees*. No one cooks like this anymore."

Several more people came to the door.

Kote was giving a mini lecture to a few of the guests. "It seems that archaeologists and developers have one of three ways of doing things. They have respect for our ancestors and leave burials in the ground or move them to a close, protected area that won't be disturbed. Or they are so concerned about development that they move our ancestors wherever and sometimes even destroy the burials. And then there are those who dig up bones to study them or put them in a museum."

"Hey, I thought I was giving the talk tonight," Charlie joked.

As if on cue, Patty came back into the room. "The rest of the food will be ready soon so now is a good time to hear your talk, Charlie. I don't want to miss it."

Charlie took a stance at the front of the small crowd. The few standing sat down. All seemed anxious to hear what he had to say.

"I'm going to talk about rock art and burial sites. How many of you have been to any of them?"

Almost everyone had. Charlie listened as they described their experiences. He could tell what they knew and what they needed to know. He talked a bit more about preservation, especially fighting early and in a concerted effort to make sure sacred sites were not obliterated by builders or vandals. Vandals worried him, especially in regard to rock art and sites with artifacts.

"So don't tell where these sites are. You are inviting trouble. People who do not understand might desecrate these sites. Any questions?"

"What if we have to talk about them? How do we do that without saying where they are?" one young person asked.

"Use their archaeological number, if you know it. It starts with the county. For example, Ven 110 for Ventura County, site 110."

The small crowd nodded in agreement.

"Now with all sites, well, first of all I try to preserve what's there. Sometimes we have rock art; sometimes we have burials, sometimes villages, sometimes just artifacts. You know tools, mortars, pestles, beads, and things like that. See they have three phases of archaeology, the archaeologists I mean. They have the surveying where they look across the ground to see if they can identify anything and if there's something identified they have an excavation, that's phase two. Now the third one is the mitigation with the local government agencies."

"Mitigation?" One of the guests furled his brow.

"Mitigation. We discuss what they are going to do with the site when they find burials or artifacts. I learned a lot from working with archaeologists. Normally we Indians are not involved so much in the first phase or the third phase. That's kind of a sore spot with me because we should have been involved with the mitigation to protect some sites."

"Burial sites or village sites?"

"Both. Sometimes an archaeologist tells a developer that we don't have to do a phase two or excavation, but if we know that it's one of our sites, we have to keep on about this. You have to make sure things are handled right and with respect. You make time. You go to the city or the park or whoever is involved."

Charlie continued to talk and answer questions for a few minutes more; then he finished, "Thanks all for listening."

Patty scurried back to the kitchen. Charlie sat down with Kote.

"Chester filed the environmental report. It was all worth it. We bought time. Point Conception sits on an earthquake fault line, so no processing plant there—ever!" Kote beamed.

Patty came in with a platter of egg cakes. "Here, try some of this. It's my mother's way of cooking."

Kote took a bite. "*Stile!* My mother cooked like this too!" Kote talked about his mother for a while and then a sudden ah ha! Patty knew Kote's mother.

"Madlyn Guevera, Mountain Dove! She worked on the fountain in downtown Santa Barbara, the Dolphin Fountain."

"She was one of the first to bring the Chumash together in Santa Barbara," Kote added proudly.

The small crowd moved to the buffet table and then sat down to eat and socialize. Kote was learning about medicinal plants from his aunt. He found that Patty, too, had an interest in indigenous medicine. Her grandmother had given her some training. A few months later, Patty asked Kote to train her in the medicine ways. She changed her name to Lin A'lul-koy or Blue Dolphin. She separated from Richard. Some years later, in 1983, Grandfather Victor married Kote and A'lul-koy at Point Conception. Kote continued to teach his new wife basic indigenous medicine but believed in allowing her to develop her own feminine way. A'lul-koy also knew some Chumash. She translated Eye of the Eagle telling Charlie, "Your Chumash name is TIQ SLO'W."

Importantly for the native community, Kote, A'lul-koy and TIQ SLO'W joined forces.

At Du-par's: reaching out to more Native Americans

Phil had finished the survey interviews and report. It indicated that people wanted hiking trails, riding trails, picnic areas, and ways to learn about the history of places they visited. In addition, Indians emphasized the preservation of nature as a part of their cultures for children of all descents. The next step in the NPS public planning process was to create the general management plan for SMMNRA, and a draft was done by the end of 1980. NPS gathered input to the draft by holding public meetings. Phil noticed that few Native Americans were speaking up. At Du-par's after one of these meetings:

"Charlie, will you look at what we have written here to go into the final draft of the management plan?"

"Looks okay, but there should be more about the Native American culture."

"I agree. But, Charlie, native peoples are not speaking up at the public forums except for you and a few others. Can you do anything to get more up to the podium?"

"I am not sure I want to make them do that."

"What do you mean? You do it."

"Yes, but many people you interviewed are uncomfortable in front of a group. We gotta come up with another way."

Phil took a few bites chewing on his thoughts. "How about if we took people I interviewed on tours to sites we're looking at?"

"Great idea! I can ask Kote to help us get the word out. I can talk to John Dawson and Sallie Cuaresma at Indian Center West. I can get A'lul-koy to help. We can make this happen."

Back at NPS headquarters, Phil told John Reynolds they needed better Native American input to the management plan and so he proposed tours. John thought it was a great idea and encouraged Phil to get it going.

Charlie's influence on me when I was at SMMNRA was tremendous— reinforced for me that Indians have a cultural background as valued as the rest of our culture. In the late 1990s, I led a negotiation for the creation of a reservation in Death Valley for the Timbisha Shoshone. Charlie's influence came into play. (John Reynolds)

All three of us had lived in our own Chumash world until we met. We all carried walking sticks. A walking stick is a rod to the earth. We laughed when we realized that we were each carrying a piece of the puzzle. I understood the earth from a woman's perspective. I helped grow food to feed us. I worried about working to support my children. When younger, I had spent a lot of time in my aunt's back yard in Ventura exploring middens. Sometimes we found bones of our ancestors and put them right back. I was already fighting for the land and the secrets it was keeping. When I met Kote, he carried tobacco as a symbol of the magic of creation. He carried a rattle. He could sing and remember old native tunes. Charlie also carried tobacco. His aunts and uncles taught him that in the Chumash world tobacco is an offering to the earth for life. Charlie had already taken a stance toward redeeming and renewing the earth and the native heritage buried in it. (A'lul-koy Lotah, Chumash Medicine Woman, July 21, 2009)

That old dog, Charlie, set the whole thing up. I was invited to a meeting at her house, by Charlie. Yes, she stole my heart through my stomach. We had Indian stew (*ki sa tho*), round bread (*atipo*), old *stile,* egg cake, and wild greens (*kelikes*). I knew it was all over for me. That damn Charlie set me up with her. I owe Charlie for a great life with her. (Dr. Kote Lotah, email September 28, 2011)

Chapter 12: Eye of the Eagle, 1981-82

A caravan of ten cars pulled onto a narrow ranch road. They'd have to move over onto the dirt if anyone came the other way. Over the last year-and-a-half, Phil had led these caravans four different times. They would visit several sites in a day, places that were or eventually would become part of the SMMNRA system, like Palo Comado Canyon, Cheeseboro Canyon, Malibu Creek State Park, Paramount Ranch, Peter Strauss Ranch, Circle X Ranch, and the Danielson property.

Now they were on their last tour. About 70 people got out of their cars, trucks, or four-wheel drives, most of them Native Americans. Some were Tongva and Chumash whose ancestors had lived in this area. Others were Apache, Cheyenne, Cherokee, Hupa, and more. Some were people from tribes very far away, who now lived in the Greater Los Angeles area. It was about two o'clock in the afternoon at Rancho Sierra Vista. They started up a trail past a small ranch house, past a man-made pond full of reeds, and then up a small knoll. It was February of 1981. Boney Mountain, with its white bluffs, towered over them.

They saw prickly pear and yucca poking their heads up through native and introduced grasses. They saw some haying equipment rusting in the grass. A few lone oaks stood silhouetted against the skyline. A rabbit scurried out from under some brambles and scampered away through the grasses. A continuous breeze brushed softly across their shoulders reminding them that they were not far from the ocean. In fact, this was prize recreational property because you could hike to the ocean through Sycamore Canyon. The bluffs faced the canyon almost as if those huge rocks could see over the hills to the sea.

Figure 32: Danielson, narrow ranch entrance (Author's photo, 2013)

NPS and Native Americans creating the vision right on site

They stopped at the top of the knoll and looked down at a natural bowl. Some people took out tobacco pouches. Phil pulled out his notes and missed seeing them sprinkle the ground with the traditional Native American honoring gift, but he knew the tradition well enough to know what they had done and why. Now, a stronger breeze, creating a soft rustling of leaves— nature's background music! The group seemed to be waiting for Phil to start, so he did. He shared a brief history about the site and asked for input on uses for this newest of NPS properties. Then he listened.

"Our ancestors must have lived well here before the native plants were destroyed. Look . . . just a few oaks left. How could we subsist now on acorns like they did?"

"We can bring the native vegetation back."

Phil was listening and writing. "Bring native vegetation back . . ."

"I am not sure the urban Indians would get out here. I think we need to have a center for them in LA."

More notes, "Appeal to the urban Indians."

"The ranching here is interesting too. Include it somehow."

"Where would people park?"

"How about using that little house we passed. The one that's a display center for Tongva and Chumash artifacts?"

Phil kept writing, trying to keep up with the ideas as Charlie moved to the very top of the knoll and began addressing the group. First he bent over and reached down.

"Feel the earth. Bend over. Touch it. You can't feel it with shoes on. This is what it is all about, for all of us. Feeling and living and sharing our culture! Look at that natural bowl down there. It was probably a gathering place and could be again! There's a special feeling coming from those bluffs! This should be for all peoples."

He looked up for a second and wondered silently if he had just glimpsed an eagle soaring past. He scanned the expanse below. It was a natural bowl soft with grasses, some native, but some buffelgrass was taking over. That mimosa tree behind the little house wasn't native either. Charlie thought to himself they could fix all that.

For a quick moment, times past flashed across the bowl below him. He saw

Chumash ancestors gathered together. They were dressed in clothes made of grass and tree bark. Their hair was straight and pulled back. Some were gathering acorns. Some were repairing aps with tule from a nearby steam. He saw some throwing dice made of decorated walnut shells. Someone was playing a flute made out of a bone. A few children were singing. Some women were starting a fire, getting ready to cook game the men had brought home—rabbits today. Two young girls were carrying water in a waterproof basket. The basket maker must have been a novice. He could see some of the black asphaltum used to waterproof it, and a drip or two. A man was counting shell bead money. He saw a Tongva visitor coming to trade. And then, quickly, he came back to today.

"I see a learning center for all Native Americans, in fact for all, to learn about our values and ways. We should all be involved here: Cherokee, Apache, Hupa, Tongva, Chumash, and peoples who are not here today."

Phil stopped writing. "Oh no," he panicked to himself, "this will never work. Native people do not cooperate with each other." And then as he listened more and watched people mesmerized by the man talking in the shadow of Boney, he had to admit to himself, "Well, at least that's what I heard."

The group walked back down the hill talking among themselves. Some huddled by their cars. A group, including Charlie, wandered behind the house. A pair of eagles in the mimosa tree peered down at the group. A red-tailed hawk flew into view and rested in the tree, and then a Coopers Hawk, then two black and white kites, and finally an osprey. "Some of these are power birds. This must have some meaning," they said among themselves as they joined the huddles by the cars.

Phil noticed that there was some scrambling and that a few people traded for seats in other cars. Phil headed back to headquarters to prepare a report for John Reynolds.

All night excitement about shaping the vision

A few cars continued all the way to the Indian Center in Culver City. These people, who had rearranged themselves, had decided to meet to assure that something happened soon at Rancho Sierra Vista. They were behind Charlie's vision, but some were worried.

"Good idea, Charlie, but can we trust the Feds? After all they took our lands to begin with."

"Tons of buffelgrass there . . . I doubt they will ever try to return that land to its original condition."

"I hope they don't have rangers tell our history. They learn it from books and get it all wrong."

"Do you think we should ask for a free burial ground on site? After all, they have unearthed so many of our ancestors."

"I still think it should just be a Chumash Center. That's who lived there."

Charlie listened. It was now about midnight.

"They'll probably put in a museum. No one wants stones and bones relics! We are alive."

"How about a rodeo area?"

"And other areas for horses."

"I still wonder how people are going to park there."

"Did you see that rusty old piece of farm equipment?"

Charlie listened. He looked at his watch, 2 a.m.

"Our urban youth don't have any idea about how their ancestors lived. They think a blade of grass growing in a sidewalk crack is nature. This would be a great place to bring them—no matter what tribe they belong to."

"We need a place that is Indian friendly. We need a place about living culture, not a bunch of rocks."

"We need to maintain control of any Indian Center."

"They need to do a better job of building and maintaining trails."

"What are they going to do about our sacred sites to keep them from being vandalized?"

"Maybe we could make it work, if we gave them a list of what we think needs to happen out there."

"You mean work with the Feds?"

"I think we could give it a try."

It was now about 4 a.m. Charlie rubbed his eyes hiding the tired, hopeful twinkle.

"What do you think, Charlie? You seem to be able to manage with the Feds."

"I think they listen," he answered. "They let me talk to them almost every day about what we need even though they are about ready to go home when I get there. Give them a chance."

And then Charlie stayed quiet.

"Will they listen to us?"

"Hey, didn't we meet John Reynolds at one of our meetings? He's one of the chiefs there. Seemed reasonable."

"They went through the trouble of the tours so they could hear our ideas."

"Well, yeah, Phil listened. He was even taking notes."

"Do they have any of us on an advisory board?"

"Charlie."

"But none of us are on the Channel Islands Board."

"Well, Charlie talks to Bill Ehorn. He and Kote stood up and got involved."

"Let's not wait to be asked. Let's form our own advisory board."

As day dawned, they had formed the American Indian Advisory Council to the Santa Monica Mountains National Recreation Area. They elected Charlie as president. They drafted and sent a letter to Superintendent Bob Chandler with a list of concerns, most of which they had dialoged during the night. They decided to hold regular meetings about once a month.

The next morning, Phil found out what the caravan shuffling was all about. He had already started his notes for John Reynolds telling him that the tobacco offering he partially witnessed meant that the group recognized the area as a sacred site. Now he added to his notes, "There is cooperation regarding Charlie's vision for a center for all native peoples at Rancho Sierra Vista."

After the first all-nighter, Phil started attending the Native American Advisory Council meetings (not to be confused with the SMMNRA Advisory meetings). These meetings would start after everyone could get to the Culver City Center from work about 7 p.m. Native interest and attendance were tremendous. Sometimes because there were so many introductions of new people attending, business did not start until around midnight. A lot of the issues that came up the first night came up again and again.

Phil kept communication flowing. He was filling in his immediate boss, Nancy Fries, and also John Reynolds. Then one day Bob called him into his office. He was working on a presentation for a native cultural center at Rancho Sierra Vista and wanted Phil's help. All those late night meetings at Du-par's with Charlie and in Culver City with the Native American Advisory Council were about to pay off. Bob was preparing for a meeting with Native Americans of any ancestry in the area.

The impact of the NPS spoken word

In January of 1982, two hundred people assembled outside near the pond at Rancho Sierra Vista, still known to some as the Danielson Ranch. They had come to hear what Bob had to say. Superintendent Chandler presented his dream for the cultural center reflecting closely what the Advisory Council and Charlie had communicated.

". . . a Native American program in the Santa Monica Mountains that involves and is developed in cooperation with Chumash, Tongva, and multi-national Indians on the Danielson Ranch."

He looked over the crowd. He could see that people were paying close attention.

". . . a demonstration village, a living museum, an interpretive trail, Native American events," he continued.

Native Americans present recognized many of their own ideas.

". . . interpretive programs by Native Americans and eventually a building."

". . . preservation of rock art and other sacred sites," he finished.

Bob did not present the impossible, such as a burial ground that would take an Act of Congress.

After the meeting, Native Americans talked among themselves. Later they told Phil they were impressed that the superintendent did not just send written ideas but actually spoke to them. Something written down by the government, they explained, does not mean much to them, but the spoken word does.

At a meeting in Culver City, the group was so hopeful that they discussed naming the center. They bantered back and forth:

"If it is out at Rancho Sierra Vista, how about naming it after the bluffs?"

"What's a Chumash word for the bluffs?"

"The Chumash word is *Satwiwa*."

Charlie's reach extends land to sea

Back to the sea! In the 1980s Bill Ehorn took Charlie, some other Native Americans, and some NPS staff by boat or helicopter several times to

Anacapa, Santa Rosa, and San Miguel. As Charlie did on Anacapa, he walked Santa Rosa and San Miguel. He saw exposed skeletal remains. Particularly on Miguel, the continually ferocious winds lashed the ground stirring up bones and scattering them over the constantly shifting sand. It was clear: Chumash ancestors had lived on these larger islands, not just visited. The boat and helicopter visitors were very concerned about preservation, especially on Miguel since it was so windswept.

Charlie advised simply, "Keep the burials and artifacts protected. Cover the bones where you can. Let those bones near the water go into the water." In time Charlie and Kote got involved with reburials on these islands.

For now, with the help of the Channel Islands Advisory Board and input from Charlie and Kote, San Miguel was protected. Visitors had to get an NPS permit. When they arrived on the island they were met and escorted by a park ranger. Anacapa, Santa Barbara, and now San Miguel had some NPS oversight; but the bigger islands, Santa Rosa and Santa Cruz, were calling for protection too. Bill was working to bring them into the Park Service.

By the end of 1982, Charlie had joined forces with anthropologists and archaeologists, park service staffs, politicians, and Native Americans of many backgrounds—all on his journey to reclaim his heritage. He started going to public agencies and arguing for the protection of habitats as part of his ancestral culture. He did not separate cultural and natural. To him, like to his native brethren, they were intertwined. Finally, people were paying attention to the Chumash as a living presence. But ranching still ran in his blood.

Rodeo: for Dad

The sea breeze floated over the rodeo site at the Ventura County Fairground on this weekend afternoon in 1982. Charlie and his partner, Steve Vonani, were waiting in the hole for their turn at team roping. Damon was in the stands close to the arena sitting next to Grandpa Cy Cooke. Charlie caught his dad's eye and said to himself, "This one's for you, Dad!" Dad's health was failing and he was no longer roping.

Charlie turned his attention to the gate again. He needed to concentrate now. He patted Blue. *Clang!* The steer broke through and Charlie was out after him. He roped the horns in a split second, so fast that he hardly remembered raising the rope. Blue had turned just as he was supposed to. It was like they were all in some cosmic synch, the man, the horse, the steer. This felt good, really good. He twisted in his saddle and saw Steve pulling the rope tight around both heels. Yeah! Yeah! They had done it. This was their best time ever. He could see Damon and Dad jumping up and down. They knew! Steve and Charlie had taken first place! They won the team roping event! He could feel the sea breeze again. "What a life!" He patted Blue again, waved at Steve, and smiled to himself, "We're rodeo champs and things are looking up for Native Americans."

There were 70 people almost all Native American. Charlie stood at the top of a hill and pointed to a site below. He said he'd like to see that site as a Native American cultural center for all Indian people in LA. I was surprised. Charlie inspired and orchestrated the energy of people to create this center which became Satwiwa and an NPS site. When we had a workday for volunteers, as many as 200 people would show up to work on the center—native and nonnative alike. Charlie's suggestion of sharing Satwiwa galvanized the Indian community. (Phil Holmes, May 27, 2011)

Some in the group meeting about Satwiwa were concerned about working with the Feds as they put it, which meant NPS. They felt NPS dictated to them. Charlie was level-headed so he said. "Let's work together. Let's see how this works out and then voice our concerns when we hear their side." (John Dawson)

Charlie is one of the most inclusive people I know. He has a lot to share but holds back until everyone has spoken. You can see him in a room with lots of ego going on—but he probably knows three times as much as anyone in that room. He makes sure that everyone has a chance to speak. (Dr. Wendy Teeter)

Charlie's attitude is we exist and need to take up responsibility. We need to put our best foot forward. What we do reflects on other Native Americans. We all have responsibility for the land. (Mati Waiya)

PART FOUR, NAVIGATING OUT OF THE PAST: Overcoming old mindsets and obstacles to defend ancient sites and to create an inclusive Native American center

Charlie is a consensus builder. He could have been bitter but chose to reach across and seek common ground. Thus he achieved greater appreciation for and awareness of the Native American story in people across all boundaries. Charlie's is a story of inclusion. (Woody Smeck, fifth Superintendent, SMMNRA, September 27, 2009).

It was clear early on. He has a gift for getting along. He does not get flush with anger. He is always calm. He has a good deal of knowledge, great self-respect, and respect for others. (Clay Singer)

Map 6: Areas of Activism on Behalf of Parks and Archaeology
(Courtesy of James Mansfield)

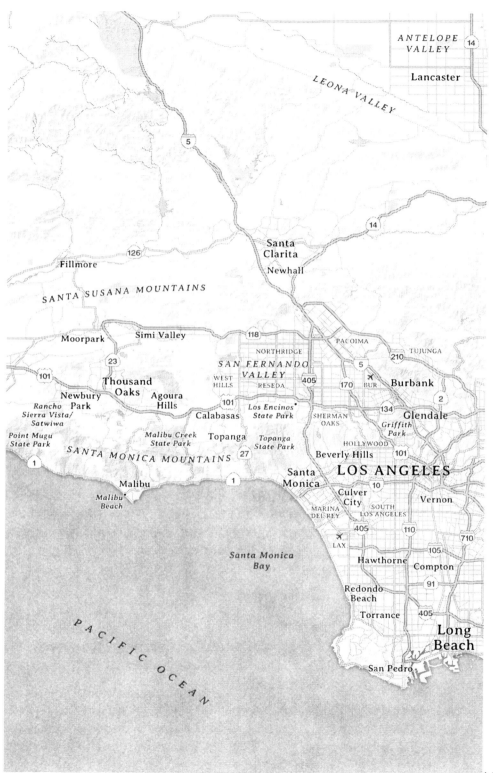

ANTELOPE VALLEY

14

Lancaster

LEONA VALLEY

5

14

Santa
Clarita

Newhall

126

Fillmore

SANTA SUSANA MOUNTAINS

Moorpark

Simi Valley

118

PACOIMA

TUJUNGA

210

NORTHRIDGE

23

SAN FERNANDO
VALLEY

5

BUR

Burbank

101

Thousand
Oaks

WEST
HILLS

RESEDA

405

170

2

Newbury Park
Rancho
Sierra Vista/
Satwiwa

Agoura
Hills

101

Los Encinos
State Park

SHERMAN
OAKS

134

Glendale

Calabasas

Griffith
Park

Point Mugu
State Park

Malibu Creek
State Park

Topanga

Topanga
State Park

HOLLYWOOD

101

SANTA MONICA MOUNTAINS

27

Beverly Hills

1

LOS ANGELES

1

Malibu

Santa
Monica

10

Malibu
Beach

Culver
City

Vernon

MARINA
DEL REY

SOUTH
LOS ANGELES

110

710

405

LAX

105

Santa Monica
Bay

Hawthorne

Compton

91

Redondo
Beach

Torrance

405

Long
Beach

PACIFIC OCEAN

San Pedro

Chapter 13: To the Beat of the Drummer, 1982-84

By April of 1982, the National Park Service had completed its Development Concept Plan for what had been property on the Danielson Ranch. As the Park Service began gathering input to the Danielson concept plan at community meetings, some residents near the site objected loudly and said things like:

"There'll be a lot of traffic. Junk cars will be parked all around."

"An Indian Center! They'll be pounding drums, singing, and dancing way into the night! We won't be able to sleep."

"Will there be drinking?"

Charlie could understand why Grandpa Fred had wanted to hide his heritage. He continued to sit calmly. He was thinking about a way to handle these perceptions. At Du-par's one evening, he and Phil came up with a plan. Shortly after, they put it to the test.

The noise obstacle

A few trucks pulled up to the small house on the Danielson property. It was about 9:30 on this June night close to the longest day of the year. A few faint stars were starting to peek between clouds in the overcast sky. Phil pulled up in his truck, still sporting the wooden toolbox seat he had installed some time ago. He reached into the box for a flashlight and then started to pull his keys out of the ignition but decided to leave his lights on for a few minutes.

Leaves brushed against each other in the soft wind. Some mice rustled about. No howling coyotes, at least not yet. Overall, it was a quiet night, so far. Charlie got out of his truck. John Dawson, an Apache and the director of Indian Center West, got out of his truck and walked to the back of it. They too left their lights on.

"Need help with that?" Charlie asked.

"I brought my guys. We got it!"

John lowered the tailgate as a few more men jumped out of their trucks and ran over to help him pull a powwow drum from the back of his truck. It was huge—the size of a small, round table.

John Dawson brought his ALL NATIONS DRUM, as they called it. John wrote it all in caps to mean not just the drum but also the drummers. John had founded this DRUM about 1975. It had 15 men in it from the Winnebago,

Cheyenne, Navajo, Arapaho, Apache, and other nations. At least one was Chumash. The men went over to their trucks and cars, opened trunks, and pulled out metal chairs—a mixture of yesterday and today.

Phil pointed. "Over there, upstream from the pond. That's where we'd have a powwow."

They turned off their vehicle lights. Some switched on flashlights. Some carried the drum, the others the chairs. Just one big drum. No other instruments. They knew this routine so well that they set up in the dark, with just their flashlights.

The men sat around the drum pounding out Indian rhythms all together with exuberance. They chanted native chants from the 1800s to present day in two styles: Southern Plains in a low tone and Northern including Canadian in a higher tone. The chant leader started each chant and then all joined in. They moved themselves to a few different places in the bowl itself where the drumming got extremely loud even though not amplified.

"Keep it up—all together," said Phil as he started walking around shining his flashlight ahead. And keep it up, they did. They drummed and chanted the whole time without stopping.

Charlie, not a drummer, followed Phil. They walked over a ridge toward Boney. It was quiet there. They walked on trails for a while. No drumming sound. They heard nocturnal animals rustling in the brush.

"Well, here goes the real test. Keep on drumming. Loud. Louder!" and Phil got in his car. Charlie edged into the passenger seat.

They rolled down their windows as they got near the public road. They looked at each other and smiled. The drumming was quieter than cars driving down the road.

They parked their car at the entrance to the ranch on Potrero and walked up nearby hills. Just a little drumming sound. They walked across the street into the 1960s residential area. No drumming sound.

With a sense of victory, the DRUM packed up and wound down the dark narrow ranch road in single file cars to home.

Later Phil decided to ask nearby residents if they had heard the drums. They had not.

Phil felt comfortable with Native Americans even in contentious situations since he had been working alongside them for a while now.

"Why," he asked John Dawson a short time after the drumming experiment,

155

"are we national park people getting so much support from the Indian community when you have issues with federal agencies?"

He knew Charlie had an effect, but was that all? The answer was that Charlie's cultural center concept was so related to the concepts of respect for Mother Earth, respect for ancestors, and to the concern for the future of our children that they all, NPS and Native Americans, wanted to cooperate. Archaeologists too! Clay Singer conducted numerous walking archaeological surveys on the Satwiwa site with Charlie, who functioned as a crew member and Native American consultant. As they walked over the area time and again, they saw surface signs of Chumash occupation: items like stone flakes probably left from making arrow heads from chert, sharp stones used as tools, and marine shells transported from the coast for food.

More obstacles

In one of the interchanges after work, Charlie suggested a powwow out at the new park site. After all, they knew the drums would not be too disturbing to neighbors. Many would even come. Indian Center West and Many Trails Powwow Club became co-sponsors. Bill Redmond worked with Charlie to plan the event. There would be all nations dancing, Indian music, and native food. They expected a large crowd so there was a lot to do.

Bill had a lot of experience with large events, but the park had a new young staff and there were no amenities out at Rancho Sierra Vista, as they were now consistently calling it. The group would need to make things up as they went. Charlie was very patient with bureaucracy, with requirements, and with the schedule for the powwow. There were a few minor snafus. Sue Nelson, one of the recreation area's early promoters, opposed the powwow at first. He mediated this and other issues that arose, always keeping a sense of humor. But then a big problem emerged.

Tony Roybal, son of Jessie Roybal, was now on staff as a ranger. He knew Native Americans well. He warned that Dennis Banks might show up and turn the powwow into a civil rights protest. Park Service authorities and local law enforcement took this very seriously. They knew that Dennis Banks was one of the founders of AIM (American Indian Movement) and one of the leaders of the Wounded Knee occupation in 1973. Law enforcement started planning for a SWAT team on the perimeters of the park.

During one of the planning meetings, Charlie weighed in with his calm voice.

"Everybody breathe. This is a family event—about culture, food, music, and traditions. It is an awareness that we are alive. People who now live in these mountains can see who lived here and what they can learn from them."

And then he enlisted his Native American cohorts including Kote Lotah, Chumash; John Dawson, Apache; and Lionel Allrunner, Cheyenne. They sent flyers throughout the Los Angeles native community billing the powwow as a family event. Down deep they believed AIM would not destroy a good thing; they would want Satwiwa and all it stood for to succeed.

Everything seemed in order. Sallie Cuaresma had charge of planning the food booth. The food had to meet Health Department regulations, and she was on top of that. Many Trails had arranged the powwow activities. People had come to the site to mow, clear, sweep, clean, and post signs. The staff and volunteers had met challenge after challenge including creating a makeshift parking lot. Charlie was one volunteer, who mowed grass for the parking lot. But then the day before the event, the fire department called. They warned that hot car engines could spark a fire in any tall grass left in the makeshift lot.

"We'll be there at 6 a.m. and if we see any chance of fire, we'll shut down the powwow."

Stars were starting to pop out over Rancho Sierra Vista. A newly married couple was pulling weeds here and there on the parking lot. That was the answer to the multi-faceted question Charlie did not know he was asking. Nancy Fries and Bill Ehorn had married in April, just a few months before.

Bob Chandler, John Reynolds, Phil Holmes, the Ehorns, and other NPS leadership and staff were not going to fail the Native American community. They had been working with them successfully now for some time. And the Native Americans were there in force: Charlie, Elder Bob Rivera and his family including his grandchildren, John Dawson and some of the drummers, Lionel Allrunner, and others. It got darker, but they kept going over the parking area, set away from the bowl as Charlie had suggested. They stayed late into the night hoeing, shoveling, and using gloved and bare hands to pull weeds and blades of grass where tomorrow they expected a sea of cars. Flashlights came out for a while. Finally, they felt they were done. Some went home. Some slept on the ground or in their cars. The over-nighters woke up to heavy dew and fog, the June gloom expected every morning this time of year. It would burn off as the early June sun came over the mountains.

6 a.m.: fire inspectors showed up as promised. They walked the parking lot. They tried to start a fire. The all-nighters held their breath. No fire. The inspectors tried again. The fire wouldn't light.

"Well, can't see any reason to shut this event down." And the fire inspectors got in their vehicles and pulled away.

Figure 33: Charlie helping prepare for a Satwiwa event, possibly the powwow, Chumash Elder Bob Rivera seen at back right (SMMNRA Archives, nd)

Figure 34: Grass cleared for parking at a Satwiwa powwow, (SMMNRA Archives, 1983)

The sun was fully up now. It promised to be a beautiful sunny day, just warm enough, just cool enough. Two people were inside the little ranch house preparing for the powwow crowd.

"Here are some *manos* and *metates*. Put them where we put them last weekend."

"There were a lot of people here last weekend. I don't know if our living room can handle this crowd."

"What are these?"

"They were used to grind seeds. Sort of like a mortar and pestle, but they were around before that. Here, put out these stone flakes, probably left over from making arrow heads a long time ago. I'll hang the map."

"Why don't we just leave that up instead of taking it down every week and then putting it right back up again the next weekend?"

Earlier in 1982, Bob Chandler had interviewed a number of people looking for someone to live as a volunteer caretaker at Rancho Sierra Vista. He chose Tongva Art Alvitre to live rent-free in the small house on the ranch close to the natural bowl. Art and his wife moved their belongings out of the living room every weekend so it could be a display area for visitors. Today, they were doing this in anticipation of the powwow gathering and really feeling the squeeze.

The powwow

"Well, the June gloom has worn off! Just enough sun today!" Marti Leicester was walking the powwow area with Charlie.

"Did you see the two golden eagles and two hawks fly over when we were getting things ready this morning? They are a good sign."

John Dawson pulled up to the small house with his big heavy drum. The drummers were waiting for him with their chairs. Off they went to set up—light and bright this time.

"All is going well. Hey, watch out for the gopher hole." Bill Redmond joined Charlie and Marti from the direction of the parking lot. He had brought to bear his experience with large events for this powwow. He had worked with Charlie on the planning. Their worries dissipated as they rambled together across the hard packed ground, compacted by the work they had done and from the crowd that was all around them.

They constantly changed course as something caught their attention—so much to see. Now and then someone stopped them—so glad there was a great turnout.

They walked by the food booth tempted by the appetizing smell of fry bread. They saw people sitting on bales of hay scattered here and there as seats brought in for the event. Some were picnicking. Some were just talking.

"What a job setting up all those bales. Thanks to the volunteers!" Bill commented as they walked near the powwow circle. Bales of hay, two rows deep surrounded the circle, about 25 yards in diameter. John Dawson's drum was center. There were other drums with their groups outside the circle.

"Looks like we are about to start," Marti noted dancers in native dress lining up east to west for the grand entrance. A master of ceremonies, as the voice of the powwow, started introducing them as they came into the circle. The ALL NATIONS DRUM started drumming and chanting. It was 11 a.m., standard start time for a powwow.

Law enforcement rangers walked the perimeter of the Satwiwa area, just in case. Marti, Charlie, and Bill kept on walking as organizers but also as participants.

People were sitting on most of the bales surrounding the circle, captivated by the colorful Indian dress whirling in All Nations dancing. Now the MC was talking to the powwow director, who managed the events. Today it was Bob Rivera, a 6-foot, 5-inch Chumash elder who could certainly oversee the events. The central drum slowed. The MC started passing the drumming in clockwise fashion outside the circle. The first perimeter drum started. Now and then, a dancer would catch and hold the eye of an elder sitting on a bale or a chair brought to the event. They were dancing and singing for themselves but also for those who could not, as was tradition.

Charlie, Marti, and Bill found themselves moving briskly to the enthusiastic drum beat. The music became spiritual at times and their pace slowed down to match it. They felt the drum rhythm as if it were the heart of the very earth they walked on. They looked up to see hikers on the trails and an occasional person on horseback.

John Reynolds' wife, Bobbie, felt a visceral connection to the whole event. She couldn't wait to sample some fry bread. That done, she and John found themselves inside the powwow circle. Bob Rivera had set aside some dances for non-Indians. Now was their chance. Mitzi and Bob Chandler joined in. So did Nancy and Bill Ehorn. They saw Phil and tried to get him into the circle too, but he waved and moved on to check the parking lot—all okay there. He was very busy with logistics. He walked out to the entrance at the city road to make sure there was no serious congestion—all okay there. He made sure there was enough water for the crowd on this sunny day. There was. He saw a few members of AIM having a good time.

Jane Cazabat, a Muscogee-Creek/Seminole storyteller, saw Charlie. "Charlie, this is fabulous. But where's your powwow ribbon shirt?"

Charlie looked down at the shirt he was wearing.

"I'll make you one." And she ran off to do some native storytelling to a waiting group.

Native people from Indian Center West in Culver City stopped to talk to Charlie, Marti, and Bill as they continued their walk. Members of the Many Trails Powwow Club joined the conversation.

"Thanks for co-sponsoring this event," Bill said to the group. Indian Center West had been involved in the planning and set up. The Many Trails Powwow Club really knew how to orchestrate powwow events. They held monthly powwows in the San Fernando Valley.

"Hi, Charlie, what projects are you working on? Any land being threatened?" Vicki Goldschlager had come by for a short while.

Charlie and Vicki talked briefly about various development projects. More and more Vicki was encountering Charlie at meetings about preserving large parcels of land, especially when native heritage was involved. Sometimes he had Clay Singer, Chester King, Alex Kirkish or another archaeologist with him; sometimes he came solo but armed with their material.

"Well, I was a little worried about all the dust and traffic and wish everyone could have come by horse or on foot."

Charlie chuckled, "On horseback? Maybe next time."

As Vicki waved and walked off, Charlie asked a man walking by, "You enjoying yourself? Where are you from?"

"Across the street, actually. This is fun."

Charlie involved the neighbor in conversation with the Many Trails Club members for a few minutes, until the man caught wind of the food booth.

The sun was starting to set, the traditional end of a powwow. Law enforcement was still walking the perimeter.

The director was cuing the MC again. Powwows take time to honor people who have made a difference. The MC called Charlie and the NPS staff to the center and thanked them for making this event happen. Then, as the sun waned —a little more drumming, dancing, and scrambles for fry bread.

Jane Cazabat stopped to talk to Charlie on her way out. She had her 12-year-old son and his two friends with her.

"Looks like you boys had a good time."

"Like we said, these urban kids need to feel the earth."

"Well, come again." Charlie said to them as they started to leave.

"Remember my shirt," Charlie teased Jane as she and the boys walked toward the parking lot.

Charlie felt a tap on his shoulder.

"Saw your old, ugly face in the paper. Came to see what you were up to." Charlie lit up and smiled broadly at his father's old roping buddy, Ben Johnson, now the movie star.

But the movie star was upstaged, "This is wonderful! Why haven't we done this before?" Charlie's eyes twinkled as he agreed with Sue Nelson.

No demonstrators, no trouble, just good family fun.

Figure 35: Powwow, Satwiwa, (SMMNRA Archives, 1982)

But some unrest was out there. Sometime after the powwow, elder and powwow director Bob Rivera visited a camp near Point Conception where a group of Chumash lived. There he engaged in a conversation with some young men that went something like this:

One asked, "Why are you elders still hunting with traps when guns are available?"

Bob did not argue this point, but instead talked about making progress while preserving the environment.

Another asked, "Why aren't we going to meetings and demanding our rights, saying what we think instead of working with all these lawmakers?"

Bob explained that many approaches have their place.

And another, "When you do a blessing, why don't you use a wand with a crystal in it, like my relatives do, instead of an eagle feather?"

Bob answered directly, "Some traditions are worth keeping. Are you aware that only we Indians are allowed to have eagle feathers? The eagle is one of the four power birds." Bob was beginning to see that this group had a lot to learn.

"And why should we recognize Charlie as our chief?"

Bob answered full on, "Because he is the one who can lead and teach you."

Some took in what Bob had to say, some didn't.

Satwiwa: the vision is named and expands

In 1983, the National Park Service and the Native American Advisory Board agreed. They would establish the Native American Natural Area at Rancho Sierra Vista and as soon as possible start construction on a new Native American Cultural Center building. They named the area *Satwiwa*, Chumash for *the bluffs*. A brown wooden sign went up on the corner of Reino and Potrero Roads in Newbury Park: Rancho Sierra Vista/Satwiwa.

Ranching would be celebrated there also, but Satwiwa was the real prize— the only outdoor national park site in the United States dedicated to all Native Americans. Volunteers and Park Service staff arranged a ring of logs in campfire style near the house. The house was a weekend showcase. But that was about it so far. A new building to replace the little house was a few years off, but there would be a ground breaking ceremony now anyway, figuratively and really putting a stake in the ground as a promise.

A'lul-koy Lotah conducted the ground breaking with a Chumash digging stick similar to those her ancestors would have used. Kote made it for her of ceanothus, better known as wild lilac. He hardened the tip in the traditional way by alternately plunging it into a fire and then quickly immersing it in water. He carved a hole in a piece of sand stone, slipped it over the handle, and affixed it with tar. He did this to add weight, which was traditional for sticks used to dig posts, exactly its use at this Satwiwa dedication. A'lul-koy also did the white sage blessing. Soon after, Charlie, as chair of the

Native American Advisory Board, started holding regular meetings to keep the promise and give the dream life.

The Advisory Board quickly took on a new name blending the Chumash and Tongva languages, *Friends of Hutast and Tugupan. Hutast* is Chumash for earth. *Tugupan* is Tongva for sky.

Discussions ensued regarding the official name for the Indian natural and cultural area on the old Danielson property. Satwiwa would be part of the name, but the Indians involved, along with others, bantered about the details over a few meetings with discussions like this one:

"We are American Indians. It should be the American Indian Center."

"I thought it would be the Chumash Center."

"But the Center is for all indigenous peoples."

"Are you saying that it is for Hawaiians and Eskimos in Alaska?"

"Yes."

"Would you include Samoans?"

"Samoa is a U.S. Territory, so sure. So we need to call Satwiwa a Native American Center."

"Some of us prefer to be called American Indians."

This bantering went on for a while. At one meeting, Charlie suggested using both terms in the name. Most agreed to the *Satwiwa Native American Indian Cultural Center*, and so it was.

Back at Cheeseboro

While the Danielson property was being converted to Park Service purposes, SMMNRA was in the process of acquiring several other properties. John Reynolds was handling some of these. Back at headquarters, Bob Chandler asked him, "How's it going with Rad and Cheeseboro?"

"Rad Sutnar? Interesting fellow. He's out there managing large residential projects and business parks—and looking out for the environment and historical sites at the same time. He has a way with private landowners."

"Eight hundred-forty acres there are slated for development," Bob continued.

"Yes, and Rad'll be involved in developing about half of that canyon, but he'll help us get the other half—four hundred acres or so."

"How long before we own that land?" Bob asked.

John was up on the details. "Congress has to appropriate funds, so first it'll

164

be sold to the Trust for Public Land. Rad's known Charlie for a while, by the way."

"That helps."

"The day I was out there with Rad, a red-tailed hawk came out of a clump of oaks and tried to land on my shoulder. He and Lisa Mc Gimsey from the Trust kept trying to shoo it away."

"A good omen, you know, according to Chumash beliefs. I learned that from Charlie. NPS will have that property by the end of 1984," Bob projected. He was right. December 1984. Four hundred acres: another large property acquired for SMMNRA.

Even with larger properties coming on board, the small Satwiwa bowl remained a focus for Charlie and NPS. In 1984, the National Park Service held three public meetings for the Rancho Sierra Vista Development Concept Plan that year. The plan was for a unique cultural program with the cooperation of federal, state, and local agencies as well as Native American and nonnative organizations. Charlie was there. The first meeting was very negative. For the second meeting NPS changed the map so the Indian natural area was the same size as the demonstration farming area and much of the opposition died away. The successful powwow contributed, of course.

Charlie was now immersed in Native American projects, especially Satwiwa. His rodeo days faded. He traded the rodeo arenas for mountains, canyons, seashores, islands, and meeting rooms throughout Southern California.

Figure 36: Charlie speaking in an NPS meeting room, (SMMNRA Archives, 1982)

Figure 37: Charlie, the cowboy, as he starts to focus more on Satwiwa, (Photo by Roger Hardy, News Chronicle Collection, Thousand Oaks Library, 1982)

At Du-par's: storytelling roles of Indians and rangers

Phil hesitated and then decided to be blunt. "A few rangers have been stopping me in the halls at headquarters saying things like, 'Are Native Americans really going to be doing interpretations at Satwiwa? I spent my life learning how to interpret Native American culture, I am a professional. Are you really going to have amateurs do it?' "

"Tell them I'll be glad to sit with them in nature or in the office and share what I know about our native culture. We can learn from each other."

"I'll see if I can set that up."

"But," Charlie continued, "we need to tell our own stories passed down to us, not out of books written by someone with ancestors from a different continent. I can't tell people about their culture. It goes both ways. Let's just get this started. How about if we call it the Native American Guest Host program?"

Charlie was an instrument of peace in the Native American community and helped NPS build trust. He is an open man. He talks with you, shares with you. In a tense, angry situation, he is calming, sometimes by being direct, sometimes just by his presence. He would tell people to slow down, talk about this; and they would. He attracted people. People gathered to listen no matter what he was talking about. He could be very serious if a line was being crossed. He made no bones about it. (Bill Redmond)

Right from the beginning, I saw Charlie as approachable. He was not intimidating, didn't push his agenda. He was there for a purpose: to represent Chumash values and traditions in the park. He was fun to work with. I wanted to get to know him because he had knowledge I needed, and he was himself willing to learn. He was patient with the bureaucracy, requirements, and schedule for the powwow. He knew we were a new, young staff challenged by a park with no amenities. He educated the staff about Native American culture and traditions. He was there. He had the network. He got us in touch with all kinds of people that enriched our understanding of the Native American heritage on parklands. (Marti Leicester, first Field Ranger, SMMNRA, June 14, 2011)

Charlie involved people in conversations, whether he knew them or not. Everyone was a potential friend. (Sallie Cuaresma, Site Supervisor and second Director of Indian Center West, Cherokee/Creek, October 12, 2011)

NPS had a history of thinking they know what people need to hear. Charlie set a model that needs to be replicated: let native peoples tell their own stories. (Woody Smeck)

I learned more about Chumash culture when there as superintendent. Early on I got blank stares from people when you'd mention Chumash. I myself had no idea about the Chumash at first, but I learned. Charlie is a good person, solid guy, seems to promote what he believes and is dedicated. I never heard anything negative about Charlie. His focus was to expose and promote Chumash values. (Bob Chandler, first Superintendent, SMMNRA, February 25, 2010)

Chapter 14: Monitoring the Monitoring, 1983-86

"The Lost Village in Encino! Where is it? Who lived there?" Charlie thought about these newspaper headlines and questions as he parked his 1969 green, fast-back Mustang along the road, got out, and walked to a development site in modern Encino. He had known the ancient village was there for a long time. A number of people were walking ahead of him. Some were behind. All around him now, swarming toward a gate, he saw men, women, and some children. Some were calm. Some were agitated. There was a hill behind him, where in the past he had dumped cement for luxury condominiums. He looked up for a moment, wondering what he had done.

Charlie's friend, Tom Hoskinson, an aerospace engineer and an avocational archaeologist, had found burials where some old structures on the hill had been and told Charlie. Also, some of his professional archaeologist buddies had told him that the rumors he'd heard from cement mixer drivers were true. The seven thousand-year-old village site below the hill did have burials in it, and they were being desecrated.

He was in the middle of all the excitement at Satwiwa. But he had to fit in some time on this situation.

Figure 38: Charlie with Kote Lotah and Tom Hoskinson (SMMNRA Archives, c. 1992)

The Encino burial site demonstration

First Financial Group (FFG) was planning a commercial building on this site and was ready to start construction in 1983. But the heavy earth moving equipment stood idle, stopped temporarily, partly because of the California Environmental Quality Act (CEQA) passed ten years earlier. CEQA required mitigation measures for significant environmental impact, including impact on historical resources. The site had been recorded as a prehistoric site as far back as 1960 when Dr. Charles Rozaire from the Los Angeles County Museum of Natural History observed artifacts on the surface of the area. So now, the City of Los Angeles was requiring First Financial to conduct an archaeological excavation.

It took years for cities to create the implementation plans for CEQA, so it was not until the 1980s that the demand for independent archaeologists in California accelerated. Until then, mostly university teams conducted the archaeological surveys and related work on Native American sites. But now private firms were getting involved. FFG hired such a firm headed by Roger Desautels. Back in 1978, the firm had conducted a surface examination for signs of artifacts in sight of where Charlie and the crowd were walking. They had found evidence that this might have been an Indian site.

The Desautels firm knew it needed a most-likely-descendant on site to monitor the excavations. The firm's full-time ethnographer, Page Talley, tried to find appropriate Native American descendants to monitor at the site daily, which would have been descendants of Indians who had lived at the San Fernando Mission. She went to that mission and other outreach Indian places but could not find any Fernandeños to come and monitor so they hired Sparky Morales, chief of the Gabrielinos and some of his relatives. Gabrielinos descended from Indians who had lived at Mission San Gabriel, about a 30-mile drive southeast of Mission San Fernando. They were Tongvas, who had also lived at Mission San Fernando.

Because the site was at a busy corner, the developer eventually fenced it in to prevent vandalism. That's what Charlie found when he arrived one January morning in 1985, around the same time as about 30 other Native Americans. A blur of orange chain link stood in front of them.

"What's all the noise?" Sparky looked visibly upset.

Roger had passed away in 1982. His widow, Dr. Nancy Desautels, an archaeologist herself, was now leading the work. She looked toward the orange fence and then went into a building to phone Sparky's son and nephew to come and help out, but neither was available. The newspaper articles had caused a flurry of reactions to the site. On top of that, Nancy was dealing with more work than she had anticipated. Few had expected the quantity of artifacts being unearthed at the site.

Sparky could hear shouts from the other side of the orange fence.

"You won't let my child visit the cemetery of his great, great grandmother!"

"Let us in. You are on our sacred ground!"

Sparky looked more and more upset. Because he was about 80 years old, Nancy started to worry about him. She walked over to make sure the gate was locked. She noticed one man standing near the front of the crowd quietly assessing the situation. He started to speak to her.

"We would like a word with you. I am Charlie Cooke."

She nodded with recognition. "Nancy Desautels. I heard my late husband speak of you, Charlie, as a chief. He told me that you worked on some digs with him."

"Sorry to hear about Roger." Charlie talked a few more minutes about Roger and the work they had done together.

"So you are in charge here, Nancy. I am related to people buried in there. So are these people here with me. We are Fernandeños." Nancy noticed a firm but respectful tone.

Charlie looked at her directly. "Surely, you understand. We have a right to visit the cemetery here."

"Charlie, you know that I cannot allow so many people to come in at one time; that would threaten the integrity of the excavations. Certainly, it would be disrespectful to those buried here."

Charlie and Nancy talked some more about what would be respectful. Charlie knew from work with the Native American Heritage Commission that the work was supposed to be monitored by Native Americans, if possible a most-likely-descendant. In this case that would be a Fernandeño. Nancy noticed that the crowd behind him had quieted and was listening.

"I'll contact Chief Little Bear, Rudy Ortega, for you. He is part Chumash and part Tongva. Now he is chief of the Fernandeños." Charlie did not bother to explain that he had been the founder and leader for the San Fernando Mission Band and that it went dormant in the 1970s after the rolls were closed. Rudy was resurrecting it.

"I thought you were a chief."

"I am a Chumash chief," he explained. "I know you understand the history here. Several tribes lived at the San Fernando Mission. Our heritage is something of a jumble. The village here—it was a cross-over area between the Chumash and Tongva. I am an example, part Tongva, but San Fernando Tongva. Contact Rudy. See if you can get him to monitor. I don't have time off from my job, but he does now and then."

Nancy offered, "I can let you in ten at a time."

Some of the group dispersed. Some took Nancy up on her offer. She could hear some rumbling and knew the work at this site would be challenged constantly.

"Our ancestors should not be excavated ever," she heard.

In her mind, archaeologists had a role in moving cemeteries, especially when there are no ways to stop impact. She saw their work as preserving native culture. She got in touch with Rudy, who started monitoring when not working at his regular job. He sat on the same hill with Sparky. He gave Sparky permission to monitor for the Fernandeño people when he was not there.

Time passed.

Observing monitoring

It was about noon in the San Fernando Valley on a warm summer day in 1985. Again, Charlie parked his Mustang near the busy Encino corner where the FFG project was continuing. He watched for a good opportunity to get out safely in the zooming traffic. He jumped out of his car and felt a twinge. He was going in for a gall bladder operation soon but couldn't sit home. He could feel the midday Valley heat bouncing off the pavement. He walked across the sidewalk and through an opening in the orange fence onto a dirt path. He saw activity ahead so left the trodden path and made his way though some native California scrub brush and then onto flat, brown ground which seemed to have been scraped clean of vegetation, the archaeologists' pathway perhaps. The Desautels firm was starting Phase Two, the archaeological process of excavating for artifacts and burials.

Charlie had come on this summer day in 1985 to see what was happening to the ancient native site on behalf of the Chumash, Tongva, and other Fernandeño Indians. No one had told him to come, but rumors were floating about possible disrespect to native ancestors interred at the site. Who was at fault was unclear and didn't matter. Now, even more than at Alcatraz and Point Conception, he knew that not only did he have to be here, but he had to do something to make the situation right.

He wiped his forehead and felt glad that there was still one shady oak standing. He looked behind him and up a small hill at luxury condominiums.

He remembered delivering cement there in the 1970s and hearing rumors of Indian burials nearby. There had been a restaurant and a smoke house on the street at the bottom of the hill. They were gone now.

Charlie looked around. There were about 90 people on this 2-acre site working at 2 by 2 meter excavations, basically square digs, sampling the site. He had worked with Clay Singer, Chester King, and Alex Kirkish enough by now to know what was going on all around him. He saw people with shovels and other digging implements at about 75 holes. He saw the site as strained—too many findings, too little monitoring.

He watched some workers digging carefully with small implements so as not to damage any artifacts in the ground. Most holes had only one person at them. Charlie walked around talking with the crew. He asked several individuals what they were unearthing.

"Remnants of food."

"Pieces of pottery and baskets."

"Burials of dogs and birds."

"Some stone tools, and look a piece of ceramic."

"I think these are floral remains."

Some holes had two or three people at them. He walked over to a group of three. They were looking at charred bones.

"That means they were Chumash and Tongva here," he said. "You know that the Chumash buried and the Tongva cremated—at least in this area."

Charlie walked on and noted more than one worker where there were human remains, as should be, but he saw a few bones strewn around. Again, too much going on for a single monitor. To do the job right, he would have to be in several places at once.

The developers had agreed to wait for burials to be moved and artifacts to be collected. The heavy equipment stood idle for now.

He watched a young man and woman looking at the soil in a wheelbarrow they had pushed into the shade of the huge oak. They crunched old, dried acorns under their sturdy work boots as they talked, almost as if punctuating their excitement about their findings.

For a few fleeting moments Charlie thought about the size of this tree. "It must be over three hundred years old," he guessed. In his mind's eye he saw his ancestors collecting acorns from oaks of all types throughout these hills. He knew this tree was a valley oak, a deciduous tree. It was summer now so the tree was full of leaves. He thought about other oaks in the hills. Some, such as live oaks, were green all year round. Natives cooked the acorns and used the wood from valley oaks for firewood. They used the harder or more flexible wood from other types of oaks to make bowls, bows, and even hoops for a game.

Another big crunch under the tree and Charlie turned his attention back to the two young people. They talked quietly as they looked at the soil in their wheelbarrow. The bubbling sound of the natural spring nearby would have been background music to their conversation in a time gone by, but today it was the traffic.

The young woman started pushing the wheelbarrow to the corner of the site that had been set aside for water screening. Charlie walked along and talked with her. She was a student. She was jumping up and down in synch with the bouncy wheelbarrow, excited about finding lots of artifacts. At the screening table, he watched and listened as a crew of four took her soil, poured it on a screen, and then sprayed it with a hose.

"Look, here's another one."

"Here too."

"How many artifacts does that make today?"

"Lots. There was so much Indian activity here on just these few acres. Look at the vegetation all around us. The food sources and the spring must have brought people here."

Charlie watched them bag and mark the artifacts for a while and then started walking around again. Everywhere Charlie looked, archaeologists were digging and screening. Some were students like the excited young woman. Some were seasoned. "There are an overwhelming number of artifacts," he thought. He continued walking around. The work looked professional, but the monitoring situation disturbed him.

He almost bumped against the spiny pads on a variety of prickly pear. He knew enough to know that this giant was 300-400 years old. He imagined his ancestors using the fruit and pads for food when it was young and tender or the thorns as needles at any age.

He knew that this Encino area had been the hub of the Southern San Fernando Valley for thousands of years. Here both Chumash and Tongva peoples lived and intermarried. In 1843, when the Mexican government dissolved the California missions, three Mission Indians, Ramon, Francisco, and

Roque, received 4,460 acres that became Rancho Los Encinos. Over the next decades, descendants subdivided and sold off pieces of the property. The Indian village was obliterated as cattle ranching, sheep herding, and some farming took over. In 1949, one of the final owners of a small piece donated five acres to the state along with an adobe typical of a rancho. The parcel became Los Encinos State Historic Park, close to the building site, the two acres that had been sold to a developer.

Charlie looked around for Roger's widow, Nancy. He had been hearing rumors about the site that bothered him. He had come by to touch base with Nancy and to make sure that Indian heritage was being respected, but she was not there today.

Charlie asked around for the site supervisor and found him. "Where are the Native American monitors?" he asked.

The supervisor pointed toward the large, old, valley oak, the only oak on site. Like most people in the archaeological community, he probably knew Charlie's reputation for working untiringly to preserve native sites and heritage.

Charlie saw Sparky Morales, the Gabrielino Tongva elder, walking over to sit under an umbrella by the big oak tree. Charlie talked to a few more of the crew. Sparky stayed under the tree sipping on lemonade.

Charlie walked back to supervisor. "Where are the other monitors?"

He told him there were no others.

"Sparky must be tired," thought Charlie. "He is the only monitor with 90 or so archaeologists digging all around him. How can he monitor all this work by himself? I wonder what happened to Rudy. Probably didn't have many days off, or maybe he comes when I am not here."

Promoting representative monitors

Two weeks later, after his gall bladder operation, Charlie was back. He was sore but forgot that as he walked onto the site. Sparky was in the same spot under the same umbrella by the same ancestral tree.

Charlie started coming several times a week and saw the same situation again and again: many burials, what looked like millions of artifacts, and one monitor. Charlie, remembering the days of observer training with Vince Ibanez, wondered if Sparky had been trained on what was expected of him. It seemed to him that Sparky, a well-meaning and respected elder, was in an impossible situation. Possibly, Nancy was too. The extent of the

174

lost village had erupted as a surprise to all involved.

At one of his visits, Charlie found that Nancy was at a Mexican restaurant nearby. He went there and sat down with her.

"I hear you are doing a great job cataloguing all the artifacts you found," Charlie started.

"Yes, there are a lot. Many fragments, which makes this even harder."

"I could see that. This site is too rich and dense for one monitor. We need at least three. Besides, Sparky is a San Gabriel Mission Tongva."

Nancy knew Sparky's heritage.

"This is the San Fernando Mission area where a different band of Tongva and the Chumash lived. You can tell that both were here."

Nancy was an experienced archaeologist and knew that at least in this area the Tongva cremated and the Chumash buried.

"We need monitors who represent their San Fernando ancestors. And we need more. There is no way Sparky can monitor all this work by himself. This site is full of artifacts that should be preserved. Our dead need to be better respected."

Charlie had learned a lot about the site from John Romani and others at the Northridge Archeological Research Center. He added, "Do you know that some of these burials date back to 500 BC?"

Nancy agreed to more monitors. Charlie was happy for the moment.

He drove up again and again over months. Still, he saw only Sparky monitoring. He talked to the workers. Eventually, they began to know him.

Some of the people working at the site started calling him. One night they called to tell him that the burials were going to be moved.

He went to the site the next day. One of the crew told him that the coroner would be coming to remove the burials. Charlie looked for Nancy, but she was not there so he told the supervisor not to do anything until a Native American Heritage Commission representative came from Sacramento. He also told Sparky. The following day, the coroner did come and did take the remains. As soon as he saw Nancy, a few visits later, Charlie told her the way the burials were being handled was disrespectful to Indian heritage, and it was wrong—and to talk to the developers about getting more help to do the job right.

About a week later, as he drove up, he noticed a security guard.

"Hi there, fellow. What's new? What's going on?"

"Sorry, sir, but we can't let you in."

"This is not over," Charlie said to himself.

A special ride

Later in 1985, Charlie, Damon, and a group of seasoned rodeo cowboys and cattle wranglers rode into the hills of Antelope Valley, many miles from Encino. Charlie was balancing a box on his saddle. Damon was riding next to him.

"Damon, this is a Tataviam and Kawaiisu area. I'm part Tataviam."

"How do you know?"

"Well, I grew up in this area. My grandma was a Mission Indian and some of the Mission Indians came from here."

"So why aren't you Kawaiisu?"

"They weren't at the San Fernando Mission as far as I know."

They rode quietly for a while. Charlie held onto the box he was carrying tightly and almost reverently. In the background the others were laughing and remembering good times in these hills.

Finally, the group dismounted. Charlie stayed astride his horse.

There were hills and trees all around. A small stream gurgled by. Right in front of them was a rock shelter, not quite a cave, but a roof of sorts, no less. Ancient rock art covered the walls.

"Here," said Charlie. "My dad liked it here. We used to ride up here when I was younger than you, Damon. His brother, too."

"Uncle Izzy? I wish I had met him."

"Yes, Izzy was a ranch hand around here as long as I can remember—stayed in the area until the day he died. He told his wife a few days before he died, 'If I die tomorrow, I hope they bring me back as a cowboy.' Died young in his corral. This place had meaning for our people." And then he rode over to the rock shelter, turned the box upside down, and let Cy Cooke's ashes flow out to meld with the soil, the rocks, the stream.

Charlie dismounted, pulled out a conch shell, dried sage, and an abalone shell from a sack attached to his saddle. The cowboys and wranglers looked at him and saw the son of chiefs. He called the spirits by blowing the conch shell four times facing the four winds. Then he lit the sage in the shell, waited for it to smolder, turn white, and then wafted it with an eagle feather over all who were with him.

"I learned a lot from him about the land and how to live on it." They all stood silently together for a while and then walked back to their horses and rode off down the mountain, again laughing as they remembered all the good times with Cy Cooke.

Figure 39: Charlie with his dad, Cy Cooke (Courtesy of Linda Cooke, 1985)

Organizing a meeting to argue the cause

"There's gonna be a Heritage Commission meeting at Los Encinos Park about the work near there. Can you come?"

"Charlie, I need to use the phone."

"Okay, Linda, just a few more calls."

By 1986, Charlie was back at work. He had healed well after his gall bladder operation. He started making phone calls every night. He called Chumash, Tongva, Tataviam, and other Indian groups whose ancestors had lived at the San Fernando Mission. He contacted Loretta Allen, the executive secretary of the Heritage Commission, and Dr. Chester King, by now an archaeologist respected for his Native American expertise. Charlie invited them all to a Heritage Commission meeting on the Los Encinos Park site. About 60 Indians attended. In all, about seventy-five people came. State Senator Alan Robbins was on site and asked to speak to Charlie. Charlie told him he would talk with him once he was done with the meeting. The senator did not wait.

The meeting was held in a small, 15 by 15 room in the old historic De la Ossa Adobe. Most people stayed outside along the fence and talked about the site's long history and its many archaeological finds. Phil Holmes was among them. Inside Charlie was explaining the importance of the site to Commissioner Allen. In the end, the group assembled succeeded in getting the Heritage Commission to express disapproval of the work at the site, but the building would go up. The developer did agree to re-inter the burials and to employ representative monitoring.

Figure 40: Los Encinos Park site, large prickly pear, historic adobe (Author's photo, 2010)

After nine months of archaeological work, the crew uncovered over a million artifacts. The burials were re-interred. Charlie had asked that all the native tribes in the area be represented at the burial, but Sparky Morales presided over a small ceremony. Few, including Charlie, knew about it. The developer did not hire any more monitors. Some believed, and a newspaper article reported, that Nancy held the artifacts, waiting for funds the developer owed her firm so she could archive them properly.

"This is not over," Charlie again said to himself.

The time came in 1987 to pour the building foundation. Charlie told the dispatcher not to send him there with cement for the foundation.

"I am not against progress," he explained, "but I would be a hypocrite after all that happened there. I was fighting for our heritage and ancestors."

Livingston Graham respected his position, but they sent another driver. The commercial building went up.

Charlie sees all in a holistic view. Land affects people; people affect land. He will fight for both. He works with natives and nonnatives alike. He looks at a project—how it will affect everything. Charlie is important because he bridges Native American backgrounds. He is both Chumash and Tongva. The 80s were tumultuous in regard to Native Americans. Some were aggressive. The Chumash and Tongva wanted him to side with one or another: Charlie very carefully and strongly embraced both. In fact, he bridged and represented several Native American cultures. (Dr. Nancy Wiley, AKA Desautels, archaeologist, June 15, 2011)

Chapter 15: Contrasting archaeological approaches, 1986-88

He'd park his cement truck down at the work site near the beach at the end of the day, chat a few minutes with fellow truck drivers, edge into his Mustang, and then zip his Mustang along the Pacific Coast Highway, up Malibu Canyon Road, past the Howard Hughes Research Lab overhanging a cliff facing the ocean. He'd look up right about then, watching for any boulders that might let loose. A friend of his had gunned her car to outrun one of those not too long ago. It smacked down right behind her and she just kept going.

On he'd go through two tunnels. He'd curve along the outside edge of the road—a steep drop down and then pass into grassier terrain where Malibu Canyon Road morphs into Las Virgenes Road. He'd slow down his Mustang as he passed an archaeological site near Malibu Creek State Park. If this were a day when his cement runs had ended early, he would stop there, otherwise home or to a meeting somewhere.

This was Charlie's daily commute to and from his home in Newbury Park, some 30 miles or so one way. He was based at Livingston Graham's Santa Monica site in the late 80s, delivering cement from there to Los Angeles, the San Fernando Valley, Hollywood, and Malibu.

Malibu Creek as a contrast to the Lost Village

In 1987, the Los Angeles County Public Works Department started to widen the turning lane into Malibu Creek State Park right on Charlie's commute. This was the same general area Charlie had monitored when the parking lot was enlarged, ten years before. Charlie got involved with this project while he was still involved with the Lost Village in Encino. The two projects overlapped in time, showing up their differences. The way they were handled was affected by the fact that one was on public and the other on private land.

The Malibu Creek property belonged to the State of California and the road in front of it to Los Angeles County. Since the parking lot had been enlarged ten years earlier, Dr. Chester King and others had done archaeological surveys at and around the Malibu Creek site. As a result, the state now knew much more about the Chumash village of Talepop that had existed in the area. In order to mitigate effects of the road widening on any possible Indian burials and artifacts, State Parks contracted with the Northridge Center for Public Archaeology (NCPA, formerly NARC) to conduct excavations on the west side of Las Virgenes Road. An anthropology professor at California State University at Northridge (CSUN), Mark Raab, was the principle investigator. Lynn Gamble, a graduate student in archaeology, was the lab director for the project.

The dig was right at the edge of the roadway in plain view of all the passing traffic. As the NCPA crew made their way through the canyon to the site in the early morning, they drove through mist, typical of spring in the area. Art Alvitre, fitting this in between his Satwiwa responsibilities, was part of the digging crew. The crew was lucky that they did not have to work around the constant summer beach traffic: busses and cars with bikes and surfboards attached.

Few busses, but there were cars. As people slowed down on this section of road, they saw surface scraping at test pits right at the road's edge with a worker at each pit using trowels and small brushes to remove any top layers of material, workers sketching the objects in pits, right in place—right as they were found, someone photographing the objects before they were moved, and now and then the crew sweeping dirt into a kitchen dustpan and putting it in five-gallon white buckets for analysis in a lab set up nearby.

On some days, an early morning coyote lingered in the area, and then with no food in sight, moved on. Deer walked into the area, froze when close to the test pits, and then noticing no threat, glided away. Hawks flying overhead soared on—nothing in sight to swoop down and capture.

Figure 41: Malibu Creek State Park (Courtesy of Bryn Barabas Potter, 2013)

As the sun moved high in the sky, the crew started putting items into small brown paper bags, labeling them with standard archeological information. Two or three monitors walked around from pit to pit, conversing with the diggers and making notes. Charlie stopped often enough that people driving by would see him.

Sometimes traffic stalled while crew vehicles slowly pulled out to take heavy buckets down the street, very close to the pits. The buckets were filled with water and dirt scooped in, a flotation method teasing seeds and other plant materials to the top. The hardened crew took buckets out of the vehicle and carried their dead weight to a screening area at the park site.

There screeners poured dirt through successively smaller screens. Bryn Barabas, a CSUN student, was one of these. The students talked excitedly from time to time, "Look, some large shells! Here are some flaked stone tools. Oh, here they are—small shell beads!" The crew knew the importance of these beads, which the Chumash and Tongva in this area used for money. By evening a few items were left on the last screen, air drying before being transferred to paper bags, finally ready for the field lab.

Science on an historic movie set

Like so many sites in the Santa Monica Mountains, the Malibu Creek site shared the drama of Native American resurgence and that of the burgeoning Hollywood industry. Lynn Gamble set up her NCPA lab inside a prop for the 1948 Cary Grant movie, *Mr. Blandings Builds His Dreamhouse*—a house slightly scaled down to make Cary Grant look taller. The crew went through slightly shorter than normal doors and worked at folding tables under the low ceiling of Mr. Blandings' living room. The sizing had the effect of making Charlie look larger than life, but then some people on the crew already thought he was.

Inside the lab the crew was at work using dental picks to move dirt on brightly-lit cafeteria trays. They moved the soil from one side to the other as a sifting method. Once in a while, someone would put a finding into a small container. Charlie would walk into the makeshift lab on his visits, talk to the workers, and look at their findings. He was always learning as well as teaching.

For the most part the lab crew was quiet in concentration. They were doing exacting work. Now and then though, an exclamation! "An otolith! Show Lynn." And then the explanation to a new crew member. "Lynn is very interested in these. Ear bones of a fish can tell us what species we have here."

"More small beads! Chester will want to know about these." And then to the new guy, "Chester knows native beads better than anyone."

A computer sat on one of the tables. One of the CSUN students had developed an archaeology data logger. Bryn took her turns entering findings onto the logger's database, cutting edge field technology for 1987.

At the end of the day, the crew pitched tents on the park site and spent the night. They were grateful for the onsite shower.

The team worked from Tuesday through Saturday. On Saturdays, there would be a barbecue on Mr. Blandings' patio. Charlie came by for these social events. There were several paid Indian monitors, but Charlie would stop by in his role as a native leader. He would get around to a lot of people while a few of the crew started cooking on the grills.

"How is it going, Art? Must be interesting to you since the Tongva as well as the Chumash were here." A little more chatting with Art and then Charlie would move on.

"Hi, Lynn, good to see enough people at every pit—and several Indian monitors here. Let me know if there are any hurdles I can clear up for you. I see the artifacts in storage boxes. I hear they will go to the center at CSUN."

"Hey, Charlie, how are you, friend? What's going on in your life? How's Linda?"

"Thanks for asking about her. She's great. We're thinking of moving—want better horse property. Hey, how do you like this staff? Linda gave it to me."

"Wow, where did she get that? I like the carved eagle's head."

"From an artist at the Renaissance Fair, out there at Paramount Ranch. But I'm using the one Kote made for me too."

He'd stop and converse with one or two people for a while.

"Hey, Bryn lady, glad to see you are working here."

"It's fun, Charlie. Things seem to move smoothly here."

"No burials here at the side of the road; that does make it simpler in a way."

"But even so, this was a long occupied site. I am privileged to work on it."

"Me too," Charlie agreed with Bryn. As the sun started to set, the barbecue grill sent smoke signals to come and get it. The crew relaxed, savored the food, and enjoyed their camaraderie.

Since Arden Edwards' days of adventuresome collecting, archaeology had become a science. Charlie had learned much of the science along the way, but his role was to help that science be responsible and respectful, so soon he was back to the Lost Village situation.

Unfinished business with the Lost Village of Encino

Sometime in 1988, Charlie stepped out of his Mustang in balmy Santa Barbara to attend a quarterly Heritage Commission meeting.

An old car drove up. A familiar woman stepped out. She looked worn out to Charlie, but he recognized her as he was walking into Santa Barbara City College. It was Nancy Desautels. She had been struggling with the developer over paying her firm for its work at the Encino site, which turned out to be a more extensive excavation than originally anticipated.

On the agenda tonight: the Heritage Commission would decide if it would back an assembly bill that Senator Alan Robbins was proposing. The bill would set aside state funds to pay for a summary report on archaeological work done at the Encino site and for managing the collection of the findings. Developer funds had not been adequate to pay for finishing the work at this dig.

Nancy was there with her two brothers-in-law. Perhaps, the Heritage Commission would use their influence to move the bill along or push the developer to pay her for all the work her firm had done and still needed to do.

Charlie started talking and summed up the situation as he saw it. The monitoring at the site was inadequate. There should have been three or four monitors. In addition, ancestral artifacts had been moved. Where? They needed to be preserved properly.

Other testimony included statements that described the situation from a number of vantage points.

"It is not right to hold our ancestors hostage."

"There was a large crematorium, and some bones were strewn around. We need to treat burials with more respect."

Nancy weighed in. She said that she knew there were scathing reports in the papers regarding the burials and reburials. It was a dammed if you do and damned if you don't situation. She pointed out that her firm was the first to rebury a major Indian cemetery. Before this time burials were sent to universities for study. She also stressed that they had listened to the Indians.

In the end, the Heritage Commission decided not to support the Robbins bill. They saw the situation as a developer issue. Eventually, some artifacts came under the control of Palomar College. The Fowler Museum at UCLA rehabilitated some others and moved them to a vault elsewhere. Los Encinos State Park housed some others. Nancy Desautels kept the field notes and catalogs. Nancy sued the developer for payment. A compromise was reached by the courts and all Desautels employees were paid outstanding salaries in full. Nancy received the satisfaction of knowing that the collection was safe but no funding for additional sorting or cataloguing, which is why other institutions took over housing and cataloguing the collection.

There remained another issue in the Encino area. A subterranean garage being planned as parking for a new grocery store was threatening to ruin the natural water system in the area, the very water that had sustained the ancestral Indians in these parts. Charlie and others fought the garage. They won. The store went up, and that was okay. Charlie was for progress and preservation, a dichotomy to some, but made sense to him. In the end, the artesian well was preserved; the ancestors were re-interred, but what a journey!

Differences between the Lost Village and Malibu Creek excavations

Because the Malibu Creek property was publically held by a state and its roadway by a county government, more environmental and cultural preservation regulations came into play than were the case at the Lost Village. There the property was held by a private corporation with commercial goals. The Malibu Creek project was managed by a public university with a philosophical approach to archaeology that promoted Native American involvement. Several native monitors were on site and engaged as part of the team. Charlie was welcomed and allowed to contribute. As a contrast, the Lost Village philosophy and related funding allowed for compliance. There was usually only one monitor. Charlie had to fight for his principles regarding artifacts and human remains. Very importantly, the roadside Malibu Creek site harbored no burials so how they were handled was not tested and made the entire situation easier than at the Lost Village where the burials made the situation volatile. Both projects moved the field of archaeology forward. The Lost Village provided a learning lab for future projects on privately owned land with burials. The Malibu Creek project provided a learning lab for a number of students who went on to other projects with a mindset that included Native Americans as part of the archaeological process.

At Du-par's: monitoring guidelines, Satwiwa's reach

"This can't happen again," Charlie stated as he continued to eat his late dinner.

"Huh?"

"The way the monitoring went at Encino. We all learned some lessons there. To be fair, that was a tough situation. I mean with burials and so many artifacts, but we need to be ready for the next time."

"I'm working on some guidelines for our park here," Phil answered, now deeply into his National Park Service Native American liaison role, which was about representing NPS to the native community.

"Well, to start with, make sure the monitor represents the culture that was there. Oh, and needs to be a part of the team—and needs to be listened to—and needs some training."

They talked about monitoring a while longer. They paid their bill and walked out to their trucks. They chatted for a few minutes under a giant old oak that reached across several parking spaces.

Figure 42: Giant Oak at Du-par's (Local History Collection, Thousand Oaks Library, nd)

"The other day, John Reynolds called me into his office to ask me how things were going at Satwiwa. His brother, Bob, is superintendent at Mount Rushmore. They had a special ceremony there with a number of tribes involved. After the ceremony one of the Indians came to his office and asked why they didn't have something like Satwiwa. I think he was a Sioux."

"Mount Rushmore? How did he find out?"

"Well, Charlie, you met at Indian Center West while the Satwiwa idea was forming—you know how you said a place for all Indians. Certainly, there are Sioux at Indian Center West. Maybe a Sioux from Los Angeles went back to visit at Mount Rushmore and, well, just talked about what he had seen or heard here. I am very proud of this."

"The Sioux—or any Indian—they are welcome here at any time." And Charlie added, "I'd like to learn more about their ceremonies."

The stars were studding the dark sky as they pulled out of the Du-par's parking lot, Charlie in his red truck and Phil in his white truck, still using a tool box as his driver's seat.

They continued meeting at Du-par's and more formally at NPS Headquarters and other places. As the Santa Monica Mountains Recreation Area took shape so did new monitoring guidelines. Phil started to include the guidelines into contracts with Chester King and other archaeologists who consulted with SMMNRA. At the same time, word was spreading about Satwiwa.

Charlie is atavistic or displaying the kind of behavior that seems to be long since suppressed by society's rules. For example, he views the land as his ancestral Chumash did—not owned but borrowed. Life is not linear, but cyclical. We are part of one large interconnected system. Mother Nature is not segmented. Man is just a part of this system. (Dr. Alex Kirkish)

Charlie is unique, combining several native heritages, never living on a reservation. He could see both sides of arguments and carefully embrace what made sense in both. He bridges groups. He taught but also learned from everyone. By the time I met him, I felt he could have run an archaeological investigation himself. Charlie is very public about his desire to preserve as much of the holistic world as he can. He spent a lot of his own time and energy, from what I saw always in a very respectful manner. Always a gentleman! Charlie made a difference in how I handled the situation in Encino. (Dr. Nancy Wiley)

Chapter 16: Involved, Involved, Involved, 1982-90

By the late 1980s, Charlie found himself everywhere, out to the islands, to developer sites all over the Southern California area, and on trips to Sacramento to meet with the California State Parks Advisory Board and the California Indian Legal Services Board, on which he still served. He was constantly invited to conduct Chumash blessings at major events like the opening of the new Thousand Oaks City Library. He found himself the subject of many newspaper articles and local radio and TV talk shows.

An island for sale—or not

Superintendent Bill Ehorn continued walking the islands with Charlie and Kote now and then. For years, Bill had been working with the owners of Santa Cruz and Santa Rosa to bring those islands into the park system.

Dr. Carey Stanton owned the west end of Santa Cruz, which was 90 percent of the land on that island. The Gherini Family owned the remaining 10 percent on the east end. Bill called Dr. Stanton in 1976 and asked if he could bring his bosses, regional director Howard Chapman and NPS national director Gary Everhardt, out to meet him.

"Sure, we'll have lunch around the pool," Dr. Stanton extended his invitation. He also invited his friends, the Vail brothers, who were part owners of neighboring Santa Rosa Island.

Once the NPS staff and the Vail brothers arrived, Dr. Stanton took them all on a jeep trip around the island and then to its center where he had a stately two-story ranch house that even had its own chapel. The pool was off to the side and that's where the Vail brothers relaxed as the others talked.

"Why don't you give us the islan—"

"No, and hell no!" Dr. Stanton reacted sharply before Director Everhardt finished his last word.

"The government can't take care of this island as well as I can—"

The director tried to counter but no chance.

Dr. Stanton hardly took a breath, "—or as well as any private citizen for that matter. You guys come and go, come and go."

The NPS visitors went back to the mainland defeated. Bill knew that the doctor was quite annoyed by the lack of attention to the islands from past NPS administrations. He kept visiting and improving the relationship, but Dr. Stanton continued to be wary of the park service so started working with the Nature Conservancy, a private organization not to be confused with the Santa Monica Mountains Conservancy.

Bill's phone rang at his Ventura beachfront office in 1978.

"Well, I just sold to the Conservancy. I hope you are pleased."

"If that helps preserve the island, yes, but I hope we can work with the Conservancy."

"I don't see why not." Dr. Stanton and Bill both hung up, but that was not the end. Their relationship strengthened over the years.

NPS lost its chance with most of Santa Cruz in the 1970s. Charlie's involvement with the Channel Islands was primarily with NPS so other than visiting Santa Cruz, he had little to do with it. However, he and other Native Americans were involved with the other Channel Islands that had once been inhabited by the Chumash.

The oldest Indian on the island

Santa Rosa, the other large island, was still a prize to be had for both its ranching and native history. Vail & Vickers had started cattle ranching on Santa Rosa in 1902 and now had up to 6000 head and 200 gorgeous quarter horses on the island. They ferried calves from Port Hueneme, a deep-water harbor and naval base on the mainland. The marine cowboys would push the cattle off the barge as it neared the island shore. The calves would swim to start two years of grazing in this pristine place. Then they'd be ferried back and shipped off to market on the mainland. Why would anyone go through all this trouble? Why not sell this island and raise cattle on the mainland? Vickers, the silent partner, and the Vail brothers knew that the island's rich grasslands made it perfect for fattening cattle; and perhaps more importantly, that its isolation made it disease free. Vail & Vickers beef became known as the best in the U.S.

Bill had an ongoing relationship with these island ranchers. In 1982, Bill asked Charlie to come out to Santa Rosa to help him figure out how to handle what the ranch foreman had told him was the oldest Indian on the island.

"We're getting close, Charlie."

"I can feel it. I don't want to go any farther."

"Okay, but I'm going on. I'll be back soon." Bill continued on for a few minutes to a cliff along the ocean and then he returned.

"It's still there. I can see the whole skeleton, but it's eroding into the ocean.

What shall we do? Some people want to study it. I met with Grandfather Victor in a sweat house out at Santa Ynez."

"What did he say?"

"I'm not sure I got a direct answer. What do you think we should do?"

"Kote's seen it. I agree with him. Let nature take its course." Charlie was definite about this.

They lightened up, walking back to the helicopter, through ranch land.

On December 31, 1986, Vickers and Vail sold Santa Rosa to NPS. People would ask, "What about the east end of Santa Cruz?"

"Not yet, but we're working on it," would be the answer from those involved. Truth was one member of the Gherini Family was holding out with their 10 percent and would do so for years.

Figure 43: Cattle on Santa Rosa Island (CINP Archives, nd)

Changes for Charlie and Satwiwa

Linda wanted a new house with horse property. They found the perfect place in Acton and moved there in April of 1988. They were back in Charlie's childhood haunts. Leona Valley and Newhall were not too far away. Coincidentally, Acton is in Santiago Canyon, named after Charlie's great, great grandfather.

Family lore was that people in the area considered Santiago Garcia a chief. He was chopping wood with some other guys near Little Rock Dam close to Acton, almost in Palmdale. He came across a bear with cubs, and to protect himself and the others he swung his ax killing the grizzly. The next day the crew was back. The same grizzly, evidently resurrected, came growling at Santiago and mauled him badly. The other guys took him by horse-drawn wagon down the canyon, but it was too late. He passed away at the bottom of canyon. People told this story as one of courageous leadership. Santiago's fighting and protective spirit lived on, certainly with Grandma Frances, Aunt Mary, and now Charlie. Charlie's reputation for leadership had spread across Southern California. Even though he lived in Acton, he was called upon in many places to lend his knowledge.

Although Charlie frequented many Native American and park sites, Satwiwa continued to be his primary dream. He would drive there on weekends to lead walks or come just to be present at an event.

In 1987, right before Charlie moved to Acton, *Hutast and Tugupan* changed its name to *Friends of Satwiwa* with Charlie as president. The Friends incorporated as a 501(c)(3) nonprofit organization made up of enthusiastic Native Americans and nonnatives alike. Their mission was promotion of Satwiwa, ongoing programs, and fundraising for a new center building and just in time. Art Alvitre had moved on in 1990 leaving the little house empty for a short while.

At Du-par's: turning a Satwiwa loss into an opportunity

"Some people think the programs will die without Art Alvitre." Phil paused, waiting for Charlie to comment.

"It's an opportunity to get more people involved. How about if we emphasize the guest host program, invite Indians of any tribe to come on Sundays, talk to people, show their crafts, read their poems, talk about tradition, sing their songs . . ."

"Great idea! The rangers can staff the house, introduce the guests, including you, Charlie, when you lead walks."

"We'll work on it with the Friends of Satwiwa."

The Guest Host Program becomes a hit

Between the Friends and NPS, Satwiwa started buzzing more than ever. Rangers started running programs out of the little house for school children during the week. Guest hosts from many different tribes came on Sundays to talk about their cultures and show their crafts, play their music, tell their stories, all in an interactive way with park visitors.

In addition to Charlie, guest hosts spanned the knowledge and talents of: Dr. Kote Lotah, who talked about Chumash traditions and medicine; William Oandasan, a Yuki poet; Bill Neal or Elk Whistle; Cherokee flutist; Kat High, Hupa storyteller; Richard Bugby, a Diegeño specialist on building aps; Running Grunion, a traditional Diegeño mime; Sallie Cuaresma, a Cherokee community leader and service provider, famous for her fry bread; Qun'Tan Shup, recognized for his knowledge of Chumash traditions; and Jane Cazabat, the Creek/Seminole story teller who still owed Charlie his powwow shirt, but she was busy taking her stories and the story of Satwiwa to many states across the country.

Sallie's fry bread demonstration was an example of Sunday visitor enthusiasm. It was raining hard, but about 20 people hung around hoping. Phil announced that the fry bread demonstration was off, but 20 hardy souls were insistent. They stood in the rain, held their umbrellas over Sallie and the hot oil until they sampled the fry bread.

Figure 44: Danielson Ranch house which was used in the 1980s and early 90s as the Indian Cultural Center at Satwiwa (Author's photo, 2013)

Figure 45: One of Sallie Cuaresma's fry bread events, (SMMNRA, 1993)

Topanga Oak Tree Mystery

Elsewhere in the Santa Monica Mountains, there were other programs to which Charlie gave his time. The Topanga Canyon Docents formed in 1988. They held full weekend training sessions twice a year. Charlie presented for a half day at many of these. He gave an overview of Chumash culture, plants, and cosmology.

Rosi Dagit was one of these docents. She was also a biologist working for the Resource Conservation District of the Santa Monica Mountains. One of her projects was to solve the mystery of why oak trees in the mountains were not regenerating well. She talked with Charlie.

"The Chumash depended on the oaks for food. They must have known how to keep them healthy and regenerating. How did they do it?"

"Rosi, they set fires, not big ones, what we would call low intensity fires or controlled burns. The fires cleared away pests. They also got rid of plants that shouldn't be there anyway, and they made room for the sun to warm the soil so that seeds could germinate."

"Anything else?"

"They knew that scrub jays dropped seeds throughout the mountains, and of course the mother tree did too. So they used fire and cleared the ground where they saw jays nesting and flying to make it easy for the seeds to sprout."

Rosi added this information to her regeneration plan. Charlie continued to work with both state and national parks.

Charlie can talk to all sorts of people. He moves from a leadership role to a role as member of a community. He has good medicine—personal power, charisma, presence, in modern parlance—mojo! (Dr. Alex Kirkish)

I worked with Charlie and others as I researched issues around the regeneration of oaks. Charlie had a lot of relevant knowledge that he willingly shared, but also a lot of questions which led to good scientific discussion and exploration. (Rosi Dagit, March 23, 2012)

Chapter 17: A Chief's Leadership Style, 1990

By 1990, clearly, Satwiwa was popular. The little house strained to provide for all the visitors. The Friends started to fund raise in earnest. At the same time, some students at the UCLA School of Architecture and Urban Design wanted a project. Satwiwa seemed perfect. While they were designing a new energy efficient cultural center building, Charlie and the Friends were planning fundraising events toward its construction.

At the picnic table: listening, talking, action

A shiny black BMW was kicking up some dust as it wound its way cautiously down the old, narrow Danielson Ranch road. Charlie and Phil were sitting at a picnic table outside the small house with a few Friends of Satwiwa board members on a Sunday afternoon.

"If this ends up with as many people as that powwow . . .," Phil started to say and then he saw a man in a suit get out of his BMW. He was walking toward them.

"Looks lost," he thought and got up to redirect him.

Frank Rocha showed Phil a flyer.

"Oh, we're just planning that fundraiser."

"Can I help?"

Frank sat down with the small group that day. He told them his roots were Chumash but he wanted to know more.

"Well then," said Phil. "Learn about your heritage and be a teacher for us all. Charlie could use some help."

"How are you going to make any money with this event?" Frank, the businessman, waved the flyer.

"We'll collect donations. The Santa Monica Mountains Conservancy will match whatever we can raise."

"Toilets! What are we going to do about toilets for so many people?" Frank put the flyer down on the picnic table and pointed to it. "A lot of these are out there."

"Hmm. What have we done about that with big crowds before?"

"We use Porta Potties on our construction sites." Frank owned a successful construction business with all its amenities.

"Yeah, good idea," said Charlie.

"I can arrange that and some other things like barriers where we need them," Frank volunteered.

Charlie listened and talked and listened. The afternoon was waning. The meeting was winding up. Now he summarized.

"Okay, then. We'll go over this at the next Friends of Satwiwa meeting. We'll have storytellers, dancers, and a flute player. We know people from different tribes we can invite to perform. I'll do a walk. Some of us will put out donation jars or walk around collecting. We'll set up a picnic area but people will bring their own food. We'll have the living room open with some displays. We'll put some more displays outside. And Frank, you'll take care of the potties."

"And barriers," Frank reminded.

They talked a little more. Frank told the group that he knew very little about the Chumash. In fact, he said that sometimes he was embarrassed to admit he was Indian at all because of reactions he would get. Charlie and Phil encouraged him to learn and then teach.

At the conference table: collaborative decision-making

Charlie drove back and forth from the new Cooke home in Acton to guest host at Satwiwa on weekends. Some weeks he came on a work night to chair a Friends of Satwiwa board meeting as the board president.

There he was, at the head of a long table in the Park Service building nestled at the bottom of a hill, a new headquarters now in Agoura Hills, between Los Angeles and the Conejo Valley. Phil sat a few chairs down, next to Dolores Rivera, an Indian with several tribes in her ancestry. Dolores worked all night as a medical transcriber and then worked tirelessly on behalf of Satwiwa in her off hours. She was the secretary and also the guest host and volunteer coordinator.

"Here's the agenda we talked about. Maybe this will help." One of the Friends, dressed in a business suit, briskly handed Charlie a typed paper. She had just come off the crowded freeway from work at a major corporation.

Charlie took it and added it to the top of his pile of notes. "Thanks," he said to Mary Gordon, his vice president.

The Friends Board was ten directors strong. Most were American Indians. Mary, as part of her day job, had been working to make corporate meetings highly productive, which in those days meant bring data, adhere to an agreed upon structure, and speak your turn. She couldn't help but wonder about the free flow of the Friends meetings. They followed *Roberts Rules of Order* and worked from a list of items to cover, but it had all seemed a bit too loose for her. Well, tonight there would be a structured agenda.

"A few items to talk about tonight . . ." Charlie looked at the agenda and started to follow it when he noticed a new member coming in.

"Glad you could make it, Frank." Charlie had invited Frank to join the board soon after he crashed the outdoor meeting at Satwiwa.

Some side conversations: two members, Ernest Siva, a Cahuilla/Serrano, and Kathy Kimberling, Seneca/Cherokee and Irish/English, talking about possible activities at Satwiwa, Dolores asking Phil about what to put in the minutes, and Ron O'Neill, a nonnative board member, listening.

"We have a lot of conversations going on. Where are we on the agenda?" Mary asked in her best facilitator voice.

"Some of us talked out at Satwiwa a week ago." Charlie shared the discussion under the trees outside the little ranch house. Members interjected with what they had all done on the fundraiser since the last regular meeting.

Then again, some side conversation: tables for a potluck out at Satwiwa. Could we make it part of the fund raiser? Maybe not a potluck, ask people to bring their own picnics.

Charlie was listening and waiting, "Picnic, good idea!"

Charlie continued, "We're down to details. Frank, any news about the Porta Potties?"

"Details? Hardly! We got them. No charge to you."

"Wow, thanks," a number of members chanted in unison. Funds were always an issue for the board. NPS helped with basic support, but anything extra was up to the Friends.

"I think we need to put up barriers."

"Why?"

"Do we want people driving down that narrow ranch road? Even if they could with cars coming the other way, where would they all park once they got there?"

Phil weighed in quickly "Oh, we need to keep it open for handicapped people so they can park where they usually do in front of the little house— you know, close to the activity."

"I can bring barriers to make the handicapped area bigger," Frank again offered. "There are not a lot of spaces there."

Charlie listened to other options erupting in conversation. Soon, it seemed to him they were all agreeing. "Okay, then, let's put up a sign that says *Handicapped Only* on the road there where everyone else should go no farther."

"That means we need to direct all other people to the dirt parking lot by the ranger residences . . ."

"Or to the state parking lot. They can walk in from there with no problem."

Charlie broke into the discussion, "Frank, you bring barriers and set them up. Phil, you'll tell him where and deal with the parking situation. Okay?"

"We normally arrange handicapped parking. It's park policy, and it's law. I'll help work out the details."

"Wait a minute," Dolores interjected. "What about our elders? They might not be handicapped, but out of respect we need to give them good parking spaces."

"Dolores, let's you and I get together to work out how to do that," Phil knew that he and Dolores could solve that quickly.

Figure 46: Dolores Rivera and Phil Holmes in a planning session (SMMNRA Archives, early 1990s)

Some more bantering back and forth about storing things in the little house for the event! Mary tried to bring that conversation to some closure, but to no avail.

Charlie listened for a while and then finally said, "How about if you come early that day, if you need to put things into the house. Can we have a ranger there to let us in?" He looked at Phil. Phil nodded yes.

"Okay, then. That's the way we will handle that?" Charlie asked for motions and seconds on all the topics they had discussed—all made and passed quickly. He glanced at the agenda and saw "Treasurer's Report."

"How's our money?"

Eva Larson, the treasurer who was a Navajo, read out numbers. "We're doing fine."

The editors of the newsletter, Natasha Zazhinne, a Russian immigrant, and Ayesha Jamal, Cherokee, reminded everyone of the story deadline.

Joan Genter, one of the nonnative board members, reminded all that the contest for the Satwiwa logo had started among local artists.

"Will we be ready to vote for the winner soon?" Rhonda Campbell, another nonnative member asked.

"Next meeting should be okay," Joan suggested and all concurred.

Charlie reminded them about an upcoming meeting when the UCLA architecture students and their professor would be coming to show their design.

With most business covered by now, he started to wind down the meeting.

"Dolores, thanks for all the calling you did to get volunteers out at Satwiwa to help with the clean up around the house."

"I cold-called a lot of people. It was scary for me, but most said yes right away so now I don't mind."

"But for this event, we all need to help get volunteers."

"I can share my list," Dolores offered. "I'll get it to you all."

More discussion on the details of the list and then Charlie asked for a motion to adjourn, which was made and seconded quickly.

The board members talked with each other as they streamed out to the dark parking lot. Mary hung around waiting for Charlie to finish gathering up his papers.

"Charlie, what happened to the agenda?"

"I used it. Thanks. We covered it all."

Dolores overheard this. "Look, I have it all here. I'll type it and get it to you, Charlie."

Charlie put on his jacket. It was cool in these mountains at night.

"You don't mind all the side talking? I think you could get a lot more done if we could get that under control."

He stopped what he was doing to give Mary his full attention. "In a meeting like this, I hear what they are really thinking. I get all the information, and in the end if I have to, I make the decision." They talked a while longer. Mary began to see the merit of Charlie's style when all voices needed to be heard out loud as soon as possible. They walked out together and joined other conversations in the parking lot under the late night sky.

The Friends chose Navajo artist Marvin Phoenix's very symbolic logo. A condor flies over Satwiwa—the Chumash ultimate power bird. A hoop encases the scene, representative of continuous life. Four feathers hang at each quarter point of the hoop, representative of the four directions and of the stages of life: infancy, childhood, adolescence, and adulthood. An oak tree with its life giving acorns represents the tie to Mother Earth.

Figure 47: Satwiwa Logo on a T-shirt (Courtesy of Dolores Rivera, c 1992)

The 1990 early summer fundraiser was crowded but went off perfectly and made a good sum of money. The Friends had decided to publicize in the media. A steady stream of people came though and donated cash, putting it in jars, as much as $200 in one case. They also asked for donations in the Thousand Oaks city water bill and got quite a bit.

Figure 48: UCLA graduate students and local citizens reviewing new center model in Satwiwa exhibit shelter, (SMMNRA Archives, nd)

The architecture students came to one of the next meetings and listened as Charlie and the Friends suggested ways to make the building fit the landscape better. Frank became more and more involved with Satwiwa and native causes in general. He took on Charlie and Kote as mentors. When the City of Malibu was established in 1991, Charlie took him to participate in the blessing and started involving him on boards in the Malibu area. Eventually, Frank changed his name to Mati Waiya, Little Hawk.

Charlie was and is effective because people trust him. He does not have to say a word—just walk into an environment whether it is tense or not. People felt comfortable with him. He's head of the Southern Chumash and he did not require drums to announce his presence. You knew who he was and who he represented. He comes across as a nice guy who has come to talk about what he has to say. (Bill Redmond)

He pools people, not just those in front of him, but gets them to enlist others in order to continue what he believes in and to create an awareness of the history before written history. (Dolores Rivera, Mescalero Apache/Pasqua Yaqui/Picuris, Charter Member of Friends of Satwiwa, October 31, 2011)

Charlie was instrumental in creating a venue that helped various Native Americans springboard to roles in their communities. The rangers helped me a lot as a guest host. Satwiwa opened doors for me. (E. Jane Cazabat, Muscogee-Creek/Seminole Storyteller, October 15, 2011)

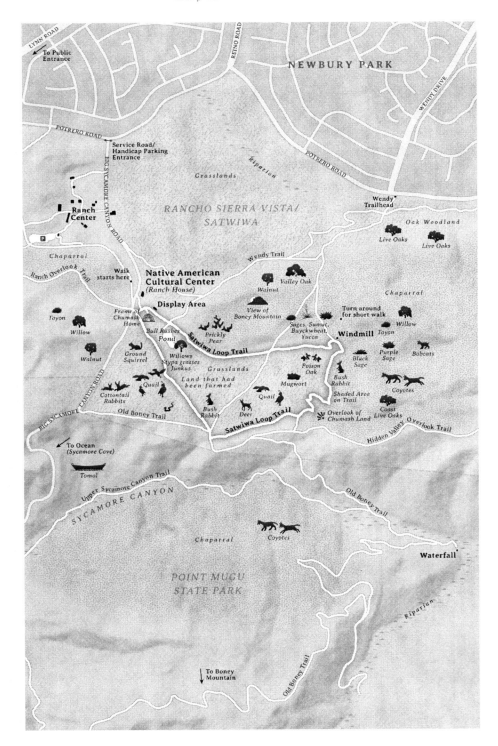

Map 7: Satwiwa Loop Trail in the 1980s (Courtesy of James Mansfield based on sketch in Loop Trail brochure by John Detlie and Mary Gordon, 1986)

Chapter 18: Talks on the Walks, 1990

Ernie Quintana pulled his car into a space on the graveled parking lot, a short walk from the Satwiwa bowl. "Why are there so many cars here?" he wondered. Ernie was the chief ranger in charge of law enforcement, fire, interpretation, and education programs for SMMNRA at the time. He had seen an article in the *Los Angeles Times* about the walk this Sunday. "Maybe I should have come in uniform," he thought. But it was his day off. He was coming just to enjoy Charlie's guided walk. Phil was not there. He was on NPS business in San Francisco. Art Alvitre had moved out about a month ago. A lone ranger had opened the little ranch house used as the Satwiwa Native American Cultural Center.

Charlie, well-known and a draw

Ernie started walking toward the Satwiwa site. It was Sunday, March 18, 1990, a perfect ocean breeze day at Satwiwa. It was only 10 a.m., but he could see people already exploring the grounds and looking at displays in the Center. A few were leaning on a fence and talking. Some were sitting at picnic tables under shade trees to the side of the house.

Ernie saw Charlie driving his truck up the old ranch road, open to guest hosts and handicapped people. He quickly walked off to meet Charlie. He told him, "I parked in the public lot—fuller than usual for this time of the morning."

They talked about what they would do if a lot of people showed up. Ernie went into the little house and called Tom Young, the head ranger for Satwiwa.

Charlie talked to small groups of two or three as they walked by on the paved road in front of the little house. Some people were in hiking boots. Some had on sneakers. A few had on city shoes, even high heels. A few children were running in circles enjoying the fresh air and open space. Charlie was smiling and joking, seemingly unconcerned about the growing crowd and about his knee that was bothering him. Most of the visitors were first timers at Satwiwa, but not all. Every once in a while, someone would walk up excited to see Charlie. The women would give him a hug, the men a hardy handshake. Charlie reciprocated in kind, only his hugs were bear hugs. His handshakes were friendly and firm.

Tom Young arrived with additional rangers just as the walk was about to start with an overflow crowd. One of the rangers gathered as many people as he could in the road in front of the house where he knew Charlie would want to start his walk. He introduced Charlie as the Chief of the Southern Chumash and a walking geography book. "He knows more about this land and what lives on it, plant or animal, than anyone I know," he said.

Interweaving nature and heritage

Charlie lowered his eyes, a little embarrassed. "Okay, follow the book," and he raised his walking stick and pointed to the side of the paved road.

"Look here. What do you think that is?" he asked a boy squeezed between his parents. He took a leaf. "Looks like a holly leaf—like Christmas holly. This bush even gets red berries," he chuckled. "What's your name?"

The boy answered softly as he tried to maintain his position at the front of the crowd. Now Charlie noticed that there were a lot more people walking from the parking lot and joining the group. He worried that some could not hear him.

"How about if you let the kids come up front. I'll talk loud. So is this holly?" Charlie asked the little boy again who just shrugged his shoulders.

"No, it's not. Fooled you, huh? It's toyon." He took a branch. "This is really hard wood. So what do you think it was used for?"

"Arrows," said the little boy.

"Good, yes, yes. And walking sticks and cradle frames. Your mom would have carried you on her back when you were a baby? Fun, huh? What about the berries?"

"You ate them?"

"Well, yes, but not raw. The Indians who lived here knew what was poisonous or just did not taste so good. They knew how to remove the toxins, usually by boiling." Charlie noted a confused look on a child's face. "Toxins, poison."

The crowd was getting bigger. Charlie shouted louder. "We are on national park land," he explained. "But over there," he pointed toward the ocean, "out of sight but close, that's Point Mugu State Park. The rancher who used to own this land owned that too. That park and this one border on each other. That's another good hike, all the way to the beach." He looked at some teenagers. "You taken that hike, or the beach bus?"

"The hike. The beach bus." He heard in soft chorus.

"Some days the beach bus is the way to go especially if you are carrying a lot of things, you know, maybe a surf board. But the hike will show you nature all the way. It's a long trek down so wear good shoes, bring water . . ."

A middle-aged woman interjected. "I did it, Charlie, but I had my daughter come to pick me up at the bottom—at the park site there on the Coast Highway."

Figure 49: Charlie leading a walk at Satwiwa (SMMNRA Archives, nd)

Charlie smiled and turned back to the trail they were on. "See this willow tree right here. Did you know you could make baskets from willow and boil berries in them?"

"But the water would seep out. Wouldn't it?" A young woman in heels said.

"Hmm," mused Charlie. "We used yop," he smiled at what he knew was an unfamiliar word, and then looked at the little boy, "Yop, can you say it?"

"Yop. Yop."

"You know what that is? We were lucky to have asphaltum around here, a gooey substance that oozed out of the ground."

The little boy's eyes widened as Charlie talked. "And we made pine pitch—from the oozing from pine trees, of course. We mixed the two and then we coated the inside of the baskets. We'd fill a basket with water and then put two or three hot stones in it."

One of the rangers appeared. He was wishing he had a bullhorn to give Charlie, but Charlie was on his own with his booming voice and chiefly presence.

The group followed Charlie off the pavement, past the Center, and onto a dirt trail. They could see a windmill up the hill. Charlie stopped to explain that at one time this had been a working ranch, but now the National Park Service was working with the Native American community to return it to its natural state.

They walked by a man-made pond full of bull rushes. "Ranching was part of the history of this place, so you'll see things like the windmill and even old ranching equipment, but not in this natural area," he explained.

"See those valley oaks, just a few over there," he pointed to a knoll. "There used to be a lot more. Acorns were a mainstay of our diet."

Then he looked at a group of teenagers. "Any of you eat acorns these days?"

Head shaking and several no's from the crowd.

"But you do eat foods that the native people ate. A lot of the food in the world came from here in the Americas. Do you know what some of them are?"

"Tomatoes, I learned that in school."

"I think avocadoes?"

"Yes, and chilies, beans, chocolate, potatoes, melons, squash, peanuts, corn," Charlie added.

"Berries?"

"Yes, blueberries and cranberries, which do not grow around here, but strawberries do. Actually there was a type of strawberry in Europe at the same time we had them here. Any of you go to the Strawberry Festival over the mountains there in Camarillo?"

A lot of heads nodded yes.

They walked on for a while with Boney looking down on them. Up the trail into a woodland area they went. Charlie leaned on his walking stick. By now, the line was so long that people at the end could not hear even with his booming voice, but they stayed with the walk, even the few in high heels. Some people passed Charlie's messages down the line.

"Watch out for poison oak. It has three leaves. Look, it's right there." A few people moved back.

"Just stay on the trail and you'll be okay. See that plant there. It's mugwort. See the top of the leaf. It's green, but look underneath. What do you see?"

"It's silver," a few people chimed in.

"Mugwort is the antidote for poison oak. The ancient medicine people knew exactly how to use it. Not all of us do, and we could make things worse."

Then he told the story of hiking with Dr. Krupp who had a rash from poison oak. He told the good scientist to rub mugwort on the affected area. The next day it was worse. "It was my fault. I had forgotten exactly how the ancestors, including my Grandma Frances, applied mugwort which was not just rubbing it on. So don't try this unless you know what you are doing."

Even though the group spread out, some still could not hear. There were just too many of them. A few who had walked this trail with Charlie before moved back, giving others a chance to see and hear better. The line was getting longer and longer, and no one was leaving.

Charlie wanted to go on, but this had to be the end for this large crowd. The trail would become a narrow path hugged by trees on both sides. He turned them around to go back down hill to the Center.

"Thanks for coming. I am sorry some of you had a hard time hearing."

And then he turned around and gave the walk several more times. At the end of the day, he raised his walking stick in a gesture that said thanks to the rangers. They had used their special clickers and counted one thousand people!

Phil was coming to the Center almost every weekend. For a few weekends after he got back from San Francisco he heard things like:

"I couldn't hear a word he said, but it was so wonderful!"

"I'll come back another time to hear him."

"It is wonderful that the Chumash are talking to the public in nature, not in a building."

Giving voice to what was and still is

Charlie gave more walks in the coming months with smaller groups. On this particular day, they had been on the trail for a while already. It was warm. They were in full sun as they craned their necks to watch the old windmill spin.

"Now we leave signs of the ranch and get into woodland." Suddenly, it was cooler and felt a little moist. There was small rivulet, really just a muddy line where water had run after a light rain a few days ago. Branches and leaves arched overhead. They lost sight of Boney.

"These are called live oaks because they never lose their leaves. They are evergreen, kinda like a pine tree. The Spanish word is *encino*. Keep watching for poison oak. This wooded area is more like what Cabrillo found when he first encountered the Chumash people in 1542."

They started up some stone steps that the park service rangers and volunteers had installed over the years. They came to a stream. They stepped across the little bit of water.

"That could have been a Chumash village water supply. They tended to live near water. Makes sense, of course."

Charlie walked on and then stopped. He heard rustling in the underbrush.

"Listen carefully. Quail lay their eggs on the ground under these types of bushes. Of course, there are rabbits here."

"Coyotes too?" someone asked.

"Usually you won't see them during the day. They don't like you any more than you like them. Come up here with your family. Be very quiet and you will hear the wild life even if you don't see it, maybe a red-winged black bird, maybe a hawk! But today, well . . . ," he nodded his head, smiled at the crowd, "We're the wild life and I think we scared everyone else way."

Charlie walked on. He had forgotten that his knee hurt the other day. They all looped around to a point where they were looking down on the Satwiwa bowl.

"The Chumash and Tongva inhabited these mountains. I am Chumash and Tongva. The Chumash lived on the west side of the mountains between Topanga Canyon and Oxnard Creek. The Tongva lived on the east side. Both lived on the Channel Islands—but not the same islands. The Chumash lived on the more northern ones that are now a national park. The Tongva lived on the islands more to the south, Catalina for one. But they went back and forth. Both made carved wooden bowls and waterproof baskets. Do you think we spoke the same language?" he asked a little girl.

"Maybe" she wrinkled her forehead.

"Well, we had ways of understanding each other enough to marry, trade with each other, and even make money that we could use with each other," he said to the child on the behalf of everyone there.

He turned to a preteen boy who was digging the toe of one of his sneakers in the dirt. Charlie took that as a cue that the language discussion lost him. "How long do you think people have been here?"

208

"A long, long time?"

"A very long, long time, more than ten thousand years. Do you know how many grandmothers you would have to go back ten thousand years? Great, great or great, great, great . . ."

The boy squinted trying to figure that out. Charlie remembered trying to understand the greats to get back to Aunt Candelaria and let the boy off easy especially since he had reengaged him. "So many, it might take this whole hike to say them all, and then I wouldn't get to talk."

He pointed to the distance, "They could take off on a different trail—over there—and get to the ocean. Both tribes made a seafaring boat. They traded up and down the coast with it and out to the islands." He looked at the little girl and leaned over, "But we spoke entirely different languages."

Charlie started the trek down and then stopped. "See that dome down there? Remember we passed it coming up here."

People craned their necks. Some let others in front to take a turn at looking. "Remember I told you that's the frame for a Chumash home. It's called an ap. I forgot to tell you that you can sign up to help finish it if you want. It has a hole in the top, kinda like a chimney. At one time there were villages of a thousand people in these parts, full of those aps. Before the missions, the Chumash and Tongva people had the most people and were the richest of the native groups in California." Charlie continued talking about the native peoples of the area.

Figure 50: Chumash ap under construction at Satwiwa, part of the Loop Trail to the left (SMMNRA Archives, nd)

"Look, the big mountain again," someone exclaimed.

"Yes, it's always there even if we don't see it. The Chumash celebrated winter solstices up there, but you can feel its power right here."

Close to the end of the walk, "Did you notice that you left civilization behind? Do you hear any cars or trucks, any horns blowing? When you leave here, you will be back in the city." Charlie looked up at the bluffs and then back down at the earth. "Before we get back on the road, bend down and touch the earth. Get a little in your hands? That's Mother Earth. She's here, but out there we forget. Don't forget."

Figure 51: Chief TIQ SLO'W at Satwiwa (© 1990 All Rights Reserved, Tom Gamache)

Some Native Americans would like people to stay away from sacred sites. But he's a teacher. He leads walks to teach people about nature—the native uses of plants, respect for the land the way natives respected it. He does not say you can't come out here, but rather let's teach people how to appreciate the land as Native Americans appreciated the land. (Dr. John Johnson)

Charlie had the inclusive idea that the Santa Monica Mountains should be a teaching tool so all could learn about Native Americans, so that all could have a connection to the land. (Bill Anderson)

NPS was still listening to Charlie years after Chandler and Reynolds were gone because he was sincere. He wanted to make sure we didn't lose interest. He came to us. He made it easy for the Park Service to learn his story which he presented in a friendly, personal way. He wanted to make sure the Chumash people and in fact, Native Americans in general were portrayed accurately. He was careful that he couldn't speak for other tribes, yet common messages came across for all Native Americans—common themes whether Hopi, Navajo, Apache. By bringing attention to the Chumash he created attention for other native cultures. (Ernie Quintana, Chief SMMNRA Ranger, November 1, 2011)

I would watch him lead walks with many people—could be several hundred at a time. He would draw you in—lead you on a journey back in time to what Native American culture was and still conveys what it is today. (Joan Genter, Charter Board Member, Friends of Satwiwa, October 16, 2011)

I took my goddaughter on a Satwiwa walk with Charlie in 1994, when she was four. He made sure she was upfront. He held her hand for some of the walk. He put chia seeds in her hand as he explained their importance to native people. You could see the wonder and admiration in her little eyes. (Vicki Goldschlager, Environmental activist, Thousand Oaks City and Ventura County representative to the Santa Monica Mountains Conservancy, January 15, 2012)

PART FIVE, THE FUTURE TAKES HOLD: Building on accomplishments and mentoring new leaders

He stands his ground as a chief, a WOT.

He is representative of our Chumash ancestry in the time that I am. (Lin A'lul-koy Lotah, Chumash Medicine Woman)

Map 8: Indian Centers and Monitoring Sites
(Courtesy of James Mansfield)

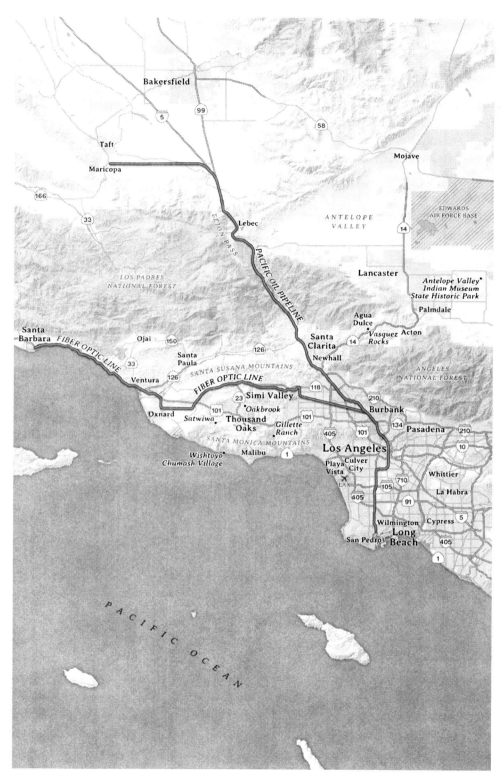

Chapter 19: Blessing at the Bluffs, 1991

"Chumash and proud of it!"

Ed Krupp laughed to himself as he read the bumper sticker. He reached into his car for his camera. "I should have known," he said to himself as he took some pictures of the back of the truck parked next to him. He had just hiked back from the rock art site. It was summer solstice again, this time on June 21, 1991. Charlie and others had been with Ed to watch the sun strike a rock that Chumash astronomers had lined up so exactly for the solstice centuries ago. It was pre-dawn when they had arrived, but now, a few hours later, Ed could see the bumper sticker plainly. He put his camera away and got ready to leave.

Charlie emerged from the hills with some others.

"Thanks again, Ed. See you next year."

"I hope not that long." Ed waved from his car. "Hey, you've had that bumper sticker for several years."

"Yep, Chumash and proud of it!" As he climbed into his truck, Charlie tipped his hat to Ed. Ed noticed that it said CHUMASH in big, bold letters across the front.

While in fact, Charlie's ancestors came from several different California tribes, by now many people thought of him as Chumash due in part to his tireless efforts to promote the Chumash people and their heritage as alive and active in today's society.

Figure 52: Bumper sticker (Courtesy of Dr. Ed Krupp, 1991)

Solstice at Satwiwa

A large group was gathering around a log circle surrounding a fire pit at Satwiwa on Sunday, June 23, 1991, right after the June 21 solstice. Some were just walking into the area. Some were sitting on the logs talking to each other. A few were standing and waiting. A partially built ap stood to the side. Tule hung across the bottom rung all the way around. The rest was still open. A few people were examining the tule thatching to see how it could possibly be waterproof. A young couple and their two toddlers were walking in and out, imagining living in the small space with a family. Well, at this time of year, the family did its cooking outside and slept inside at night. Finally out of the ap, the mom started urging the two little guys toward seats in the log circle while the dad was running interference, holding them back from taking off in another direction.

Figure 53: Unfinished ap at Satwiwa (Author's photo, 2012)

Long before today's visitors to Satwiwa, ancient Chumash shamans climbed the steep white cliffs above the bowl to hold their private, five-day winter solstice ceremony. Today's Chumash hold abbreviated and public summer solstices on the mountain floor in the shadow of the bluffs. That's what was going on today.

The sun was high. It was about 11 a.m. Charlie motioned for everyone to come into the circle. He waited for the young couple to catch up with their two little boys as they ran, tripped, giggled, and then plopped, each on his own little log. Charlie went over and asked them if they had good enough seats. Their parents answered for them, "Yes, thank you."

He smiled and walked into the circle right to the fire pit. "Please stand up, everyone," he addressed the whole group.

As had become his way, he asked everyone to touch the ground and remember who they were, where they came from, and to respect and care for Mother Earth. Members of the Friends of Satwiwa Board were standing close. Joan Genter, one of the nonnatives on the board, thought about her own grandfather picking up a handful of dirt and reminding his grandchildren to stay close to nature. A teenage girl looked up at the dirt trails she often ran in these hills. The toddlers were stirring the soil with their chubby fingers.

Charlie waited for the young couple to wipe the soil off little hands and shirts. Then he asked everyone to join in a Chumash welcome song easy for people to sing. It repeats the same phrase over in different tones, as a melodious chant. Spelled phonetically and with a steady marching rhythm, they all chanted:

O hia unga wah, O hia unga wah, O hia unga wah, O hia unga wah . . .

Then he introduced Chumash doctors, Kote Lotah and his wife A'lul-koy, who had come to conduct the solstice ceremony. Kote had positioned his staff in the ground. It told him that it was close to noon. Mati Waiya watched Kote carefully. He was now studying with him to learn Chumash traditions.

Kote drew a prayer ring around the fire pit, then stooped to the ground and played a small flute. He stood up, raised a conch shell and blew it, sounding to each of the four winds. He picked up an abalone shell, put white sage into it, lit it, waited for it to smolder, and then handed it to Charlie.

Figure 54: Kote Lotah stooped at the prayer ring, A'lul-koy Lotah with her back turned, Friends Board members from left: Charlie Cooke, Mati Waiya, Eva Larson, Joan Genter, Ron O'Neill, Kathy Kimberling, Mary Gordon, Dolores Rivera (Courtesy of Rodney Genter, 1991)

Charlie started blessing each visitor one by one, wafting sage over them to share a renewal of spirit and closeness to the earth.

When he got to Joe Edmiston, he did his usual with him.

"Joe, I need to give you an extra blessing. You're trouble," Charlie winked and chuckled, "and need extra cleansing."

Joe smiled. He knew Charlie would say this. But today the extra blessing had an extra meaning. Joe Edmiston was there as the Executive Director of the Santa Monica Mountains Conservancy. By the late 1980s, Satwiwa events were drawing more weekend visitors than any other SMMNRA site, and the staff at the Santa Monica Mountains Conservancy, a funding agency, knew it and so had approved a challenge grant.

Figure 55: Joe Edmiston at one of the many sage blessings Charlie gave him (SMMNRA Archives, nd)

Sharing the fund raising success

Blessings done, Charlie moved to a cloth-covered platform the rangers had set up for the day and picked up a microphone. A red-tailed hawk soared into the area and lighted on the unfinished ap very near the platform. Charlie thanked all who had worked toward this day. The hawk stayed put through all the congratulatory speeches made by leaders of local organizations. Carole Stevens, Chair of SMM Conservancy, came to the platform and handed a $50,000 check to Charlie. Charlie accepted it for the Friends of Satwiwa. They had done it! With this check and the $50,000 they had raised through special events, the water bill insert, and a large gift from an anonymous donor, they now had enough money to start the new Satwiwa building. Charlie shook hands all around.

Then Charlie led a walk through the Satwiwa Hills. About forty-five people followed him. He started by saying, "I hope you all noticed the red-tailed hawk. He came and sat on top of the ap during the ceremony. He is a symbol of good things to come."

Good things indeed. A lot of people were noticing and wanting to be part of the Native American resurgence. The local newspapers reported that other people were declaring themselves Chumash or local native chiefs. Charlie just kept doing what he was doing. The Park Service and many Chumash continued to recognize him as chief and his work as chiefly.

Figure 56: Dennis Washburn, mayor of neighboring Calabasas presenting certificate of appreciation to Charlie Cooke at Satwiwa. Others on platform: Mary Gordon, Superintendent Gackenbach, (Courtesy of Rodney Genter, 1991)

Figure 57: Carol Stevens, Chair of SMM Conservancy, and Charlie Cooke showing the replica of the $50,000 check, Satwiwa (SMMNRA Archives, 1991)

Figure 58: Red tailed hawk on ap at Solstice Ceremony, (Courtesy of Rodney Genter, 1991)

Rodeo: A widening rope

At the end of the summer of 1991, Charlie and Linda went to visit Bill and

221

Nancy Ehorn up in the Redwoods. Bill told Charlie that he was going to a rodeo soon. Charlie flashed back in time. Standing in the Ehorn driveway, he showed Bill how to hold a rope for lassoing calves and steers. But that was it, no more team roping. Back in Southern California, Charlie's communication skills had become his rope thrown high and wide as he participated on many teams to save the environment and his heritage.

By his persistence over the years, he made recognition of Chumash contributions an essential component of the National Recreation Area. (Joe Edmiston)

I remember this event. Charlie took us on a hike. He showed us the yucca, that you can eat the root. To this day I tell people that when we go hiking there. He talked about how kids these days think food comes from the grocery store and not the earth, and how we need to change that. He also talked about how Native Americans are still alive today—that just because you drive a truck and live in an apartment does not mean you are not Native American. He specifically said that all cultures evolve, and ours [Native American] did too. We do not live in teepees anymore, but we are still Native American. Europeans do not live in stone castles anymore, but they are still European! I remember this so well because about two years later I wrote about him and that idea for a college entrance exam. (Rebecca Lubitz, MD, former Satwiwa teenage hiker, quoted from email of November 7, 2011)

Charlie is a very unusual person in terms of his Native American involvement—before it became fashionable to be Native American. He was involved way back in the 60s maybe even 50s. And now since the 70s a lot of people have gotten involved, because it's become fashionable, plus there's money to be made. Charlie wasn't in it for the money; he always just wanted to give of himself, his time and energy to help out the Native American movement. He's just concerned. (Dr. Alex Kirkish)

Charlie does blessings at land dedications and other events with unusual humility. He is conversational, not lecturing. He brings an abalone shell, tied up sage, his staff, and humorously, a cigarette lighter. I have seen him bless everyone individually even when there are 60 people there. He is very patient having each one turn around and lift their feet up. He tells you to reach down and pick up the dirt to remind you where you come from. (Suzanne Goode, California State Park Service Senior Environmental Scientist, March 7, 2012)

Chapter 20: In the Mind, 1992

"Eleven thousand years old?"

"Yes, Charlie. It was that skeleton on Santa Rosa Island," Bill Ehorn was excited.

"Remember we reburied that skull on San Miguel."

"Yes, but this—on Santa Rosa—it was that skeleton that was visible and eroding into the ocean and now it's gone, but not before—well you remember Dan Morris, our Channel Islands anthropologist. He sent some bones to the University of Arizona to be analyzed. They're eleven thousand years old. That makes that skeleton the oldest known human in the western U.S. so far."

"Yep, we've been here a long, long time—and still are."

Mission Records and DNA

This conversation happened in the early 1980s before Bill Ehorn left Channel Islands in 1989 to become the superintendent at Redwood National Park. Back in the late 1960s, Professor Jack Forbes told Charlie that he might be Chumash. Did he have any connection to those eleven-thousand-year-old bones? Was he an islander or a mainland Chumash? What about the other tribes he knew were in his heritage?

In 1992, another scholar, Dr. John Johnson, who had been the curator of Anthropology since 1986 at the Santa Barbara Museum of Natural History, met and talked with Charlie at a California Indian Conference held at UC Berkeley. While working on his Ph.D. in anthropology at UC Santa Barbara, he started researching mission records as one input to his work on Indian genealogy. He was now interested in mitochondrial DNA, especially because it made it scientifically possible to trace ancestry back through the female line. Dr. Johnson had been studying mission records for years, able to prove some lineage but leaving others in question.

"We ought to trace your DNA, Charlie." John explained how it was traced.

"But you're telling me it has to be traced back through my mother. She was European."

"Yes, but we can go back through your grandmother's maternal line on your father's side."

"Grandma Frances—she died in 1947."

"Does she have any direct female relatives still alive?"

"Aunt Lida! Yes, yes." Charlie was excited. "She was my dad's sister, Grandma Frances's daughter. Go see Aunt Lida. She'll have plenty to tell you. She is in her 90s but still sharp."

Dr. Johnson called Ted Garcia, Sr., a nephew of Aunt Lida's, who took him to her nursing home. There he found a lively 90-year-old who gladly gave him permission to take some of her hair follicles. He also took a few follicles from Ted. Sometime later, he called Charlie.

"I got the results. Aunt Lida has a very unique DNA sequence. We checked it out with Ted's hair, and another of your cousins. They all match."

"Unique, what do you mean?"

"It is different from other samples found in the Americas."

"But I am Indian, right?"

"Yes, Charlie. Remember, I worked on your family tree from mission records. I am not sure what this DNA result means yet, but the sequence is so distinctive that eventually it should shed light on your heritage."

Several years later, Dr. Johnson spoke to Charlie again regarding his DNA sequence.

"Charlie, you know that Indian burial in the Palmdale area that was over a thousand years old—on that site that we know is about three thousand years?"

This sparked Charlie's ire. "Yes, there were about fifty-five burial sites in that area. Palmdale was growing fast. Chester and I tried to get monitors on the development sites. I'm not trying to stop progress, but we should not disturb our ancestors."

"As I understand it, the city gave the okay to build there and yes, they found burials. The archaeologists on site asked some of your relatives for permission to extract DNA from a tooth. That DNA matched Aunt Lida's with the same very unique sequence. My examination of mission records shows that she had Vanyume, Tataviam, and Tongva ancestry. Since Aunt Lida was Grandma Frances's daughter and your dad's sister, your dad would have that DNA."

"What about me?"

"You wouldn't, because it is passed from the mother. But remember we know who your relatives are. We know that they have DNA identifying them as Indian, and we know some of their mission ancestry. So from all that together we can say that like them, you are Vanyume, Tataviam and

Tongva."

"So at least part of my ancestry was here on the mainland, not the islands. What about the Chumash part?"

"I cannot say."

"Professor Forbes told me I could be Chumash."

"He is a well-respected scholar. You might be, but I cannot say that from this DNA sample or from mission records. What I can say is that you are the first most-likely-descendant proven to be a most-likely-descendant."

"Huh, please say that again."

"You know that by law, a most-likely-descendant needs to be on site once native burials are found or suspected. Well, a descendent as much as possible. How do we really know? But now we do, in your case. You are a most-likely-descendant of the Vanyume, Tataviam, and Tongva peoples."

It was clear that Charlie's Native American roots went back thousands of years. But Charlie still felt Chumash after all the work he had done on their behalf over decades. He welcomed the DNA findings, in fact, was excited about them. But in relation to his inner core, who he was as a person, he remembered his bantering back and forth years before with Clay Singer, especially the point about the spirit of cultural heritage:

"Culture is transmitted in the mind."

At Du-par's: NPS perspective on who is Indian

At Du-par's, now moved out of the dark corner and into a new strip mall, Charlie talked with Phil about his ancestry.

"Dr. Johnson cannot certify that I am Chumash from mission records."

"But how do you know the mission records tell the whole story?"

"I don't. Jack Forbes did research here in this Ventura area and said my family might be Chumash. After he told me that, I talked to a lot of people with Chumash ancestors and found relatives. I also remembered that Grandma Frances said she had relatives from Pitas Point."

"Right here along the Ventura Coast?"

"Yes, some relatives. But it's all confusing. On Grandpa Fred's side, well, my family tradition is that we took the Cooke name from a Lt. Cook. No letter *e* at the end of his name by the way—that came later. Fremont put Indians in camps in the mid-1800s. The family story is that my great-great-grandfather was held at Fort Tejon with other Indians. Lt. Cook was a guard there. He was a nice guy and treated the Indians well, so Great-Great-Grandfather took his name. Clay Singer told me that he actually came across Lt. Cook's name in an account about Fremont. But that's another story."

Figure 59: Charlie, Satwiwa Display Room with drawing of the ancestral Chumash village, Humaliwa from whence came the name Malibu, from a set commissioned by the Malibu Surfriders (News Chronicle Collection, Thousand Oaks Library, 1991)

"Charlie, here is how the Park Service here determines native ancestry: First, your relationship to the land. You are a walking geography book in the Santa Monica Mountains area. All the rangers know that. Second, you are accepted by other Chumash, in this case Grandfather Victor among others. Third, you identify yourself as Chumash. And Number Four, you are in the California rolls as Fernandeño which includes Chumash and Gabrielino."

"We use Tongva now instead of Gabrielino. Some Tongva were at Mission San Fernando and some at San Gabriel. The missions made us theirs and confused who we were."

"Yes, and finally, Number Five, you share activities and cultural orientation with other known Chumash—no question there."

Their order came and they moved onto other topics. They walked out to the parking lot earlier than usual. Charlie wanted to get home to Linda and the boys.

Charlie and Linda's boys were teenagers now. They saw other kids in affluent Newbury Park getting cars for their birthdays, but knew that was not going to happen for them. Charlie, like Cy Cooke, expected his boys to work hard and act responsibly. The boys started earning money to buy a car.

The Native Plant Garden

Many of the original Santa Monica Mountains NPS staff had moved on and up to other assignments in other parts of the country. Bob Chandler was superintendent at Grand Canyon National Park. John Reynolds was the manager of the NPS Denver Service Center in Lakewood, Colorado. Bill Ehorn was superintendent at Redwood National Park. Daniel Kuehn and then David Gackenbach had taken over as superintendents at SMMNRA. The Recreation Area and Satwiwa continued to grow under them. Charlie stayed involved.

Back in 1991, a new young landscape architect had come onto the scene. One of Woody Smeck's first jobs was to design a native plant garden at Satwiwa. He worked with Charlie on planning and putting the garden together.

"You know, Woody, it would be good to have some of the plants I talk about on the walk in the garden, as an introduction."

"And for people who can't make the walk," added Woody. "We'll plant what the Chumash and Tongva used in their daily lives."

"But make it traditional and contemporary."

Woody met with Charlie and the Friends of Satwiwa periodically as he worked on the garden over a two-year period. He developed a database of plants organized by use such as medicinal, tools, and edible. Woody tapped into Charlie's incredible knowledge of plants as the basis for the design of the garden.

"Make the garden small and easily accessible," Charlie suggested.

"And we'll put signs along the way that tell the Indian uses of the plants. And benches—benches so people can sit down and just enjoy the garden."

"Or rest if they're getting older like me."

Woody worked hard to make sure the garden would have the right plants and ethno-botany stories. The garden layout, design details, and preparation of construction specifications took several years beyond the two-year database development, and then several more years to raise the funding, to negotiate the construction contract, and finally to award the contract to a small business vendor—who happened to be an American Indian.

Instead of Du-par's: a visit and a gift

One weekend instead of meeting at Du-par's, Phil went over to Charlie's house to talk. The conversation veered away from park business.

"It's been sitting in my driveway for years now."

"You mean that white truck you had with a box for a driver's seat?"

"Oh, no. I'm talking about my 1963 22S Volvo. That was a good car. I bought a new motor for it, but with all the public meetings and everything else, I'll never put it in."

"I have a solution," Charlie said, and he called to Damon.

"Too big a job," said Phil. "You have to put in the new motor. It's too hard for one person. It's expensive at a shop."

Damon answered quickly and hopefully. "I know Jason paid to fix up that 1969 Mustang of yours, Dad. But I am good at fixing things. I'll get my friend, John, to help me put in the new motor. We can do it. Really, let us try."

"Okay, you convinced me." Phil gave Charlie the car to give to Damon, who in the end after really working hard for it, did get it running.

Growing up as his son, I saw him in a different light from archaeological and park-type people. I just saw my dad as a regular dad, not a Native American. Dad had his genealogy done. He is tied to San Fernando Mission where tribes were grouped together. The information there is not really accurate. I don't know why it matters. Dad does not pretend to live like a Native American before Spanish contact. He lives as an American citizen. Reality and tradition—that's a balancing act. It's a shame that the coastal areas were stolen from the Chumash. But they have integrated into society. They are trying to preserve what they can. Dad focuses on sharing history and heritage.

Dad tried to teach us normal American values, especially a strong work ethic. Dad did not like kids trying to get out of work. Dad worked a lot. He left before we got up. He sacrificed his personal time to work on Native American stuff. Somehow, he was home several nights a week. On weekends, he was always around. He coached my soccer team when I was six or seven. I wanted to make my parents proud. By the time I was a teenager, I liked fixing cars. I am a mechanic now for the fire department. (Damon Cooke)

Not a week goes by when I do not try to learn about my family. One great-grandfather had 13 children, but when I trace back to the other great-grandfather, I find a line, just a line where his name would be. Oral history is that he refused to be baptized so there is no baptismal record of him in the New Mexico Mission records. Oral history says he was a native man; that he wore a chongo, a long bundle of hair wrapped at the base of his head at his neck, as Pueblo men wore. It is hard to trace my ancestry, in fact, feels impossible. I come to a wall, but no door in the wall—not a lot was written down. And now there are few elders you can learn from. It's a puzzle. Charlie is preserving pieces of the puzzle—trying to keep pieces intact. He spent half his life at meetings trying to preserve what's left—both the visible history and oral history. (Dolores Rivera)

Native people have knowledge that nonnatives find hard to understand. It's like my Polish grandmother stories—the nuances that are difficult to convey to others outside the circle of shared ethnic experiences. And regarding mission records, what's missing? It's possible that some people were underrepresented in the Registers, namely young unmarried men, doctors and shamans, and political chiefs. It is clear that many people refused to have anything to do with the missions and simply went away to find/make a new life. (Clay Singer, January 10, 2011, March 11, 2012)

The mission registers are nothing more than a list of folks who chose to belong. Lots of folks passed and moved on. (Kevin Feeney, Curator, San Fernando Mission, March 12, 2012)

Chapter 21: Proud of It All, 1990s

"Say Al, do you know about Satwiwa?"

"That's a great cultural center over there in the Santa Monicas, but have you been to the cave paintings here in these Santa Susanas?" Al volleyed back at Charlie who volleyed right back.

"In the Santa Susana Mountains and some others. Are you familiar with the Encino site?"

Al answered yes to both questions. This was beginning to feel like a test.

During the 90s, archaeologist Al Knight had been working with the Santa Susana Mountains Park Association, trying to establish a state historic park in Chatsworth. Charlie had been one of the Indian consultants for the association and the state. Al called him to come out and see some of the newer found archaeological sites and features that his team had identified.

"Charlie, what's your take on the Agua Dulce site?" Al thought he had him.

"That's a Tataviam area. I'm part Tataviam."

Al asked him what he knew about the Palmdale area in Leona Valley.

Charlie talked on and on about Leona Valley where he was raised.

Al began to think he would never be able to trump Charlie, but he tried a few more times. When Al told him that he had helped an old Kawaiisu Indian place a beautiful pictograph cave in the western Mojave Desert on the California Sacred Lands list, Charlie finally looked impressed. Al suspected that Charlie knew the southwest Mojave Desert better than any other living person.

"Well," Charlie paused and then said, "you know your way around. Okay, I guess we should get together and see what you found."

Getting involved with a Kawaiisu Cause

Al decided that Charlie should meet his Kawaiisu friend, Elder Andy Greene who did not like fake Indians and was not afraid to show his distaste. The introduction threatened to go poorly until Andy asked Charlie if he was related to Izzy Cooke.

"Uncle Izzy!" Charlie exclaimed remembering some of the roping he had done with him and his dad when he was a kid.

"Izzy and I worked at the cement plant in Tehachapi Valley. I got into a fistfight there. The other guy pulled a knife on me. Izzy pulled his gun and told the guy to git outta here and the guy git. Izzy saved my life! He was my best friend. Too bad he's gone now, died too young so many years ago."

The only time Andy ever mentioned to Al that he "wondered a bit" about Charlie, was whenever Charlie told him about spreading his father's ashes around the Birthing Cave.

"Why did he use the maternity ward as a cemetery?" Andy would ask Al, with a laugh! Then he'd comment about Indians living in the southwest Mojave, "Those southerners also knew about the cave but not what it was all about."

At the same time, the Tehachapi Heritage League was working with Andy, Al, and others to create another state park. When Andy learned that Charlie had extensive experience with California State Parks, land acquisition, and management issues, Andy asked Charlie if he would speak up at meetings on behalf of the Kawaiisu. Charlie did. Andy was grateful for Charlie's contribution so, even though Charlie had no Kawaiisu in him, he asked the California Native American Heritage Commission to list Charlie as Kawaiisu. They did. Charlie continued to work in the Kawaiisu area with Al Knight to preserve Vasquez Rocks as a county park site. Its jagged sandstone formations, slanted up to 150 feet long ago by earthquakes, formed stunning backgrounds for *Bonanza, Star Trek, Flintstones* and other TV shows and movies. More importantly to Charlie, it was an ancestral Tataviam site.

Figure 60: One Pinnacle at Vazquez Rocks County Park, Eagle Overhead, (Author's photo, 2010)

Figure 61: Charlie with Andy Greene, c 1997-98 (© 2008 California State Parks)

The bantering that started Al and Charlie's relationship happened because Al was enlisting Charlie to join with a group of people to preserve an area within the Santa Susana Mountains. During the mid to late 1990s, the work that the Santa Susana Mountains Park Association, Al, Charlie, and dozens of other people had done came to fruition as the Santa Susana Pass State Historic Park.

Linda's heritage

While Charlie had been working with Al Knight and others, Linda started looking at travel brochures. In 1992, she and Charlie flew to Scotland. They toured Edinburgh, Loch Ness, Sterling Castle, and Loch Lomond. Charlie was curious about the culture and asked the tour guides a lot of questions. The answers made him think back to mission days.

"Hundreds of years ago, under English rule, clans could not wear their tartans."

"They weren't allowed to speak their language or sing their folk songs."

Back in California, Linda discovered from looking at a family scrapbook that her family had Scottish names. In fact, they had come from the Scottish Highlands to Castle Rock, New York, in 1880, before Ellis Island.

After the trip, Charlie went back to his mixer truck and to monitoring. He stayed involved at Satwiwa and took on several more Native American efforts. Linda continued exploring her heritage and looking at travel opportunities.

At Du-par's: the ins and outs of official tribal recognition

Off and on over the next few years after an event like a fundraiser, a ground breaking, or a Satwiwa Sunday, Phil and Charlie would stop in at Du-par's. Sometime in late 1993:

"Phil, where's your uniform lately?"

"It's a cost cutting measure. People like me who are not in the field all the time had a choice."

"I like the suspenders."

"They were often part of my off-duty garb. Sorry to hear that your mother passed away, Charlie."

"She was not in good health, but proud of us, the German and the Indian to the end."

"There is a strong movement to build a Chumash Museum out at Oakbrook County Park. We'll support it and encourage cooperation." Phil was holding on to his suspenders wondering what Charlie was going to say.

"Well, the more chances for people to learn about Native Americans and the environment, the better."

"I'm okay with that, but what's all this in the papers about another person or two claiming to be a Chumash chief?" Phil wondered.

"Could be. There are different bands. And I guess we have made it okay to be Indian!"

Charlie picked up his glass and started to say more. He hesitated. "I hope it's not that the developers are courting them. Kote and I are still pretty strong, you know, about leaving burials where you find them—or rebury them close by. Some developers don't like us for that."

"What's this about a new leader for the San Fernando Mission Band?"

"Rudy resurrected the group for a while. They elected John Valenzuela. I lost. They want to go for recognition. I filled out the papers."

"But you are recognized."

"By California. We want federal recognition."

The waitress put Phil's and then Charlie's order on the table. "Thanks, lady," he said.

"Haven't seen you around much lately; what's keeping you away?" she challenged.

"Oh, I moved to Acton—community affairs in Acton—gotta be a good citizen you know. If I could hear better . . ." and he put his hands to his ears where he was now sporting a hearing aid, "I'da said yes to being on the town council. But hey, I got to ride in the Acton parade!"

Andy Greene was the last who knew well the northwest part of the western Mohave Desert, south of the Tehachapi Mountains. Charlie is the last who knows the southwest Mohave Desert, north of the Transverse Ranges. (Al Knight, Archaeologist, May 15, 2009)

Charlie bridges contemporary times to the past. He is visionary and greatly respected by a broad scope of people. He is tenacious. He sat in many meetings, willing to work with others. He is a true friend. (Nancy Fries Ehorn, Planner and then second Assistant Superintendent, SMMNRA, June 8, 2011))

Charlie's leadership changed Native American lives. Although negatives remain even today, now it is not a bad thing to be a Native American. Charlie is very spiritual. You see it in his connection to the earth and culture. He believes in Mother Earth, spirits, nature, being in balance with things. There is a deep spiritual core in that man. Just look in his eyes. (Dr. Kote Lotah)

Chapter 22: Park to Park, 1989-2003

Yes, Charlie had ridden in the Acton parade, but that was not all. Acton was near the Antelope Valley. Charlie had not said a word that night at Du-par's about any of his involvement there to promote Indian culture.

Supporting Indian culture in Antelope Valley

"Edra, I think you should look at that job. The state bought that place from a private owner. With new laws coming into play soon, they need someone with your background."

Edra Moore was talking with one of her professors at UC Davis. She had seen a flyer advertising a position at the Antelope Valley Indian Museum. It was 1989, on the eve of NAGPRA, the federal law that would regulate the way public entities handled Native American artifacts. Edra was working on an advanced degree in anthropology. She hesitated.

"Go, take a look. Let me know what you think." So Edra went.

The person in charge was actually a maintenance person. They walked around outside for a while. The museum was located on the round shaped Piute Butte, one of several buttes in the Antelope Valley.

"The rock formations here are striking," she said as she took in tall gray spires sculpted by the wind, large boulders that had rolled down the slope of the butte, and some anthropomorphic stone shapes. "And quite rugged over there," she added.

Figure 62: Piute Butte, Amphitheater Area, (© 2008 California State Parks)

They went inside and started through several rooms. Grace Oliver had bought the property from Arden Edwards, the adventuresome collector, who had set aside a display area in his house back in 1933. Grace had converted the entire Edwards house to a museum and added her own collection. Edra noticed rat infestation. She read display labels that disturbed her cultural sensitivity. One described cosmetics that belonged to a Dawn Maid, that name made up. The cosmetics were what a European woman would have used: her rouge, her hairpin, her powder. She saw a sacred pipe used in healing labeled as a cigarette holder. She was taken aback by the lack of understanding of the prehistoric Indian culture. "Where is the native context?" she wondered. Then the maintenance person and Edra sat down to talk. He told her she was overqualified.

Back at UC Davis, Edra shared her visit with her professor including that she did not think the job was for her. He told her, "It could be a good job. The artifacts do need to be properly identified and catalogued. You could do that."

Somewhat to her surprise, since she was more qualified than required, the State Park system hired her anyway as its very first and only museum employee. Since the state had purchased it in 1979, a volunteer staff had been running the museum. In May of 1989 they welcomed Edra. Many of the volunteers were Grace's friends. They showed Edra around with pride.

"Aren't they interesting? Grace got them on a trip through the Southwest."

"She brought that back from Alaska."

"That came from Taos, New Mexico."

Edra noted that there were no comments about the Native American people tied to these artifacts. She walked around the site and saw that it needed some serious renovation and clean-up. She noted artifacts from the Southwest, the Great Basin, and California. She noted a Hopi wedding robe on display and asked about it.

"Well, an Indian man was so grateful to Grace for her help that he gave it to her," one of the volunteers said. Since a Hopi woman wore her wedding robe on the day of her wedding, to celebrate the birth of her first child, and when she was buried, Edra was skeptical.

"Is there a catalogue of these items?" She asked. The volunteers told her there were cards, but no one could find them.

Edra was driven by an inner desire to turn the museum from a Sunday afternoon curiosity into an authentic interpretative and educational museum. She knew she needed some Native American input and said so to Grace's friends.

"How about Charlie? Everyone liked him when he came for our wowwow."

"Wowwow? You mean powwow," Edra Moore answered.

"Oh, no, wowwow. The state wouldn't let us have a powwow on this site. But Charlie was understanding. He came and started everything off well with an Indian blessing. He lived in this area when he was a child and knows it well."

"Yes, I knew him before he was Indian, when he was Mexican," added another volunteer.

Edra said to herself, "I have a lot of educating to do, and learning myself." She called Charlie, and like with everything else to do with heritage and sites, he came right over.

Edra and Charlie talked and talked over many meetings. She listened to his many stories. He helped her with concepts Indians held of their historic world and with their perspectives on their current world. Edra noticed that when the well-meaning docents made unwittingly condescending comments, Charlie acted as though he did not notice and stayed on his point. Charlie continually supported Edra with information on her path to create programs that would inspire visitors to explore the cultures behind the displays. By 1992, after cleaning up the rodent infestation and recovering from a related illness, Edra settled into cataloguing the museum items. The museum audience widened.

Figure 63: Edra Moore in Kachina Hall at AVIMSHP (Photo by Geraldine Ray, 1993)

One day Charlie told her that Piute Butte on museum property was a sacred site. Edra began to investigate, first just by looking. Her anthropology background helped her understand features in the rocks that suggested Indian ceremonial use. She noticed offerings being left there. She knew the area had been inhabited by at least the Kawaiisu, Kitanemuk, Vanyume, and Tataviam, peoples who came out of the missions and blended into the local population. There were no designated reservations, rancherias, or other lands in Antelope Valley set aside for the current Indian populations. However, American Indians from tribes across the United States had moved to this valley just as they had to Los Angeles. Many of these individuals sought out any landscape that was considered sacred by any tribal group, and used it for their own spiritual rituals. This could make protecting the site complicated or it could provide strength in numbers.

Edra contacted NAHC, who contacted Charlie, who contacted other American Indians in the area. Charlie helped the museum petition for the property to be classified as a sacred site. NAHC gathered statements from Charlie and his circle of local contacts from many tribes. They won. NAHC declared the butte a sacred site.

The museum's displays were expanded and given cultural context. All along, Edra had been dealing with artifacts subject to repatriation laws. One piece especially disturbed her. It took a while to do the proper examinations of the item and complete the paper work required by NAGPRA and related laws. Finally around the year 2000, she had the process completed. Off she went to Second Mesa on the Hopi Reservation in Arizona, where she met with Lee Lomayestewa, the Repatriation Coordinator for the Hopi Tribe's Cultural Preservation Office and put the wedding robe into his hands.

Back in Antelope Valley, Edra realized the museum was ready to support research and disseminate information. "We are going to hold a symposium and invite native speakers," she told the volunteers and the small staff she now had. "It will be on Southern Californian Indian cultural practices and traditions."

She started to contact well-respected Native American speakers representing many different native cultures. Charlie got on the phone to help recruit speakers and to spread the word. Twelve speakers came and shared their practices and philosophies from the most seasoned to those who had recently made their mark. Cahuilla Historian Katherine Siva Saubel, one of California's most revered Native American leaders, came from the Morongo Reservation. Mati Waiya came and shared his recent work, which was focused on reclaiming Chumash heritage. Mati had also recently been named the first Native American Ventura County Coastkeeper. In that role, he talked about protecting and restoring the environment on Ventura County land and coastline. The all-day event at the Palmdale Cultural Center was a clear sign that the museum had moved from being a private collection to a public educational asset with a strong native presence.

But there was still work to do. One day an elder came by to see Edra. He was a Plains Indian. "Mrs. Moore," he started gingerly, "the butte here on your property, I go there to worship. Those off road vehicles nearby are intruding on the spiritual presence there. I see other activity too on those boulders there."

While Edra had been busy transitioning the museum to its educational and interpretative focus, somebody was mapping part of the butte.

"Mrs. Moore, we are planning a bouldering event on the butte. We've made the maps and are ready to go." One of the entrepreneurs shared his excitement.

"Bouldering?"

"A very challenging form of mountain climbing. We need your permission to use the site."

Edra looked at him in disbelief. "This is a sacred site," she told him. But he and his group persisted.

Edra called the state park superintendent, but the resounding "no" she expected did not come right away. The state was interested in providing recreational activities and bouldering was appealing. The state decided to hold a hearing on whether or not to classify the buttes as a recreational area. Charlie again called on his wide circle, especially native leaders, and they came: John Valenzuela, in his role as Vanyume leader; Harold Williams, who had taken Andy Greene's Kawaiisu leadership role; and others. Charlie enlisted his archaeology colleagues, people like Al Knight, who also came ready with information to support the site's historical value. The state ended up ruling against the recreation area and instead, in 2003, created AVIMSHP, the Antelope Valley Indian Museum State Historic Park.

Back in the Conejo Valley

While Edra was embarking on her museum journey, other Indian projects were in the making back in the Conejo Valley. In 1993, before construction started, Grandfather Victor and Charlie blessed the site of the proposed

Oakbrook Chumash Museum at a barbecue held there. After that, a group of local Chumash took over its development.

The Chumash Indian Museum at Oakbrook County Park in Thousand Oaks opened in December 1994 with funds from both developers and Ventura County. You walk from a well-paved parking lot past posts with Chumash rock art symbols on them. You quickly come upon a sizable impressive stone and glass building filled with artwork on the walls and display cases throughout. A mile or so down a trail takes you to a reconstructed Chumash village. As you visit inside and out, the mission of this museum becomes clear as stated on its website: *Restoring and preserving an awareness of the Chumash people and their historical, cultural, material and present-day influence as well as the natural environment and historical significance of this site.*

About nine months later, on June 1, 1995, the new UCLA-designed cultural center building opened at Satwiwa. The evening before, the Park Service hosted a walk, Native American games, and stories. The next afternoon, Charlie gave the new center and all those there the traditional Chumash blessing. Sallie Cuaresma was there from the Southern California Indian Center, a merger of Indian Center West and the Orange County Indian Center. Again, Sallie made her famous fry bread but this time under a blue sky. At the ceremonies, she gave the new Satwiwa Center a gift: a rain stick from Central America. Friends of Satwiwa were there, proud as could be that they finally opened the new center. Charlie conducted the Chumash blessing, and then took the podium at the back of the fire ring and spoke to the group assembled. Again, a red-tailed hawk soared into the scene, lighted on a bush very close to Charlie, and stayed for the speech.

"Welcome to Art Eck, who is taking over as superintendent next month, and thanks to David Gackenbach, who was here with us as we built this new building." Charlie waited for all the clapping to subside and then continued with words similar to those he still says.

> Satwiwa brought so many people into my life, not just the Chumash people or the Tongva people, but all Native American people, and non-Native American people as well.

> This natural and spiritual place has helped impress upon people that Native Americans are still around and not extinct. It has helped a lot of people feel they're part of our culture, to make them feel, in many cases that they are now the protectors of our culture, the same as we are. Getting people involved out here shows people what they are a part of—Mother Earth. Satwiwa is a learning center for all people no matter who they are or where they come from; and it's worked out pretty well.

Figure 64: Sallie Charisma presenting rain stick to Charlie at opening of new Satwiwa building, (SMMNRA Archives, 1995)

A few weeks earlier, the *Los Angeles Times* had interviewed several board members of Friends and quoted them.

Dolores Rivera, Friends secretary and Pueblo/Apache, told the *LA Times* that the small ranch house could be easily overlooked by visitors, "Many people were unaware the center was there." She added in regard to Satwiwa, "It's kind of a jewel."

Eva Larson, Friends treasurer and Navajo, told the *Times*, "People don't realize there are so many different Indian tribes." She was talking about the Los Angeles area. "Just getting that across to some people is a great accomplishment."

From the beginning when Bob Chandler and Charlie started talking, the Center at Satwiwa was to be more of a gathering place than a museum, a place where the public could interact with Native Americans of many ancestries. The UCLA architecture students designed a new twelve hundred square foot building to fit in with the natural surroundings. A big picture window looks out onto the bluffs. Inside, under the high ceiling and open rafters, visitors look at a few displays. They peruse and buy books related to the Satwiwa area and its first inhabitants. Children and adults pick up and handle seeds, stones, and other Satwiwa natural items. Rangers and native guest hosts interact with the public in the building, on its redwood deck, at the campfire a short walk away, or on the trails. An ap sits framed, but not finished, near a powwow area—on purpose, so people can help build it. The tule for its covering grows in a pond a short walk away, near the beginning of the Loop Trail, a 1.5 mile trail that circles back to the Center. The Friends, with support from Conejo Future Foundation and the Santa Monica Mountains Conservancy, created a self-guiding brochure for walkers of this trail quoting Charlie, Kote, Art, and other local Indians, but the brochure never replaced Charlie's walks.

At Du-par's: understanding Chumash bands

By the mid-90s the Chumash had formed a number of bands along the coast and inland. Charlie and Phil talked about this now and then at Du-par's, now accustomed to its new location in the strip mall.

Charlie shared his viewpoint, "Bands are a modern day re-creation of what we Chumash believe to have been alliances, maybe among villages, but we are not sure. They overlap. You can belong to more than one. For me, well, Jack Forbes said maybe I had ties to the Chumash in Ventura. They are part of the Ventureño/Barbareño Band, but some might also be members of the Coastal Band."

"How far up the coast?"

"All Chumash living north of Los Angeles."

Phil asked, "And some from these costal bands might also belong to the San Fernando Mission Band. So they are Fernandeños too, right?"

"That might be. Indians intermarried among tribes." Charlie smiled. "And, of course, just like anyone, we moved around and sometimes found love in new places. You know, I am also Fernandeño."

Back when the new Du-par's strip mall location was being readied for its move, Phil and Charlie got into the habit of going to Denny's, a chain restaurant. This particular one was right off the freeway exit, close to Satwiwa. So once Du-par's reopened, Charlie and Phil traded off between the two restaurants. They went to Denny's, especially when it was more convenient for a late meal and some discussion.

"What about the islands? There are island bands even though almost no one lives on them now." Phil picked up the discussion about Indian bands that they had started some nights earlier at Du-par's.

Charlie nodded. "Chumash lived on some of the islands but not anymore. Now it's just a ranger or two."

"Yes, that's right—there are some rangers on the islands."

Charlie continued, "Bands can be from more places where we really don't live any more, like the Tecuya Chumash used to live in Tecuya Canyon among the Tejon Chumash, but the Tecuya may be Kagismuwas. The Kagismuwas territory is now Vandenberg Air Force Base. Maybe a Chumash Airman or two lives there, but you won't find a Chumash Village. There's Chumash rock art in that area. We've preserved that."

"And the Santa Ynez Band. They are the only federally recognized Chumash Band and the only one with a reservation."

Charlie nodded, and then mentioned more formal or informal bands such as the Malibu Chumash, Monterey Chumash, and San Luis Obispo Chumash—descended from the northwestern Chumash. He finished with, "And there are overlaps with them too."

Phil waxed professorial, as they started eating their late dinner, "So because of the disruption of their traditional lives by the missions, the Gold Rush, and general immigration to California, the Chumash and other native societies around here got muddled."

"Yes, *muddled* is a good word."

"But we know that pre-contact Chumash inhabited the central and southern coast of California, from Morro Bay in the north—to Topanga in the south—and inland to the western edge of the San Joaquin Valley. And three of the Channel Islands: San Miguel, Santa Rosa, and Santa Cruz."

"You sound like an anthropologist, Phil."

"Well, I am; but I think Grandma Frances had it right. Remember you told me what she said. 'None of this really matters. You are Indian.' "

A special Topanga Canyon tree

Charlie was very serious about native heritage, but being Indian and sharing it could be just plain fun—and with another grandmother.

In 1994, Charlie injured his shoulder and could not do any lifting. By 1995, he had to retire from his cement mixer job. He volunteered time with the Topanga Canyon docents. Like Malibu Canyon, Topanga Canyon wound from the Conejo Valley to the ocean with homes and parklands along the way.

One day that same year, Rosi Dagit, the senior biologist for the Resource Conservation District of the Santa Monica Mountains, a California state agency, found herself sitting under a severely damaged oak tree. She knew it was over three hundred years old from examining the rings in a fallen branch. As she sat imagining all the seeds this tree had dropped in its day, she felt a strong urge to write the tree's story, an urge that felt like it came from the old oak itself. So she set about doing just that. She formed a group of consultants. Charlie was one of them. Dr. Chester King was another. The group met in Topanga Canyon at the tree, off and on for several months.

"Why is this tree still here?" Rosi asked. "It would have been cut down for firewood, at least until we got electricity around 1900. After that, it would have been spared, but then it would be about 130 now, not 300."

Rosi, Charlie, and others bantered about ideas.

"Why waste energy cutting it down? It was hollow, so who would want it? Lightening ruined that tree."

"Yes, but we don't know when lightning struck. It may have been good firewood and about to be sawed down before it was hit."

"So then why is it still standing?"

Charlie started to weigh in, "It probably produced a lot of acorns. Chumash and Tongva families passed down trees like that."

Charlie pointed off in the distance, "And over there is a sacred site. Elders may have come from there to sit under this tree. That would have made it important."

"But," Rosi thought out loud, "once the Indians left the area, then what?"

Charlie reached back into his ranching days. "Lore lives on. The Trippet Ranch here was a Spanish Land Grant. The ranchers probably knew some of the Indian traditions and protected the tree."

Rosi had enough to start her book. She wound the story back in time to its Indian days. She used information Charlie had shared on plants, animals, and Indian ceremonies. Soon she was ready to bring on her illustrator, Gretta Allison. Again, the group met, now to look at the drawings. Chester King and Charlie Cooke looked at every single one. They were beautiful and just right—almost.

"That plant—it wasn't there then." And Charlie made some suggestions on what would have been in the scene.

"The ranchers had different cows then, right?" Chester looked at Charlie who nodded a yes. Charlie knew the ranching history of the area well.

Gretta made the changes. In November of 1996, the local population came en mass to Topanga State Park for an all day celebration. Children made acorn necklaces, clappers, rattles, walnut dice, and had fun with Chumash face painting. Charlie led a hike to the scarred old oak and did a blessing there. The children on the hike crawled into the hollow. Lightening did not ruin this tree for them. It had made it fun. And now the tree was famous. It had become the central character in Rosi Dagit's book, a book that taught conservation but also Native American traditions. The day had celebrated the publication of the new children's book, *Grandmother Oak*.

Collaborating on preservation in state parks

Since the days of Dennis Dobernick, the California State Park System had grown and reorganized, consolidating areas into districts. In 1988, Dan Preece took over as superintendent of the Angeles District encompassing much Southern California land.

Back in 1980, when Dennis Dobernick had recommended Charlie to the State Parks Native American Advisory Board, Mr. Preece had just been appointed that board's executive secretary. So he knew Charlie, had seen him in action, and did not hesitate to call on him, especially in regard to land issues. The Angeles District encompassed some of the most valuable private property in the country. Anyone could see construction projects of all kinds erupting every day. Over time Charlie and Dan engaged in conversations about minimizing environmental impact that involved the parks.

"Charlie, you know we run into cultural resources when we are developing or upgrading our parks."

"Sure do, all the way back to rerouting the entrance there at Malibu Creek."

"The need for public facilities is growing. We are going to run into native resources as we buy or repurpose land."

"We can minimize the impact. Like at Malibu Creek, the park needed the new entrance, but you did not have to take it right through an old Chumash site. We rerouted that entrance and did not disturb the burials," Charlie recalled.

"That's what I mean, we need to look for alternatives. Charlie, you have been at many county hearings over land development issues. What do you see?"

"It's about mitigation," Charlie echoed his talk at Patty Garcia's house years ago.

"And avoidance," added Dan. "Like changing location or changing the material involved . . ."

"The size or configuration of the site . . ."

"Engineering to avoid an ugly visual impact, like burying a pipe . . ."

"Replacing what's lost . . ."

"We can do that with a tree, but not so easily with an ancient cultural site." Charlie stopped to draw from his large store of experience. "In that case we save it entirely or if not possible, we capture artifacts and information we can and minimize the footprint of the impact. Sometimes we cap a site with extra soil or concrete and move on."

"By the way, Charlie, the Ransbottom property in Santa Susanna is for sale. What should we do?"

Charlie said simply and clearly, "Buy it."

These conversations went on formally and informally for years. In addition to advisory meetings, Charlie would drop in to talk to Dan, or come in response to his calls. Dan and Charlie were of similar minds: they did not want to frustrate developers but did want them to act responsibly whether they were public developers like the parks or private land owners. Dan learned that Charlie's advice was to the point and wise. The Ransbottom property turned out to have a significant archaeological site on it. Dan also noticed the enormous amount of time Charlie was spending at meetings, hearings, and volunteering at park sites. He recommended him for a significant and rare award given for volunteer excellence, an award referred to as the State Parks Medallion. In 1992, the director for State Parks, Donald Murphy, summarized Charlie's achievements from the words on the medallion at a ceremony at Point Mugu State Park adjacent to Satwiwa.

> California State Parks presents this medallion, the Superior Achievement Award to Charles Cooke, Chumash, for his 12 years of dedicated and exemplary volunteer service, which has involved interpretation and work on the following committees: Advisory committees to the Santa Monica Mountain District State Parks, Santa Monica Mountains State Parks Citizen Advisory Council, and State Parks Native American Advisory Council. He is also the founder and leader of Satwiwa.

By 1995, Superintendent Preece realized Charlie should be on staff. He hired him as a part time interpreter at Malibu Creek State Park. He gave him a desk in Mr. Blandings' house, now that park's office. But Charlie was not at his desk much. He led many walks for school children with a headband around his now long hair and dressed in a ribbon shirt (not yet the one Jane Cazabat had promised). Suzanne Goode, a park senior scientist, and other state parks personnel noted that the children were enthralled. He also enthralled the park staff with his after-hours stories, sometimes inadvertently slowing them down from their hurried lives. The superintendent thought it was just the medicine they all needed.

Figure 65: Charlie with Dan Preece at King Gillette Ranch (Courtesy of Dan Preece, 2012)

Linda's wish

Charlie had spent decades by now working for native causes of all kinds. For quite some time he had been the Native American voice heard most loudly in the Santa Monica Mountains. Even though other Chumash leaders had emerged in that area, a strong contingent of native and nonnative people still regarded him as the chief of the Southern Chumash, crossing bands and barriers. He was still called on to attend meetings and do blessings at events, but his Native American activity was slowing down some. The boys had grown up and were on their own. Charlie and Linda were starting to have more time of their own.

"Get the phone, Charlie," Linda called to him, happy he was home for dinner.

Charlie picked it up, "No, no. I know you think it's a good deal. No, I can't do that. Thanks," and he hung up.

"Not again," said Linda.

"Yes, another developer wants to give me land so he can build a casino on it."

As it became clear that Native Americans had rights over land they owned, some nonnatives wanted to give people like Charlie land. So that he could build a casino, one investor offered to give Charlie seven thousand acres. Another investor offered eleven hundred acres so that he could build a casino on a different property. Someone else wanted to build a casino near a lake and offered Charlie lakefront property. Charlie recognized that casinos had improved the lot of many Indians but his focus was on the heritage, not the casinos, so in all cases he declined. But also, these callers really needed an Indian from a federally recognized tribe, like someone from the Santa Ynez Reservation. After all the work Grandma Frances, Alvin, Charlie, and others did on the California rolls, the non-reservation Chumash and the Fernandeños in general were still awaiting Federal status.

"Charlie, I have been looking at travel brochures. There's a special island I want to go to."

"An island?"

"The Island of Skye off Scotland."

"Speaking of islands, Francis Gherini is still hanging on to the east end of Santa Cruz."

Linda looked at him.

"Yes, Linda dear, we'll go to Skye!"

He has a unique story—about a human being but also about a non-corruptible native politician. Charlie's life—one big positive thing—one adventure after another. People will find bits and pieces in their own lives. (Dr. Kote Lotah)

I have great admiration for Charlie Cooke and all other American Indian leaders and consultants who work to keep their cultural traditions alive and share them with the non-Indian population. While there are fewer challenges and barriers now than there have been in the past, these "ambassadors" still encounter, (in interactions with individuals and groups not familiar with deeply imbedded American Indian values), incidents of condescension and lack of total respect.

Charlie is one of those diplomatic persons who has always taken such incidents in stride and carried on with what he believed to be important. Charlie helped win some significant battles toward establishing authentic and viable representation of American Indian peoples at AVIMSHP, as he has done in so many areas in which he has been involved. His contributions, in building so many bridges of cultural understanding and goodwill are beyond estimation. (Edra Moore, former Curator, Antelope Valley Indian Museum State Historic Park, March 15, 2012)

Charlie is a leader who can be shrewd with efforts to prevent destructive development activities. He's the first guy you'd think of if you heard about a pending development. He's also the first guy you'd think of if you have visitors from Sacramento or D.C. He'd dazzle you with information, always accurate. What he said was gold because so many people respected him. (Dan Preece, former District Superintendent, Angeles District, California State Parks, March 25, 2012)

Chapter 23: Monitoring and More into the New Millennium, 1985 On

As at the beginning of this story, I am asking you to drive with me in the Santa Monica Mountain Range but at this point we're driving along the beach to get our bearings and for some historical context. As we drive along the coast, we find ourselves on a windy road flanked by cliffs on one side and huge surfer waves on the other. We're on the famed Pacific Coast Highway. Looking up, we see expansive, expensive homes perched on mountaintops, yes, the ones that can come sliding down with earthquakes and heavy rainfalls. Looking the other way, we see surfers in wetsuits riding the waves—yes, the same cresting waves seen on movies and TV shows.

Hundreds of years ago, we would have walked the beach, looked up and seen dome-shaped huts fashioned with toyon and covered with grass, blending into the canyons. Looking the other way, we would have seen families welcoming home the young men paddling the tomol, bringing fish, abalone shells, and clams to shore. They might have also been carrying steatite, soapstone, from a Tongva island, what is today the island of Catalina, one of eight islands off the Southern California coast, but not part of Channel Islands National Park. Steatite would be made into heatproof bowls, the Chumash version of corning ware. We are in Malibu, which was the prime real estate of the Chumash people, but today it is just plain prime real estate!

Malibu, Land of the Ancient Coastal Chumash

By 1985, land developers were everywhere in Southern California, especially along the coast. Nancy Desautels was leading excavations for a residential site in Malibu. Charlie was a monitor on the site. She noticed that he had his own field notebook, was taking notes, making his own inventory, and comparing with the archaeologists on site. He knew enough to describe finds at each excavation level and the excavation unit wall stratigraphy. He made sure what they got out of the ground went to the Chumash when the excavation was done. He was also monitoring in Agoura at the same time and operating in the same way there. Charlie had learned over the years from working closely with people like Clay Singer, Alex Kirkish, and Chester King.

When the federal government passed the Native American Graves Protection and Repatriation Act (NAGPRA) in 1990, they sparked an even greater demand for Native American monitoring on development sites all across the nation.

One day Charlie got a call about another Malibu site needing monitoring. "Meet us at the property." A'lul-koy and Kote were asking for Charlie's help.

He was hesitant. "Kote, that property—I mean that mansion they're building on the mountain there in Malibu—it falls outside the laws." But Charlie came. Together several Native Americans and some archaeologists slowed the excavation, giving time to consider what was in the ground.

By the mid-90s, people were building on beautiful spots everywhere in the Malibu area, an area inhabited by the ancestral Chumash. Some Malibu projects were large 20,000-square-foot homes, which at the time fell outside laws that protected cultural resources. To address these situations, Charlie started the Malibu Native American Cultural Resources Study Group (NACRSG). A key role was to review proposals concerning developments that would impact Native American cultural and heritage preservation within Malibu City boundaries. The actor, Edward Albert, son of Eddie, chaired the committee. Charlie, the vice chair, ran the meetings for him. Kote, Chester, Phil, A'lul-koy, and Mati were original committee members.

The Malibu Interim Zoning Ordinance at the time required that plans for archaeological testing involving excavations be submitted to this study group before city approval. NACRSG influence resulted in a city moratorium on building, including large homes, until the city had a permitting process in place that included archaeologists on large as well as small constructions when warranted. Dr. Chester King, the Malibu City archaeologist at the time, wrote that process. NACRSG became the Native American Cultural Resources Advisory Committee (NACRAC), which continued to exist and work with the city through 2012.

Monitoring across many tribal lands

"Come with me to monitor work on some pipelines." It was Kote again.

Charlie started working at archaeological sites full time in 1996, starting with the 138-mile Pacific Oil Pipeline stretching from Maricopa near Bakersfield to Wilmington near Long Beach. On the pipeline, he worked for Kote's Owl Clan Consultants, the first Chumash-owned cultural resource company. The pipeline went through many different tribal lands. Anything the consultant group found, they photographed, recorded, cataloged, and returned to the rightful tribal owners. Charlie and the rest of Kote's consultants walked most of the 138 miles. At the end of the line, Kote laughed to himself, "That old goat, Charlie, he held his own."

Later, Charlie monitored the fiber optic line being installed from Burbank to Santa Barbara along the tracks of the Metrolink and Southern Pacific Railroad. It had been a long, long time since Dad had gotten after him for walking a pipeline. He had to chuckle. Here he was, doing it again, and again.

"There are cultural resources where they're going to put the houses, Charlie." This time it was a Tongva elder, Robert Dorame, calling on him.

Charlie's experience with professional archaeologists came into play at Hellman Ranch near the City of Seal Beach where construction was beginning for a housing tract. There he helped to identify thirty-six burials and cremations along with sandstone bowls, pestles, and other Indian artifacts. The findings were saved and the housing tract went up.

University lecturing

In the late 1990s, Professor Wendy Teeter, Curator of Archaeology at the UCLA Fowler Museum, launched a new class, California Experiences in Native Cultural Resource Protection. She included Native American guest speakers every week. Charlie was among them. Charlie went on to lecture in a number of workshops and training sessions that Professor Teeter offered through the UCLA Tribal Learning Community and Educational Exchange Program housed within the School of Law. Mr. McBean had been right about Charlie being college material.

Linda gets her wish

Linda had been working now for years, driving the freeway from Acton to her insurance adjuster job in the San Fernando Valley. One weekend, Linda was leafing through the newspaper.

"Charlie, the 1998 Scottish Games are in Costa Mesa, not too far from here."

"Wanna go? It'll be interesting."

At the games, they saw clan tents. Linda knew she was at least part MacMillan so in she went with Charlie following her, under the plaid of that clan.

"You should join the clan, Linda."

"Hey, Charlie whatever happened with Santa Cruz?"

Frances Gherini held out long enough to get the twelve million he wanted from the Park Service, sometime in 1997, and then promptly died. I'd say we need to make the best of the time we have."

"I still want to go to Skye."

Linda picked up the clan application and turned it in. More investigation and Linda found that she was also a McLeod.

Later that same year, they visited the Isle of Skye, the second largest and northernmost island in the Inner Hebrides of Scotland. Clan McLeod was one of the dominating clans at one time. Charlie and Linda toured Skye and learned of its stone resources, experienced its cool climate, and heard about loyalty to the clan and strife with other clans until they bonded against England. They also visited archaeological sites, some going back almost ten thousand years. Of course, Charlie made comparisons in his mind with ancestral sites back in California. In 2002, Linda became the U.S. clan president. Linda, in her own way, had joined the quest for heritage. Charlie was all for it!

Mentoring new monitors

Charlie continued with monitoring. Some new monitors were coming onto the scene. As usual, Charlie interacted with them professionally but also on a personal level about their own stories. Pat Tumamait monitored a mile or so away from Charlie on the fiber optic line, but they connected. Charlie heard a familiar strain. Pat's third grade teacher, Mr. Boardman had encouraged Pat's pride in his ancestry. Pat's father, like Grandpa Fred Cooke, had hidden his heritage for a time. He had felt the discrimination and even the danger of being out in public as an Indian. In the last ten years of his life, he did so much work to restore that heritage that the Forest Service dedicated the Vincent Tumamait trail in his name at Mt. Pinos.

Pat and Charlie had many conversations about heritage and about Pat's dad. "Did you hear, Charlie, when my dad did the blessing of the bronze dolphin statue by the water in Santa Barbara, the entire harbor filled with dolphins?"

"I wasn't there, but I heard about it. That didn't even happen when Grandfather Victor did that blessing before."

Pat continued, "When the blessing was done, they went back out to the ocean. This was a sign to me of how strong our culture and its spirituality are."

Charlie is a huge volume of knowledge about our culture. I can call him with questions at any time. He's my answer man. We are both truck drivers. Like many native people, we know what it is like to be at the bottom and work our way through life. I can ask Charlie a life question, not just Native American questions. In my eyes he is a chief and a father and elder of our culture. Not many people could match what he's contributed. (Pat Tumamait, Barbareño/ Ventureño Band of Mission Indians, March 26, 2012)

The Native Plant Garden opens

Even though Charlie had lived in Acton for some time now, he continued to come to the Conejo Valley periodically, especially for Satwiwa events.

The Satwiwa Native Plant Garden opened to the public in 2001. It was right next to the new building the UCLA students had designed. People walked onto the small, packed dirt circle of a trail and learned from the signs: gooseberries were eaten raw or they were dried and pounded into cakes. Prickly pear pads, fruit, and seeds were eaten. The Indians used the juice to reduce swelling. Golden currents were eaten fresh. White alder wood was carved into bowls. Toyon berries were roasted and eaten or made into cakes and stored. Deer grass was essential basketry material. The Yerba Santa plant was soaked and the water then used as a wash. As they walked around again they would learn a lot more. A ranger stopped to talk with them and commented that the Chumash and other native people of the area knew how to remove toxins. Not all the plants were edible without treatment, usually boiling.

Figure 66: Satwiwa Center with garden in front (Author's photo 2013)

*Figure 67: An area in the Satwiwa Native Plant Garden
(Author's photo, 2011)*

At Du-par's: NPS monitoring guidelines

After events like the opening of the garden, Charlie and Phil still went to Du-par's. On a late afternoon, they talked about the monitoring guidelines

"We've got a handle on the guidelines, Charlie. I'm writing them into the scope of work for any monitoring done as part of an NPS, SMMNRA contract for archaeological work. Look here."

Phil showed Charlie a list.

1) Monitors are professionals to be on site as part of the contracted cultural resource team.

2) They are to represent the traditional culture of the site.

3) They are to be liaisons about the archaeology, including the process and findings, to the tribal groups.

4) They are to submit written notes and reports to the principal investigator.

They talked about how over time Native American monitoring became more and more valued.

"With some thanks to you, Charlie."

Charlie changed the topic.

"You know what? Sometimes you just know."

"Just know what?" Phil held on to one suspender.

"That building in Encino! We never got all the burials out of there. I ran into someone the other day who goes there a lot. He told me, it's a spooky place."

"You believe in ghosts, don't you, Charlie?"

"Yes, I do."

Palo Comado Canyon, the ranching tie to nature

Into the new millennium, Charlie continued on outings with NPS staff as they explored the recreation area. This day it was Palo Comado Canyon, which had become part of SMMNRA back in 1993. His cowboy days, so far behind him, were always with him.

> Woody, Charlie, and I four-wheeled through Palo Comado Canyon up to China Flats. We passed ranching structures. We stopped at a pond where cattle drank. Charlie began to tell a story about the place. He painted a vivid picture of the ranching operation. Charlie remembers the land before strip malls, tract developments, and subdivisions. He helps you see that it was special and important to preserve the key remnants. His story that day related to the roles we play and the decisions we make to sustain the land. He pointed to an inland archeological site with rock paintings. He noted food: deer, oaks, egg shaped lemonade berries, and yucca. Woody and I realized he had been a ranch hand there. To me, what was so striking that day was how vividly he could paint a picture as it was and crosswalk to today. (Phil Holmes, as part of the interview with Woody Smeck)

As the new century was taking hold, he cheered Linda on with her Scottish endeavors, clapped hard for new rodeo champs, and enthusiastically supported new leaders coming onto the scene of Native American causes.

> Some Native American monitors sit on the sidelines during archaeological work or construction. Not Charlie. He is right there where the action is, watching the work. He is truly interested in cultural resources. He cares about them. The crews like him. He tells them stories about his background while they all work together. (Barbara Tejada, Archaeologist, March 21, 2012)

> If you watch Charlie when he is monitoring, you will see him always thinking. He speaks up when he disagrees and answers questions right there on the spot. He is very good at identifying artifacts and knowing the purposes of them. You'll see him kidding around too. (Pat Tumamait)

Chapter 24: A Turtle to Court, 2003

It had been a long time since Charlie and Vince Ibanez had stuffed the pockets of the braggart with spoons, knives, and forks during a restaurant meal. In Chumash stories, coyote is a trickster. It appears that Charlie inherited some of that characteristic. Usually he was not alone on the pranks, but seemed to delight in participating.

In 2003, Rosi Dagit was researching aquatic life in creeks with a focus on the Southwest Pond Turtle. She came across a red-eared slider turtle, native to Louisiana; the same turtle kids buy as pets when they are the size of a silver dollar. This one, however, was very big.

Rosi was scheduled to attend the Ahmanson Land Development hearing at the Ventura County Courthouse. She arranged to meet and hand over the red-eared slider to the Santa Monica Mountain turtle specialist who was also attending. Rosi arrived on crutches due to a sprained ankle. She was struggling to hold on to a cooler that housed the turtle.

This was not too long after 9/11. Security checkpoints had been installed in many government facilities. The courthouse had one similar to those at airports. Rosi went through with the turtle. He checked out okay. Then Rosi asked the security guard,

"May I leave my turtle—he's in the cooler—by that potted plant? I need to go back to my car to get some other things."

The guard answered, "You may not leave your turtle unattended." No matter what Rosie said, the guard kept saying, "You may not leave your turtle unattended." To Rosie this sounded like the airport announcement for baggage. She did not know what to do next.

Right about then Charlie, Mati Waiya, and other Native Americans arrived for the hearing in full regalia. Rosi asked Charlie if he would take care of her turtle for a few minutes. He said yes and took the cooler and went right into the lobby. The guard did not stop him. Rosi hobbled out to her car. When she came back she found the Indians in a circle peering down at the turtle. The red-eared slider was in his cooler on the slick marble floor right in the middle of the formal columned lobby. The guard was straining to listen to the Indians. They could see her and continued with their banter.

"My rattles are wearing out. That turtle will make some great new ones."

"It would make a good soup."

"Look at that shell. We could shine it up and . . ."

The guard could take no more. She came running into the circle pleading, "Don't touch that turtle. Don't hurt that turtle. It belongs to this lady."

Charlie saw that the joke had reached its limits. He put his arms around the guard and assured her they would not harm the turtle. Relieved she went back to her post. Rosi, the Indians, and the turtle went to the hearing.

The mountainous Ahmanson Ranch property covered a lot of territory along Highway 101. The Chumash opposed development there because it contained sacred sites. The property also had a rare valley oak woodland. Rosi was there that turtle day to testify about the impact of any building on the trees. Others came to testify about endangered species in the area. Charlie talked about the history of the area and its cultural resources. Several hearings later, the County refused to allow the development primarily for traffic reasons. While the development was not stopped because of environmental or Native American concerns, the Indians and the scientists gave pause and influenced people to stop and think. The property was purchased by the Santa Monica Mountains Conservancy and turned into a state nature preserve. The slider turtle played no part except to relieve some stress among those testifying.

Charlie made statements at many public hearings regarding development projects. He always spoke with a great deal of integrity. He would focus on the history of the place and the environmental resources. He would caution against moving ahead in a piecemeal fashion. He did not stop developments, but he was a voice in slowing them down, in causing developers to rethink responsibly, and in some cases to affect their decisions to sell for a public park. (Rosi Dagit, Sr. Conservation Biologist, Resource Conservation District of the Santa Monica Mountains, March 23, 2012)

Charlie always has a sense of humor but will introduce serious thinking when needed. He provides a sensible and disciplined aspect without compromising the enjoyment or the spirit of the moment. (Dr. E.C. Krupp, January 18, 2010)

When Charlie sees me there is a specific greeting. We make jokes right off the bat to break tension and so hearts feel good. (Dr. Kote Lotah)

Chapter 25: New Leaders, 2005-2012

Four deep blasts from a conch shell cut the biting Malibu wind, one toward each of the four directions. Dawn was breaking on this Wednesday, November 16, 2005, as A'lul-koy Lotah stood at the center of a fire circle and started the ceremony to mark the beginning of a recreated Chumash village. She and the 20 guests around her could feel the occasional saltwater spray from the cresting waves on Nicholas County Beach in Malibu. They were on the shore of ancestors. She offered the traditional sage blessing and led a Chumash song.

A new leader and teacher of Chumash ways

Mati left his successful construction business behind as he started Wishtoyo Foundation to protect and preserve the coastal culture and resources. He had worked with the Los Angeles County Department of Beaches and Harbors and private donors to get the Chumash Demonstration Village onto the beach. So far the village had a fire circle, a sweat lodge, and a master plan. The plan was for simple Chumash aps and native gardens hidden from but amidst multimillion-dollar homes and landscaping. Surfers, daring the waves, would be close but out of sight. This village would also sit near Chumash archeological sites as old as eight thousand years. Stacks of reeds lay nearby ready for building the aps.

As A'lul-koy finished. Mati was talking to movie star, Beau Bridges, a Wishtoyo Board member, about Wishtoyo's larger mission to protect the environment. Then with great pride, he introduced Charlie as the Chairman of Wishtoyo Foundation.

Figure 68: Charlie Cooke and Mati Waiya with Beau Bridges, Wishtoyo event (Photo by Luhui Isha Waiya, 2013)

"This is Chumash land," the chief said. "We have never given up on this land. Now it will be here for all people, not just Native American people." By now, everyone knew Charlie would say something like that. Charlie: always inclusive, always collaborating, always sharing and dedicated to the core.

A year later Mati settled in to live on the re-created village site as did his forbearers—no more suit and polished shoes, no more BMW. He gave talks and conducted demonstrations for elementary school children who came out with their teachers. Differently from Charlie, when he felt the event called for it, he dressed as his ancestors in skins, firs, beads, earrings, a nose ring or pin, and the body painting that went with it. He ran weekend events for various adult groups, some of them overnight. After late night starlit talks, people would fall asleep in aps lulled by waves breaking on the shore—reminiscent of Point Conception but without the strife of that time. They had come so far since then.

> The first time I saw Charlie it was at the old house at Satwiwa. I met Phil Holmes at the same time and told him that I am Chumash. He asked me if I could teach about my culture. I told him I was there to learn. I had gotten a flyer and came to see what Satwiwa was all about. Phil said, "So when you learn then you can teach us." I now understand what he meant. You become a teacher, a steward, a protector and become obligated and committed to protecting. (Mati Waiya)

Figure 69: Charlie Cooke and Mati Waiya, Chumash Demonstration Village, Malibu, (Author's photo, 2010)

Figure 70: Longtime friends and associates, Dr. Kote Lotah with Charlie Cooke, Wishtoyo (Courtesy of Mati Waiya, June 11, 2011)

More Native American centers

Satwiwa, Oakbrook, Wishtoyo! As the decade progressed, newspaper articles reported arguments about duplication. But in reality, they complemented each other. Satwiwa: a natural area left as it was with its quiet walks, its waterfall, its seasonal streams, and its abundance of plant and animal life. It was about experiencing the land and something spiritual, something intangible left for you to define. Oakbrook: a museum full of art and artifacts and a re-created village. It offered a way to see the past and present Chumash culture with high quality displays. Wishtoyo Foundation's Chumash Village: a living village offering overnight experiences right on the beach. And the Antelope Valley Indian Museum State Historic Park? It underwent significant changes under Edra Moore and became a sparkling example of the evolution from a display center to a venue that shares true historic and living culture. Under Edra's successor, Peggy Ronning, the museum underwent a significant renovation inside and out. Charlie remained interested and involved.

Figure 71: Wishtoyo Chumash Village at sunset, (Photo by Mati Waiya, October 2012)

Figure 72: Grand re-opening, AVIMSHP, From left: Peggy Ronning, curator; Charlie Cooke; Cy Crites, president of Friends of the Antelope Valley Indian Museum; Kathy Weatherman, State Parks Tehachapi District superintendent (© 2010 California State Parks)

Charlie recognized professionally

Professor Teeter had been noticing all the work Charlie had been doing over many years and nominated him for the prestigious California Indian Preservation Award. The Society for California Archaeology presented this award to Chief Charlie Cooke at their annual meeting in April of 2008. Charlie completely fit the bill for this award: someone who gave a voice to Native American survival and sovereignty, who gave mainstream America an understanding of native culture and history, who participated at local, state, and federal levels to uphold respect for Native American ancestors, who bridged the gap between academic and traditional understanding of native heritages, who created centers that maintained and demonstrated native ways, who educated school children and grown-ups—anthropologists, archaeologists, and historians. That summed it up, a perfect description of Charlie Cooke, Chief TIQ SLO'W.

Mentoring a new Chumash chief

For several years, Charlie had been thinking about who would follow him as chief of his group of the Southern Chumash. He did what Aunt Mary had done and asked members in his Chumash extended family and talked to leaders like Dr. Kote Lotah. He mentored people whether they knew it or not. He would call one person in particular over and over.

"I'm monitoring the 126. A small burial was dug up. I need you to keep an eye on things 'til I get there."

At the site: "Did you see how to take notes on the 126?"

"I'm going to the Solstice Ceremony on Mt. Pinos in Frazier Park. Come with me."

At the Solstice, "Remember always the power of nature and that our ancestors understood it."

"There's a symposium in Palmdale at the Civic Center. We should go to it."

And then later, "What should we take away from that symposium?"

"I'm guest hosting at Satwiwa Sunday. Come out."

On that Sunday, "I want you to tell a Chumash story."

"Bring your drum to the powwow next week."

At the powwow, "Here, hold this sage. You are going to help do the blessing. Here's how you protect yourself from any evil during this offering."

"Yes, another park meeting. I need you there."

After that meeting, "How do you think we can support the ideas we heard?"

"Another city meeting tomorrow evening. I need you there to give your ideas."

"Good job last night."

"Yes, this month. December. Yes, this year. 2008. Playa Vista near Marina del Rey. There will be a re-internment and dedication of a cemetery. Be there."

Handing over the staff

Over one thousand Tongva ancestors were ready—bundled in deerskin, the traditional burial wrapping. Charlie Cooke, Chumash Chief and also a Tongva elder, blew a conch shell in the traditional four directions to open the reburial ceremony near the commercial and residential development built where there had been ancient Tongva settlements. Some of the ancestors being reburied this December were three thousand years old. Some were more recent, from the 1820s.

The Native American Heritage Commission had named Robert Dorame as the most-likely-descendant of the ancestors buried at Playa Vista. Robert was also Chairman of the Gabrielino Tongva Indians.

"Ya-way-ne-szun. My heart is lightened," said Robert Dorame in the Tongva language.

He felt relieved after his ancestors were laid to rest again near where they had been for centuries. Robert orchestrated their reburial in the same configuration in which they were found. Geo mapping made that possible. Robert had been involved every step of the way. Some of the steps had been difficult. Charlie had supported him whenever he needed another voice.

> Charlie never says no to helping with ancestors. He will drive miles. People still objectify us—treat us as objects. People have said things to me like, "Can I touch your hair." He helps stop this marginalizing of us. He has the ability to open doors and to promote us. He is what a chief should be. Younger Indians should look up to him and say to themselves that this is what I should be like. (Robert Dorame, Chairman of the Gabrielino Tongva Indians of the California Tribal Council, January 20, 2012.)

Figure 73: Charlie holding staff, with Robert Dorame, Playa Vista, (Image © 2008 Mercedes Dorame www.mercedesdorame.com)

After the ceremony, in front of the gathering and in front of the newly re-interred ancestors, Charlie took his staff in hand. He looked at it remembering when Kote handed it to him and told him to notch it for his accomplishments. He smiled to himself knowing that there were many notches missing—because of places like the Lost Village. He ran his hand

TIQ SLO'W, The Making of a Modern Day Chief

down the neat notches, one hundred of them. They had come a long way since their ancestors had lost their identities in the missions. He knew that he and people like Robert, Kote, A'lul-koy, Mati, and others, had helped to restore that identity.

Chief TIQ SLO'W nodded a satisfied nod and then handed the staff to a younger man. "This is a good time," he thought. "There are many Indians here today, and the Chumash and Tongva have had a long association."

In front of several Indian cultures, he introduced the new hereditary chief of his family group of the Southern Chumash, his cousin, Aunt Mary's grandson, Ted Garcia. Ted's Chumash name, Very Respected Bear, came from a story about a Santa Barbara Mission Chumash with that same name. SUL WAISEN ISET longed for his freedom, slipped away to the shore with his canoe on occasions, and one day did not return. As Ted took the staff, things had changed. There was still work to do, but they no longer needed to hide or run away.

> I am chief now, but Charlie is still very influential in the native community. He has spoken to so many people over the years. All I have to do is mention his name. Over this last weekend a nonnative woman who was a grocery clerk in a store noticed my native jewelry on me at the checkout counter. She asked if I knew Charlie Cooke. She said she knew of him and what he has done and would like to meet him. He is well known in the community. (Ted Garcia, Jr. Hereditary Chumash Chief, Aunt Mary's son, Charlie's cousin, June 19, 2009)

Figure 74: Chief Ted Garcia (Author's photo, 2011)

Related cultural issues overseas

The Cookes kept traveling: Scotland, Ireland, New Zealand, China, and Italy. The elderly lady of Italian heritage, who constantly asked what happened to the Indians, had an old family home in the agricultural mountains of Southern Italy. She told stories about her ancestry to anyone who would listen. Some seemed a little suspect. Through events at Satwiwa, Charlie got to know her and her family. In October of 2009, they accompanied her daughter to San Lorenzo Maggiore, a town in the Southern Apennines. Not speaking one word of Italian, Charlie and Linda managed to live there and interact with the townspeople for a full week. They could see the charm of the back-country Italian life among olives and grapes. Charlie bonded with Antonio, who did speak a little English. He'd go over to his farm down the road and the two would sit on his front porch drinking his homemade wine while the women went shopping. Another couple also came on this trip. Charlie and Linda went with them on day trips, including to Pompeii, one of the most famous archaeological sites in the world. Charlie knew that Linda loved castles so they went to see an old stone one in the town nearby.

And the daughter—every trip to her mother's town, she found out that people there knew the same stories she had heard growing up in the United States. The family men had been mayors of that town over a few generations. And that story about the Jesuit leaving the order, marrying, and leaving descendants who eventually came through Ellis Island—well that story was told on both sides of the ocean. "Wow," she later told Charlie, "If these stories can survive the ocean distance and loss of language, I can believe that Native American stories about family could survive from one side of a mountain range to another and out to the coastal islands."

Monitoring near Malibu Creek again

Back in the United States, Charlie got calls to get back on site.

"We need you to monitor. And for the first time we are going to use cadaver dogs."

Park headquarters was now in Thousand Oaks. It included a visitor center named for U.S. Congressman Anthony Beilenson who had introduced the legislation for SMMNRA and for Channel Islands National Park.

Phil called Charlie in 2010, "Yes, dogs. We're going to be moving the Beilenson Visitor Center in a year or two. We're renovating the stables on what was the Gillette Ranch. The new center will be very near the old Chumash village of Talepop."

"Right, not too far from where the state widened the road for Malibu Creek State Park some years ago. Only there were no burials there."

"That's right. Chester, Al, and some others you know will be out there at Gillette starting the archaeological survey. You've said there are artifacts there. Well, we are going to find out."

"With all the technology, the dogs are still the best," chuckled Charlie.

After a few months of work at Gillette, the archaeologists and the dogs verified burials and signs of Talepop, hard to find exactly because of all the earth moving to build, farm, and lay down roads over the years. Talepop was a Chumash village site at least several thousand years old. It had thrived in an area with much water, game, and plants. Charlie was very happy when his sister, Patricia Joyce, got involved doing some monitoring on the site along with him. She, like he, was a proven most-likely-descendant.

Figure 75: Charlie monitoring at the Gillette Site, unidentified archaeological workers, (Author's photo, 2010)

Influenced by Charlie, starting with Bob Chandler, the Park Service had involved American Indians in planning for SMMNRA sites that had a chance of having Indian history. On this August morning in 2010, a group of Indians, NPS staff, and some archaeologists gathered on the Gillette Ranch under large oak trees in an area between an old trailer that had been a print shop and stables, next to a hill. About thirty chairs made a semi-circle in three rows. They were about three-quarters filled.

The landscape architect for the Satwiwa native garden was there. He was now in charge of the great SMMNRA expanse. Superintendent Woody

Smeck introduced the project. Dr. Chester King gave an overview of the archeological findings and conducted a tour of the grounds. And there was Charlie. There was only a hint of his working-man look: his plaid shirt and jeans. But otherwise, he was looking the part of the Native American elder he had become. He was carrying the walking stick Linda had given him since he had handed over the chief's staff Kote had crafted to Ted Garcia. He sported a mustache, goatee, and shoulder-length hair. He was in the front row, but taking a back seat.

He listened intently to a lot of questions, discussion, and suggestions from the Chumash who had come to this meeting. He turned in the direction of whoever was speaking. He was now dependent on hearing aids. At one point he examined a drawing that was being passed around. He made comments about water conservation, re-internment, conducting Satwiwa-like cultural programs at Gillette, and about being inclusive of other native peoples at the next meeting. People listened when he spoke, but he was giving others their turns now, including Ted.

Figure 76: Superintendent Woody Smeck with Charlie at the Gillette Visitor Center Consultation, (SMMNRA Archives, 2010)

Preservation on a large and small scale

The Channel Islands: San Miguel, Santa Rosa, Santa Cruz, Anacapa, and Santa Barbara, were now all part of Channel Islands National Park. Over the years Charlie and other California Indians gave input regarding protection and access, which kept the islands a living history book and a refreshing respite from the mainland. The Chumash heritage is visible in nature, but that's all. You can imagine life past on these serene islands when you are there. No hotels, no food stops, for the most part no paved roads or cars. The public has access to the islands by boat and air through concessioners. Once there, visitors hike, kayak, fish, swim, scuba dive, bird watch, picnic, take a ranger led walk, watch an undersea live video, hold a dialog with the video's undersea divers, and camp overnight close to the sea, under bright island stars. Many people were involved with making these islands an unspoiled place to visit. Charlie was one of them weighing in with his preference for preserving native sites in a pristine way, which is the case on these small bits of land off the coast.

By now the Santa Monica Mountains National Recreation Area had many holdings over an area from Griffith Park in Los Angeles to Point Mugu in Ventura County spanning federal, state, local, and private property. Charlie's influence stretched that whole length and beyond, and yet the bluffs kept calling.

Satwiwa had been well established for more than a decade now. The bowl! That sandstone bowl that Vicki had brought him! The time was overdue to alternate years displaying it with the Stagecoach Inn Museum. Charlie had gone to the museum a few times to discuss sharing the bowl. Harriet was gone and the new staff could not find the written agreement. As a stroke of luck, Tim King, a young man who had worked with Mati Waiya, went to work for the museum sometime in 2011. Through Mati, he had met Charlie. Charlie told Tim about the bowl. The young man took it upon himself to find the paper work. One day around June of that year Charlie got a call.

"I found it, the paper work for the bowl."

"I knew it was there somewhere, Tim."

Tim waited for the New Year and then he took the bowl and a copy of the paper work to the NPS headquarters in Thousand Oaks. He left the dirt in it so that researchers could someday analyze it for ancient seeds and other secrets it was keeping. On January 15, 2012, Charlie visited the Satwiwa Cultural Center and there was the sandstone bowl on display. The ancients had chiseled it perfectly from a large boulder—another testament to the ingenuity and skill of the people who had lived joyfully and peacefully in the surrounding area for thousands of years.

Figure 77: Chumash Bowl, Satwiwa Native American Indian Center Display (Author's photo, 2012)

Charlie is not driven by time. The sense you get from him is take all the time you need. Don't rush. Don't hurry. Put one foot before the other. Have a focus. Have a vision. Don't rush through your life. Smell the roses. Touch the dirt. Many of us have the same dedication he has toward the earth and preserving culture. But some of us do it looking at a watch and rushing around. Charlie is a steady presence, even though he is always on the go. (Suzanne Goode, Senior Environmental Scientist, California State Parks, March 7, 2012)

Charlie had such a reputation as an important Native American in Southern California that I was intimidated when I first met him. But I soon found that he is a really nice guy who always smiles and projects good cheer. (Barbara Tejada)

"Charlie, Charlie, Charlie," a group of young children chanted at a park event. "Charlie, Charlie, Charlie." I don't remember exactly where this was, but I remember it. (Robert Dorame)

Chapter 26: Not Forgotten, Timeless

She is nearing one hundred, now sitting in the passenger seat, saying what she says almost every time she travels down these Conejo Valley roads because it has bothered her for years, "To think, the Indians lived here; they walked where the houses are; they picked berries; they sang their songs right here among these hills."

A large, white, rocky bluff rises into view as we make our way on this sunny California Saturday all the way to Satwiwa. Again I am asking you to come along for the ride. Should we take that new impressive entrance across from the huge, upscale Dos Vientos housing development rather than the old narrow ranch road? Dos Vientos had been planned as far back as the late 1970s when the Thousand Oaks Slow Growth Movement got underway. It was finally built in the 1990s in such a way that it does not encroach on Satwiwa, but it does flank it on one side. Will it be visible from the Satwiwa bowl?

We decide to take the old ranch entrance for the handicapped parking by the small house that had been the original cultural center. We squeeze our car between two trucks, a ranger truck and a truck that we recognize as Charlie's. We pull a wheel chair out of the trunk, help the smiling elderly woman into it, and move past a new colorful sign with a photo of Chief TIQ SLO'W on it. The National Park Service honored Charlie back in 2005 as a founder of this special cultural center—a learning center for all peoples, not solely for one tribe but for all Native Americans and for the rest of us.

I wheel my mother, Rosaria Contini, past the native garden. We notice hikers and bikers—lots of them. Some stop in the new building. The rangers are busily talking with them and directing them over to Charlie at the fire ring.

We see three people on horseback riding a trail up above—a reminder of the ranching days. We see parents backpacking their young children. We pick up snippets as they walk by.

> Wow, you can see really far from up there. You seem so far away from houses and cars here. That new development is close, but you can't see it. Look at those huge stones up there. That's an old windmill up on that trail. There was a ranch here once. (Satwiwa Visitors, March 20, 2010)

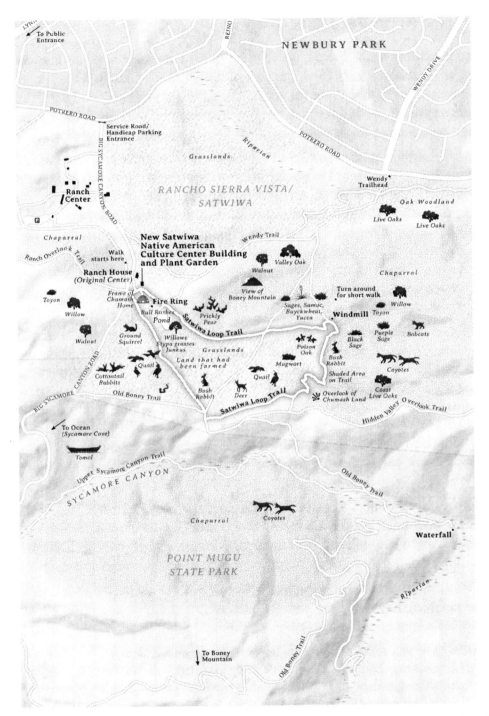

Map 9: Loop Trail after 1995 (Courtesy of James Mansfield updated from sketch in Satwiwa Loop Trail, a brochure by John Detlie and Mary Gordon, 1986)

Then silence. Some just move quietly soaking up the powerful essence of the place. Birds chirp. A loud caw caw as black wings speed by! Leaves rustle. A squirrel kicks a pebble as it scampers over the trail. Four twenty-somethings stop nearby to unload small day-trip backpacks.

> This is my favorite place—glad I live nearby. I'm far, but I don't mind driving here. Did you see the display in that building over there? I had no idea that there were Indians in California. Oh, I knew that. One came to my third grade class. He was a big guy. There's a program over there at the campfire. Glad we went all the way to that awesome waterfall! (Satwiwa Visitors)

Waterfall! They are talking about the cascade bursting over cliff-size rocks to a rushing stream forever eroding a little canyon all for itself. Lots of people make their way to the falls now, but if you hit it right you can still find solitude, sitting in the midst of the water on huge wet rocks, shaded by trees leaning off the eroded walls, thinking, meditating, or talking softy with family members.

Figure 78: Rebecca Lubitz, MD, formerly the Satwiwa teenage hiker, with her two sons and another son in utero. (Author's photo, 2009)

We look over to the fire circle. Charlie's there. We see Linda too. She is wearing a plaid baseball cap. Across it, one word in a special font: Scotland. People are still gathering so we wheel Rosaria though the plant garden. She reads every sign, smiling. We look over again. Charlie is leaning over, putting down a few things at the edge of a fire pit. There are a lot of people gathered already. His name is a draw on any program. The twenty-somethings pick up their packs and move toward the circle. We head over too.

Charlie is here this day in March 2010 for the spring equinox as Guest Host. His hair is shoulder length, and he sports a goatee. He is wearing a shirt with small rose-colored flowers printed on it, perhaps the wild roses that grow in the mountains. Rose, white, and blue ribbons stripe across the front, back and down the sleeves. Loose ribbons flow with the breeze; the ribbons could be removed and changed. From the moment Jane Cazabat finally presented him with the ribbon shirt at a powwow on the NPS Paramount Ranch site in 2001, he knew this ribbon shirt was well worth the wait so he wore it on special occasions like this one today.

> To me, Charlie's greatest achievement was the present and the presence of the Satwiwa Native American Culture Center. The present because it was a gift which spring boarded Native Americans into roles in native communities. Presence because it gave us a place we could go. (E. Jane Cazabat, Muscogee-Creek/Seminole, October 16, 2011)

Two other long-haired men, dressed in T-shirts with native symbols, huddle with Charlie for a few minutes. Then Charlie and his cousins, Chief Ted Garcia and Ted's brother Dennis are quiet for a moment.

> There is a deep inner spirituality about Charlie which comes from his selflessness. How do I know? I just believe it about him. I have been with him in quiet moments. I can sense it. It is not explicit. I have seen his benevolence and power. He has lived his life for others. (Dr. Lynn Gamble, Anthropology Professor, July 13, 2009)

Charlie, the elder, turns to the group seated on logs around the fire pit. An abalone shell, a leather pouch, a feather, a bundle of white sage, and a native rattle rest against the stones defining the pit. A red baseball cap lies in the grass by one of the stones. Across it, one word in bright capitals: CHUMASH.

That question that came up at the mission some time ago comes to mind: what do the artifacts and mission records matter to Charlie's decades of leadership? They matter because they led him to his work to restore and share cultural heritage.

The artifacts, as collected by Arden Edwards, Grace Oliver, and others in the early decades of the twentieth century, were an example of a needed change—a change toward not just collecting but respecting and understanding Native American heritage in context. Charlie took it upon himself to learn about archaeology, to work on digs promoting respect for cultural heritage, and to make sure that all Indian centers, including the one that housed the Edwards/Oliver collection conveyed cultural context.

The mission records are one factor in verifying Indian ancestry. However, the missions themselves contributed to the loss of heritage and the vagueness of ancestry. It was this very vagueness that led Charlie to search for and learn about his background, sparked by Grandma Frances's words, "You are Indian, and don't you forget it." Regardless of the details of Charlie's ancestry, he has been an effective Native American leader over decades. His ultimate goal was and is for today's residents, they themselves, to understand and to protect what is all around them. Satwiwa stands as the center of his quest toward that goal.

So, at Satwiwa, on this spring equinox, the answer to the core of the question, *What matters?*, envelopes everyone assembled. It is in the vista, in the sea breeze, and in the voices that have been playing out all around under Boney's gaze today—natural and cultural heritage hand-in-hand, restored, preserved, and shared on behalf of all who had lived on this land before us, regardless of tribal, clan, or band affiliation.

The nearly one hundred-year-old elder finds her answer too. Rosaria sees protectors of the land, some descended from those who had walked in the shadows of the sacred mountain eons ago, and many more of what Kote would call the Young American Tribe.

Figure 79: Charlie giving Rosaria Contini the sage blessing, Esther Dolyaba behind her, (Author's photo, 2010)

Charlie starts the welcome song. Then he asks everyone to stand and touch the ground. He leans over to pick up the abalone shell and sage. He lights the sage and waits for it to smolder. Dennis hands him his eagle feather. First Charlie blesses his two cousins. Then all three move to different sections of the circle and start blessing individuals one by one. Their eagle feathers send the white sage wafting over each individual steward of this earth, right here, right now, among these hills. Charlie looks toward the bluffs. The smoldering sage rises.

EPILOGUE

Charlie's Way—Leadership in Action
by John Reynolds and Woody Smeck, National Park Service Leadership

Charlie drives up to the Santa Monica Mountains National Recreation Area headquarters in Woodland Hills and parks his concrete mixer truck right in front of the front door. It is 1980, usually about 4:30 in the afternoon. Charlie has wrestled this truck around the freeways and back roads for a full day. Most of the Park Service employees are thinking that there may be only two or three more hours before the day wraps up. Like every other day in the creation of a new national park, it has been a full day.

Charlie climbs down from his high cab, grabs the office door, throws it open, and his smile and energy precede him into the room. It feels as though this late stop is the first thing he has done all day. The energy level rises as every one of us feels like we just had a Red Bull infusion (without the jitters).

An animated conversation just naturally evolves. It begins with genuine inquiry by Charlie about how each of us is doing, maybe a bit of catch-up on the last few days' activities. No one notices, but we slide easily into a focused conversation. Charlie led it there, but as is Charlie's way, no one is conscious that he did that . . . nor is he. Together, by mutual unstated consent, we are all fully engaged with Charlie's topics, which somehow, in truth, are our topics, too.

In an hour or so Charlie bids us farewell, climbs high up in his cab, shifting gears as easily into traffic as we had all shifted into the topics of the last hour. Those of us left behind realize we have just taken another step forward in achieving objectives that we and Charlie share equally.

It happens every time.

Years later there is no cement mixer but Charlie is still there. Nearly all of the other players have changed. Unaccountably everyone involved with Charlie still experiences him and his leadership in the same way.

Why? What makes him such a glue for more than thirty years with the park; longer with the Chumash people and others in the Los Angeles area?

It is "Charlie's way." It has to do with the unique way he is. Not just how he conducts himself, but the way he is.

Charlie does not operate from an agenda. Rather, he operates based on deeply thoughtful, deeply held principles based on a seemingly innate and unconscious combination of personal integrity and his connections to the cultures which created him: Chumash, and Native American more inclusively.

Yet he is also one with the cultures which surround him. Somehow he moves mentally, physically and largely unconsciously among cultures and subcultures. He seems pan-human, pan-cultural in many ways, yet always Chumash and always Charlie.

As such his personal generosity of mind and time, intellect and feeling, is seemingly limitless—the more he gives, the more all succeed, and the more he is a part of it all.

He finds the principles of others, finds the alignment of his and theirs, and moves easily, gracefully and respectfully in that space.

He never forces his way, yet he is always a part of what is important. He becomes a part of a gathering of people committed to something, some ideas are as a result of kinship and respect, never from being required.

He deals in interests before solutions. He finds and builds commonalities of interests, and allows solutions to evolve. He is not hurried, but time is never wasted. Solutions, when they come, stick. They are not decisions. They are solutions.

To describe "Charlie's way" feels nearly impossible. That is the reason for this book and the approach it takes. You have to know the man to know his leadership "style" and capabilities. Describing what a person exudes with honesty, humility, and tolerance does not lend itself well to the usual prose.

Knowing Charlie is such an honor, such a pleasure . . . for to know him and to have worked with him is to experience him, his effect, and his natural way.

Woody Smeck was the fifth Superintendent of Santa Monica Mountains National Recreation Area. In 2012, he became the Deputy Superintendent, Yosemite National Park. In 2013, he was selected as Superintendent of Sequoia/Kings Canyon National Parks. He has maintained contact with Charlie over the years.

John Reynolds was the first Assistant Superintendent of Santa Monica Mountains National Recreation Area. He went on to become the Superintendent North Cascades National Park, Manager of the Denver Service Center, Regional Director of the Mid-Atlantic and Pacific West Regions, and finally the Deputy Director of the National Park Service. Some positions after retirement: Executive vice president, National Park Foundation, Board of Directors for Chesapeake Conservancy, Student Conservation Association, and for the Presidio Trust. Chair Flight 93 National Memorial Advisory Commission. He has maintained contact with Charlie over the years.

Appendices

What Makes a Chief: Author's Comments

Driving the highways into tomorrow: Charlie was very present but looked way ahead. You scooted along a lot of Southern California freeways today, traveling from one appointment to another. You noticed something new. Signs that said Tongva area, Chumash area, Tataviam area. It's 2030. One of Charlie's dreams has come true: highway signs signaling that you are in ancient Indian Territory. Rest stops have information about the people: what they subsisted on, their housing, their traditions, their belief systems, and much more.

But that was not the only dream his many compatriots shared during the research phase of this book.

An ongoing vision built on conviction: people who know him well say he saw a future with universal respect for heritage and for Mother Earth, recognition of native contributions to modern society, better education for Natives about both worlds they live in, and for nonnatives about the world that was here before them. He constantly worked toward those goals and was able to focus opportunities.

When I, Rosaria's daughter and author of this book, asked him what he would like to see, the chief and former warrior answered with one word, "Peace." But then he told this story:

> President George W. Bush came to Satwiwa. The president and the Secretary of the Interior walked up the trail toward him. Charlie was preparing to burn sage, but the Secret Service took it away from him. Charlie wanted to talk to the president about getting our people out of Iraq, but he decided instead to use whatever moments he had differently. He knew others had given the president that message. He decided instead to tell the president that the Satwiwa was a place for all people, to please respect it, and to help preserve this place well into the future.

Unrelenting, involved, collaborative leadership: When pressed, people can give a one-word description of Charlie. The answers fall into categories of focus, interpersonal ability, trustworthiness, and charisma. What did Charlie say when asked the same question about himself? "Involved." In addition to exemplary involvement which motivates others, he demonstrates other characteristics of effective leaders.

Grandma Frances's words, overheard leaning against an old shed as an eleven-year-old, provided the **defining moment** so many leaders experience. A work ethic instilled in childhood and a focus on causes that that he deeply felt moved him **past some youthful rough spots**, He developed as a leader by taking on **experience after experience** and **through mentorship across boundaries** which included other Native Americans, anthropologists and park personnel. But that went both ways. His mentors listened to him too because he had developed **personal credibility** by constantly learning and then openly sharing his knowledge one-on-one and in group settings. As is the case with most leaders, he became a **visionary**, most graphically standing on the hill at Satwiwa. But a vision is not enough. Time after time at meetings or in the field he leveraged his **ability to work with multiple perspectives, to hear the unspoken, to communicate with humility and humor**, and to **motivate by being there** himself, thus bringing to fruition his Satwiwa vision—a vision that required working across many entities with different goals. These characteristics also played a part in saving environments and restoring heritage throughout the mountains and out to sea.

Charlie was fortunate to have worked with the anthropologists/ archaeologists, developers, civic leaders, and the Park Service staffs that came into his life. Many of them were open minded, willing to accept a California Indian even when others said they did not exist. But Charlie sought them out; that too was part of his makeup. Charlie also bonded with other Native American leaders and learned from them. Soon those in the circle with Charlie found themselves on a marvelous journey whirling together on Mother Earth from one solstice to the next.

Many CEOs and leaders of all kinds could learn from Charlie Cooke, the cement mixer truck driver, the ranch hand, the rodeo champ, the everyday family man, and the loyal friend who became the American Indian Chief and leader with the eye of the eagle, TIQ SLO'W.

Diagram of a Leader's Network

Charlie's continued involvement grew his network and the networks of others. To draw it completely as a web would make it unreadable, but here it is with its basic connections.

Figure 80: Diagram of Charlie's Network

The center is the objective or focus; for Charlie in the big picture, it was Mother Earth. In some cases it was cultural and natural resources. Sometimes it was an event such as a powwow, but even at that level of detail, the big vision of all of us together on Mother Earth prevailed.

Where Did They Go?

Following are some later positions of just some of the National Park Service (NPS) staff mentioned in this story. Others in the story, from and not from NPS, have gone on to successful positions in government and business.

Anderson, William: Left NPS in 1985 for a position in the private recreation sector as President of Westrec Marinas, a position he holds to this date.

Chandler, Robert: Superintendent Olympic Everglades and Grand Canyon National Park, General Manager of the Presidio in San Francisco. After retirement—National Parks Advisory Board. Charlie gave the Chumash prayer and blessing at Bob's Memorial Service on March 5, 2011.

Ehorn, Nancy Fries: Land Use and Planning, NPS Denver Service Center. Retired.

Ehorn, William: Superintendent Redwood National Park, Retired.

Holmes, Phil: Retired in 2011 after thirty-one years as the NPS Southern California Anthropologist. Now an NPS volunteer.

Leicester, Marti: Chief of Interpretation at Golden Gate National Recreation Area, Superintendent, Fredericksburg and Spotsylvania National Military Park, Deputy Regional Director, Pacific West Region. After retirement: writer of historical books.

Quintana, Ernie: Superintendent Joshua Tree National Park, NPS Regional Director, Midwest Region, Retired.

Redmond, Bill: After nine years with the National Park Service, Bill served as a juvenile probation officer and deputy district attorney in Ventura County for twenty-one years. Since 2008, Bill has been a Superior Court Commissioner for the Ventura Superior Court handling both criminal and civil cases.

Smeck, Woody: Deputy Superintendent, Yosemite National Park. Superintendent of Sequoia/Kings Canyon National Parks.

Reynolds, John: Superintendent North Cascades National Park, Manager of the Denver Service Center, Regional Director of the Mid-Atlantic and Pacific West Regions, Deputy Director of the National Park Service. Some positions after retirement: Executive Vice President, National Park Foundation. Board of Directors for Chesapeake Conservancy, Student Conservation Association, and Presidio Trust. Chair Flight 93 National Memorial Advisory Commission.

Some others:

Rosaria Cultrona Contini turned 100 on September 14, 2011. With mutual respect for her and each other, Monsignor Antonio Cacciapuoti and California Indian Elder Charlie Cooke gave blessings at her celebration. On September 14, 2012, Rosaria turned 101.

Ted Garcia was introduced as chief of the Southern Chumash by National Park Service Hosts of the SMMNRA Beilenson Visitor Center ribbon cutting on July 9, 2012. He offered the opening prayer to the Great Spirit and closed the ceremony with the sage blessing.

Kote and A'lul-koy Lotah own and operate a horse ranch on the central California coast. They remain active in Chumash medicine.

John Dawson left Indian Centers, Inc. in 1980 and started a public school career in supplies and purchasing. He is still doing powwows in mainland U.S.A., Hawaii, and Canada.

Sallie Cuaresma became the Associate for the Native American Congregational Enhancement within the Presbyterian Church (U.S.A.) in 1997. On retirement in 2010, she took a part time position as Site Supervisor for the Los Angeles Office of Southern California Indian Center, Inc. She remains active in her church and with Native American Ministry ecumenically.

Robert Dorame continues his work as a Most Likely Descendant when notified by the California Native American Heritage Commission to care for ancestral remains unearthed in Los Angeles and Orange Counties. He has designed a sculptural monument to commemorate his ancestors with work to commence in 2014. A master guitarist, Robert continues writing and performing original music.

Linda Cooke acquired a small horse in 2012 and started teaching grandchildren to ride and then found her horse was in foal. The colt was born very spirited on July 8, 2012. She named him Surprise.

And Charlie: He is monitoring, guest hosting, officiating at ceremonies, lending his voice at hearings, traveling with Linda, helping train Surprise, and grandfathering.

Sources: Interviews, Letters, E-mails, Voice Mails, and Observations

Recordings of interviews, their notes, and in some cases their transcriptions are being held by the author until they are archived at SMMNRA, NPS or other public archives. Also to be archived there are notes from non-recorded interviews and observations, copies of emails, and original letters. Mary Contini Gordon conducted the observations and interviews. She was the mail, email, or voice mail recipient.

Seventy-one people shared information in one or more ways: recorded interviews, non-recorded interviews, emails, letters, and photos. Their names and affiliation in regard to this book follow:

Anderson, Bill (NPS, SMMNRA)
Bean, Lowell (ethnologist)
Beck, Melanie, (NPS, SMMNRA)
Blackburn, Thomas (anthropologist/archaeologist)
Brown, Dave (community activist)
Cazabat, E. Jane (Native American)
Chandler, Bob (NPS, SMMNRA)
Chandler, Mitzi (NPS, SMMNRA)
Cooke, Alvin (Charlie Cooke's brother)
Cooke, Charlie (Native American)
Cooke, Damon (Charlie Cooke's son)
Cooke, Linda (Charlie Cooke's wife)
Cuaresma, Sallie (Native American)
Dagit, Rosi (Resource Conservation District of the Santa Monica Mountains)
Dawson, John, (Native American)
Dorame, Robert (Native American)
Edmiston, Joe (Santa Monica Mountains Conservancy)
Elison, Fran and Ed (NPS, CINP)
Ehorn, Bill (NPS, CINP)
Ehorn, Nancy (NPS, CINP)
Feeney, Kevin (curator, San Fernando Mission)
Feuer, Margot (community activist)
Folkes, Beverly (Native American)
Gamble, Lynn (anthropologist/archaeologist)
Garcia, Dennis (Native American)
Garcia, Ted (Native American)
Genter, Joan (Board, Friends of Satwiwa)

Genter, Rodney (Member, Friends of Satwiwa)
Goldschlager, Vicki (community activist)
Goode, Suzanne (California State Parks)
Holmes, Phil (NPS, SMMNRA)
Huston, Ann (NPS, CINP)
Ibanez, Vincent (Native American)
Johnson, John (anthropologist/archaeologist)
Kilday, Ruth (NPS, SMMNRA)
King, Chester (anthropologist/archaeologist)
Kirkish, Alex (anthropologist/archaeologist)
Knight, Al (anthropologist/archaeologist)
Krupp, Ed (astronomer)
Larson, Dan (anthropologist/archaeologist)
Leicester, Marti (NPS, SMMNRA)
Lewis, Bob (Thousand Oaks civic leader)
Lotah, A'lul-koy (Native American)
Lotah, Kote (Native American)
Lubitz, Rebecca (SMMNRA hiker)
Malatesta, Karen (Conejo Future Foundation)
Medeiros, Manual (NAHC)
Moore, Edra (California State Parks)
Myers, Larry (NAHC)
Pagaling, Reginald (Native American, CILS))
Phelan, Jay (life scientist)
Potter, Bryn Barabas (anthropologist/curator)
Preece, Dan (California State Parks)
Prince, Frances (Thousand Oaks civic leader)
Quintana, Ernie (NPS, SMMNRA)
Radic, Theo (artist, interested party)
Redmond, Bill (NPS, SMMNRA)
Reynolds, Bob (NPS, Mount Rushmore)
Reynolds, John (NPS, SMMNRA)
Rivera, Dolores (Native American, Friends of Satwiwa Board Member)
Ronning, Peggy (California State Parks)
Roybal, Lety (NPS, SMMNRA)
Singer, Clay (anthropologist/archaeologist)
Skei, Rorie (Santa Monica Mountains Conservancy)
Smeck, Woody (NPS, SMMNRA)
Sutnar, Rad (Developer)
Teeter, Wendy Giddens (anthropologist/curator)

Tejada, Barbara (anthropologist/archaeologist)
Tumamait, Pat (Native American)
Valenzuela, John (Native American)
Waiya, Mati (Native American)
Weil, Andrew (worked with Kote Lotah)

Other Interviews

Gordon, Mary. Conejo Conversations, TV Interview with Charlie Cooke, Thousand Oaks Storer Cable, c. 1984

Santa Clarita Television. First People of Santa Clarita Valley. Interview with Dr. John Johnson, Anthropologist, Santa Barbara Museum of Natural History, SCV Communications Group, 2003

Observations, Participation

Undocumented particpation, Charlie Cooke's walks, Guest Host Sundays, Satwiwa meetings and events, 1980s, 1990s

Notes and photos from observing team roping at the Tucson Rodeo, February 23, 2010

Notes and photos from site visits with Charlie Cooke to Calleguas Creek, Cheeseboro Canyon, Chumash Village, Leona Valley, Los Encinos State Park, Malibu Creek State Park, Palo Comado Canyon, St. Frances Dam, Topanga State Park, Vasquez Rocks County Park, Undisclosed cemetery, March 15, 16, 17, 2010

Notes and photos from observation at the Satwiwa equinox ceremony, March 20, 2010

Notes from observation of Native American Consultation Meeting, held at King Gillette Ranch, August 7, 2010

Notes and photos from visit to San Fernando Mission grounds, June 1, 2010

Notes from observing visitors at Satwiwa, February 12, 2012

Notes from observation at Beilenson Center Opening, King Gillette Ranch, June 6, 2012

Undocumented recollections from observing and working with Hutast and Tugupan, the Friends of Satwiwa, and Charlie Cooke, late 1986 to 2013

Sources: Documents, Laws, Books, Pamphlets, Proceedings, Articles, Websites

OFFICIAL DOCUMENTS ARCHIVES, SANTA MONICA MOUNTAINS NATIONAL RECREATION AREA AND CHANNEL ISLANDS NATIONAL PARK

Development Concept Plan, Santa Monica Mountains, Rancho Sierra Vista / Satwiwa, National Recreation Area / California, National Park Service, September 1984.

Ehorn, Bill. *The Establishment of Channel Islands National Park*, Unpublished paper, Channel Islands National Park files, 1989.

Environmental Assessment, Development Concept Plan, Santa Monica Mountains, Rancho Sierra Vista / Satwiwa, National Recreation Area / California, National Park Service, June 1983.

Holmes, Phil. *Preliminary Discussion Papers: Native American Programs for the Santa Monica Mountains*, National Park Service, Santa Monica Mountains National Recreation Area, 1981, 1982.

King, Chester. *Archaeological Assessment of King Gillette Ranch, Los Angeles County, California*. Malibu: Topanga Archaeological Consultants, Prepared for Mountains Recreation and Conservation Authority, June 2006.

King, Chester. *Overview of the History of American Indians in the Santa Monica Mountains*, in progress, 2013.

King, Chester. *Archaeological Reconnaissance and Recommendations for Phase 2 Archaeological Evaluation, City of Malibu File Number 94-015*. Archaeology. Topanga, CA: Topanga Anthropological Conusltants, 1994.

Letter to ACWOT, Art Alvitre, from David Gackenebach, superintendent, SMMNRA, NPS, December 14, 1989, establishing ACWOT'S last day as February 15, 1990, as a volunteer caretaker at Satwiwa. Important because establishes the date when the guest host programs started at Satwiwa.

Other Official Documents

American Memory. Library of Congress, Geographic Location of Amercian Indian Tribes. 19 May 2010. <memory.loc.gov/ammem/award98/ienhtml/tribes.html>.

California Coastal Commission. "Guide to the Collection of California Coastal Commission Liquefied Natural Gas Files." 1970-1983. *Online Archive of California*. 22 October 2011.

City of Santa Paula. "City of Santa Paula General Plan, Conservation and Open Space Element (St. Thomas Aquinas College)." 1998. *City of Santa Paula General Plan*. 22 October 2011 <ci.santa-paula.ca.us/planning/general plan>.

Edmiston, Joe. *Memorandum Regarding Grant to Friends of Satwiwa, Sketches of Proposed New Center*. Official Document. Malibu, California: Santa Monica Mountains Conservancy, March 1, 1989.

National Park Omnibus Legislation Hearing on S2856, 95th Congress, Publication 95-111, Bill to provide for NPS Land Aquisition.

Resolution of the Santa Monica Mountains Conservancy Awarding a Grant to Friends of Satwiwa, Resolution No. 89-09. Official Document. Malibu, California: Santa Monica Mountains Conservancy, March 1, 1989.

"Santa Monica Mountains National Recreation Area Advisory Commission." *Federal Register, Vol. 45, No. 111, June 6,1980, Notices.* 33152.

US Government. "National Park Service: Santa Monica Mountains National Recreation Area: Intent to Prepare an Environmental Statement and Conduct Scoping." *Federal Register, Vol. 44, No. 180, Notices.* September 14, 1979. 53581.

United States Department of the Interior, Bureau of Indian Affairs, Cooke, Alvin: Certification of Degree of Indian Blood with attached Ancestor Chart, 1972.

United States Department of the Interior, Bureau of Indian Affairs, Cooke, Charles: Certification of Degree of Indian Blood, 1972.

Laws

"American Indian Religious Freedom Act of 1978 ("AIRFA"; P.L; 95-341; 92 Stat. 469; 42 U.S.C 1996." n.d.

"Archaeological Resources Protection Act of 1979 (P.L. 96-95; 93 Stat. 721; 16 U.S.C. 470aa)." n.d.

"California Environmental Quality Act, 1973." *California Office of Historic Preservation*. 2011 <parks.ca.gov/pages/1054/files/brochure.pdf>.

"Indian Reorganization Act of 1934 (P.L. 73-576; Stat. 984; 25 U.S.C. 461)." n.d.

"Laws, Regulation, and Guidance." *Califorinia Department of Transportation*. 2009 <dot.ca.gov/ser/vol2/chap3.htm#_Toc223318705>.

"Native American Graves Protection and Repatriation Act of 1990 (P.L. 101-601; 25 U.S.C. 3001)." n.d.

"National Historic Preservation Act of 1966 (P.L. 89-665; 80 Stat. 915; 16 U.S.C. 470)." n.d.

Books, Pamphlets, Proceedings

Allen, Michael. *Rodeo Cowboys in the North American Imagination*, Reno: University of Nevada Press, 1998.

Arnold, Jeanne E. Department of Anthropology and Institute of Archaeology University of California Los Angeles. *Chumash Technology: New Discoveries of Uses of Imported Redwood and Asphaltum on the Channel Islands*, Proceedings of the Society for California Archaeology, 1993, Vol.6, pages 277-285.

Blackburn, Thomas C. (ed.) *December's Child, a Book of Chumash Oral Narratives*, Collected by J.P. Harrington, Los Angeles: University of California Press, 1975.

Boule, Mary Null. *California Native American Tribes*, Chumash Tribe. Vashon, WA: Merryant Publishers, 1992.

Campbell, Paul D. *Survival Skills of Native California*. Salt Lake City: Gibbs-Smith: 2009.

Canby, William C. Jr. *American Indian Law in a Nutshell*, St Paul, Minn: West Group, 1998.

Eagle, Adam Fortunate. *Heart of the Rock, The Indian Invasion of Alcatraz*. Norman: University of Oklahoma Press, 2002.

Ellis, Linda, ed. *Archaeological Theory and Methods, An Encyclopedia*, New York: Garland Reference Library of the Humanities, Vol 1701, 2000.

Gamble, Lynn H. *The Chumash World at European Contact*. Berkeley and Los Angeles, California: University of California Press, 2008.

Gordon, Mary Contini and Detlie, John (artist). *Satwiwa Loop Trail Brochure*. Conejo Future Foundation, Funded by Santa Monica Mountaons Conservancy, 1986.

Hudson, Travis and Underhay, Ernest, *Crystals in the Sky: An Intellectual Odyssey Involving Chumash Astronomy, Cosmology and Rock Art*. (Anthropological Papers, No. 10) Paperback, 1978.

Jaffe, Matthew. *The Santa Monica Mountains, Range on the Edge*. Angel City Press, 2006.

Josephy, Alvin M. Jr. et al. *The American Indians' Fight for Freedom, Red Power*. 2nd ed. Lincoln: University of Nebraska Press, 1999.

Krupp. E.C. *Beyond the Blue Horizon, Myths and Legends of the Sun, Moon, Stars, and Planets*. New York: Harper Collins, 1991.

Krupp, E.C. editor, *In Search of Ancient Astronomies*, New York: Doubleday, 1977.

Keller, Robert H. and Turek, Michael F. *American Indians and the National Parks*, University of Arizona Press, 1998. www.uapress.arizona.edu

Keremitsis, Eileen. *Life in a California Mission*, Farmington Hills, MI: Lucent Books, 2003.

Lamb, Susan. *Channel Islands National Park*. Tucson: Southwest Parks and Monuments Association, 2000.

Margolin, Malcolm, "Introduction," *Monterey on 1786, Life in a California Mission, the Journals of Jean Francois De La Peouse*. Berkeley: Heyday Books. 1989.

Mc Call, Lynne and Perry, Rosalind, project coordinators. *California's Chumash Indians*. San Lius Obispo, CA: EZ Nature Books. A project of the Santa Barbara Museum of Natural History, revised edition, 2002.

Mc Call, Lynne and Perry, Rosalind, (project coordinators). *The Chumash People, Materials for Teachers and Students*. San Lius Obispo, CA: EZ Nature Books. A project of the Santa Barbara Museum of Natural History, revised edition, 1991.

Pfeifer, Luanne (ed). *The Malibu Story*. Malibu: The Malibu Lagoon Museum, 1985.

Phelan, Jay. "Chapter 11: Animal Diversification," from *What is Life: A Guide to Biology*, 2nd edition, WH Freeman, 2011, (DNA discussion).

Ranch, Kohanya J. *Changing Perceptions and Policy: Redefining Indigeneity through California Chumash Revitalization*. Ph.D. Dissertation, University of California, Riverside, March 2012, (deals with issue of recognition as Chumash).

Rawls, James J. *Indians of California, The Changing Image*. Norman: University of Oklahoma Press, 1984.

Santa Monica Mountains Conservancy. "Guide to King Gillette Ranch." Santa Monica, c. 2010.

Stratton, W.K. *Chasing the Rodeo*. New York: Harcourt, 2005.

Tennesen, Michael. *Santa Monica Mountains National Recreation Area.* Tucson: Western National Parks Association, 2007.

Timbrook, Jan. *Chumash Ethnobotany.* Berkley, CA: Heyday Books and Santa Barbara Museum of Natural History, Santa Barbara, CA, 2007.

The Story of Candelaria, Candelaria Indian Council, 1973-2010. Brochure, 2010.

Weber, Francis. J. *San Fernando Rey de España Mission.* Cedex 2, France: Editions du Signe, 2007.

Weber, V. and Anderson, Dale. *The California Missions*, Milwaukee, Wisconsin: Gareth Stevens Publishing Company, 2002.

Weber, Valerie J. and Anderson, Keremitsis, Eileen. *Life in a California Mission*, Farmington Hills, MI: Lucent Books, 2003.

Welch, Rosanne. *A Brief History of the Tongva Tribe: The Native Inhabitants of the Puente Hills Preserve (tongvapeople.com/native_american_history. pdf).* PhD program. Claremont, California 91711: Department of History, Claremont Graduate University, 2006.

White, Nancy Marie. *Archaeology for Dummies.* Hoboken, NJ. Wiley Publishing, 2008.

Wright, Ralph B. (ed.) *California Missions.* Arroyo Grande, CA: Lowman Publishing Company, 1999.

Articles

(Web Site Given and Date Sourced if Accessed by Internet)

Alvarez, Fred. "A Homecoming of Sorts for Malibu's First Residents: Chumash Leaders Prepare to Build a Demonstration Village on an Ancient Site." *Los Angeles Times*, November 17, 2005, B1 and B3.

Anderson, John. "Point Conception: The Chumash Western Gate." *Point Conception: The Chumash Western Gate, 1999.* Accessed: 8 May 2010. <angelfire.com/id/newpubs/conception/html>.

Bailey, Pat. "UC Davis Scholar Jack Forbes Advocated for Indigenous Peoples," *UC Davis, News and Information*, February 25, 2011. <news. ucdavis.edu>

Berger, Leslie. "Gadfly Rallies Indians to Save Encino's Lost Village." 10 May 1990. *Los Angeles Times.* Accessed: 22 October 2011 <articles. latimes.com/1990-05-10/local/me-1666_1_lost_village>.

"Building an 'Ap Spells an 'Ap-ortunity for Volunteers." July 2004.

Friends of Satwiwa, Satwiwa News. Accessed: 1 June 2011 <satwiwa.org/archive/archive.php?choice=Ap>.

Bustillo, Michael. "2 Chumash Leaders Can't Get Together on Powwows." 8 September 1996. *Los Angeles Times.* Accessed: 30 September 2011 <articles.latimes.com/1996-09-08/local/me-41714_1_oakbrook-chumash>.

Bustillo, Michael. "Pick a Powwow: Despite Feud, Separate Chumash Festivals Bridge a Gap." 22 September 1996. *Los Angeles Times.* Accessed: 30 September 2011 <articles.latimes.com/1996-09224/local/me51900_1_native-american-festivals>.

Castillo, Edward D. "Short Overview of California Indian History." 1998. *Native American Heritage Commission.* Accessed: 6 December 2011 <http://www.nahc.ca.gov/califindian.html>.

Cheevers, Jack. "Restoring of Spread Gets Final Touches: History: State budget provides funds for work on Los Encinos State Historic Park in Encino. Area is all that remains of once vast sheep ranch." 29 August 1990. *Los Angeles Times.* Accessed: 22 October 2011 <articles.latimes.com/1990-08-29/local/me-115_1_los-encinos-state-historic-park>.

Helfand, Duke, "Digging Up Controversy: Development and Archaeology Clash on Malibu Land Where Chumash Artifacts May Be Buried," *Los Angeles Times*, July 30, 1995.

Dill, Kitty. "Long Ago Villages / Conejo Valley's Eary Residents Were Peaceful." 30 July 2004. *Friends of Satwiwa, Satwiwa News, Ventura County Star.* Accessed: 1 June 2011 <stawiwa.org/archive/archive.php?choice=Chumash>.

Gamble, Lynn. "The Organization of Artifacts, Features, and Actvities at Pitas Point, A Coastal Chumash Village." *Journal of California and Great Basin Anthropology* (1983): 103-129.

Gibson, J. William and King, Chester. "Skeletons in Playa Vista's Closet." *Los Angeles Times.* 20 January 2004. Accessed: 2 March 2012 <articles.latimes.com/2004/jun/20/opinion/op-gibson20>

Higgins, Paul. "The Tataviam: Early Newhall Residents." *Old Town Newhall Gazette.* January-February 1996. Accessed: 2011 <scvleon.com/newhall/tataviam.htm>.

Hulse, Jane. "JAUNTS: Keeping the Old Ways of the West Alive: A New Center at Rancho Sierra Vista / Satwiwa opens this summer to teach visitors about Native American skills and cultures." *Los Angeles Times*. Special to the Times, June 1, 1995.

Igler, Marc. "Lost Village of Encinos Discoveries: Senate Approves Home for Indian Relics." 12 June 1986. *Los Angeles Times*. Accessed: 22 October 2011 <articles.latimes.com/1986-0612/new/we-10442_1_artifacts>.

Johnson, John R. "The Indians of Mission San Fernando," *Southern California Quarterly*. Vol. LXXIX (79). No.3, 1997, pp. 249-290.

Klunder, Jan. "Lost Village Preservation Bill Is Opposed by State Panel." 13 July 1985. *Los Angeles Times*. Accessed: 22 October 2011 <articles.latimes.com/1985-13-07/local/me-8951_1_robbins-bill>.

Leach, Eric. "Indian Dig Turns Up the Past." Los Angeles Daily News, San Fernando Edition, May 1987, (About Malibu Creek State Park).

Lerner, Patricia Klein. "Of Relics and Rancor: Lost Village of Encino's Artifacts in Legal Limbo." 9 October 1988. *Los Angeles Times*. Accessed: 22 October 2011 <articles.latimes.com/1988-10-09/local/me-5699_1_whitney_desautels>.

Leshy, John D. "Unraveling the Sagebrush Rebellion: Law, Politics and Federal Lands." 1 November 1980. *Social Science Research Network*. 22 October 2011 <papers:ssrn.com/sol3/papers.cfm?abstract_id=1597952>.

Mason, Roger. "Summary of Work Carried Out at CA-LAN-43, The Encino Village Site." *Pacific Coast Archaeological Society Quarterly* July 1986: 9-17.

McGarry, Michael. "Lost Village of Encino Excavation: Indian Tribes to demand Reburial of Ancestors." 7 February 1985. *Los Angeles Times*. Accessed: 22 October 2011 <articles.latimes.com/1985-02-07/local/me-5329_1_indian_tribes>.

McLellan, Dennis. "Robert S. Chandler." 30 December 2010. *Los Angeles Times*. <articles.latimes.com/2010/dec/30/loccal/la-me-robert-chandler-20101230>.

McKinney, John. "A Walk in the Footsteps and Folkways of the Chumash." 8 November 1998. *Los Angeles Times*. Accessed: 29 September 2011 <articles.latimes.com/1998/nov/08/localtravel/tr-40518>.

McKinney, John. "In Step with History." 26 March 1995. *Los Angeles Times*. Accessed: 9 August 2010 <articles.latimes.com/1995-03-26/travel/tr-57206_1_white-oak-farm>.

McKinney, John. "Land of Chumash: Past and Present." 3-10-1990, *Los*

Angeles Times. Accessed: 29 September 2011 <articles.latimes.com/1990-03-10/news/vw-1881_1_national-park-service>.

Pascual, Psyche. "2 Chumash Villages May Be Too Many: American Indians: because both projects are to be in the same area, they will duplicate each other's displays and create a rivalry, critics say." 19 November 1990. *Los Angeles Times*. Accesseed: 30 September 2011 <articles.latimes.com/1990-11-19/local/me-3552_1_chumash-village>.

Pool, Bob. "Topanga Canyon's Squatters Evicted to Make Way for Club." 17 January 1987. *Los Angeles Times*. Accessed: 19 July 2011 <articles/latimes.com/1987-01-17/local/me-4959_1_eviction>.

Poss, Kate. "Newbury Park: Chumash Event to Greet Solstice." 19 June 1991. *Los Angeles Times*. Accessed: 28 October 2011 <artciles.latimes.com/1991-06-19/local/me-874_1_newbury-park>.

Potter, Bryn Barabas."Celebrating with Charlie Cooke, *News from Native California*, Vol. 19, No. 1, pp. 47 - 48, Fall 2005.

Potter, Bryn Barabas. "Chief Charlie Cooke Receives Prestigious Award," *Satwiwa News*, April 2008.

Stammer, Larry B. "Plans for LNG Terminal at Point Conception Dropped." 11 February 1986. *Los Angeles Times*. Accessed: 22 October 2011 <articles.latimes.com/1986-02-11/news/mn-22871_1_point-conception>.

"The Sagebrush Rebellion." 1 December 1980. *US News and World Report*. Accessed: 22 October 2011 <vcdh.virginia.edu/PVCC/mbase/docs/sagebrush.html>.

Vara-Orta, Francisco. "Putting to Rest Tribal Remains." 11 March 2008. *Los Angeles Times*. Accessed: 20 January 2012 <articles.latimes.com/2008/mar/11/local/me-remains-11>.

Walker, Gary. "Home at Last: Milestone Is Marked with Reburial of Excavated Ancestral Remains at Largest Native American Cemetery in California." *The Argonaut* 18 December 2008: 1+.

Weiss, Kenneth R. "Funds Approved for Chumash Musuem Artifact Aquistions: Thousand Oaks: the $100,000 allocated by county supervisors will also pay for display cases at the new facilility." 14 September 1994. *Los Angeles Times*. Accessed: 27 September 2011 <articles.latimes.com/1994-09-14/local/me-38348_1_thousand-oaks>.

Whitney-Desuatels, Nancy A. "Encino Village: The Three Faces of Cultural Resource Management." *Pacific Coast Archaeological Society Quarterly* July 1986: 1-8.

Williams, Timothy. "Unearthing a Hidden Past: Archeology: After years of controversy, Native American artifacts excavated from the Lost Village of Encino will be on display." 3 January 1994. *Los Angeles Times*. Accessed: 22 October 2011 <articles.latimes.com/1994-01-03/local/me-8148_1_native_american_artifacts>.

Winton, Ben. "Alcatraz Indian Land." *Native Peoples Magazine* Fall 1999: Redhawk's Lodge, siouxme.com.

Major Websites

Locations and organizations mentioned in the book can be found by navigating from these home pages or by searching them directly.

California Indian Legal Services: calindian.org
California Parks and Recreations: parks.ca.gov
California Missions: missionscalifornia.com
California Native American Heritage Commission: nahc.ca.gov
San Fernando Mission Archives: archivalcenter.org
Native American Heritage Commission: nahc.ca.gov
National Park Service: nps.gov
City of Malibu: Malibucity.org
City of Thousand Oaks: toaks.org
Conejo Future Foundation: clvff.org
Mojave Desert Indians: mojavedesert.net
Santa Ynez Reservation; Santaynezchunash.org
Santa Monica Mountains Conservancy: smmc.ca.org
Southern California Indian Center: Indiancenter.org

Some Specific Websites (access dates)

Burro Flats Painted Cave. 1 June 2011 <en.wickipedia.org/wiki/Burro_Flats_Painted_Cave>.

Chumash Indian Museum. 1 October 2011 <chumashindianmuseum.com>.

Conejo Valley Historical Society Stagecoach Inn Museum. Stagecoach Inn Museum. 22 April 2012 <http://www.stagecoachmuseum.org/>.

"Los Encinos Docents Association, The History of Los Encinos." Los Encinos State Historic Park. 14 November 2010 <los-encinos.org/history.html>.

Play Vista Archaeological and Historical Project, Marina del Rey, Los Angeles County, California. 2 March 2012 <sricrm.com/projects/playa_vista.html>.

"Point Mugu State Park." CA.Gov Parks and Recreation. 11 March 2012 <parks.ca.gov/?page_id=630>.

Radic, Theo. "Anthropology Answerable (Issue of Recognition as Chumash) 1999-2009" . Anthropology Answerable. 22 October 2011 <angelfire.com/sk/syukhtun/anthro.html>.

"Sagebrush Rebels." 1 June 2011 <en.wikipedia.org/wiki/Sagebrush_rebels>.

Schwartz, Stephanie M. 20 August 2008. A Brief History of Ribbon Shirts. <silvrdrach.homestead.com/schwartz_2008_aug_20.hTml>.

Shalawa (Hammond's) Meadow, California. 24 January 2011, 4 April 2011. <en.wikipedia.org/wiki/Shalawa_Meqadow,_California>.

Society for California Archaeology, Bylaws. 27 August 2012 http://www.scahome.org/about_sca/bylaws.html

Southern California Indian Center, Inc. 29 May 2011 <indiancenter.org>.

Thousand Oaks, California. 5 July 2011 <en.wikipedia.org/wiki/Thousand_Oaks_California>.

Wishtoyo Foundation. 31 August 2012 <Wishtoyo.org>.

Wikipedia. Native Amercian Name Controversy. 27 August 2012 <http://en.wikipedia.org/wiki/Native_American_name_controversy>.

Acknowledgements

It has been a joy to get up in the morning for over four years and work on this book. The story itself and the people involved made my day, every day. I put these acknowledgements at the end because at this point the reader can better appreciate what so many contributed.

Charlie Cooke is a marvelous, deserving subject and a font of knowledge. He has an incredible memory for people, events, and dates. "Ask Charlie," people would say when I asked for specifics. What he told me checked out time and again with newspaper articles and other sources. He readily shared his knowledge with me when we met or anytime I called. Linda, his wife, was always gracious, hunted for photographs, gave me her part of the story, and helped set aside time for Charlie and me to connect. While Charlie is knowledgeable about Native American and related topics, he does not talk about himself readily. So I reached out to many of his family, friends, and colleagues. His son, Damon, added the dad perspective to Charlie's story. His brother, Alvin Cooke, sent wonderful letters about and old photographs of a time gone by. Alvin was willing to talk long distance whenever needed.

Phil Holmes, National Park Service anthropologist for SMMNRA, helped me understand both the NPS and Native American backdrops to the story. Who knows how many questions he answered for me—certainly a lot. His deep knowledge of Southern California Indians, their issues and heritage, came into play many times. On the practical side, he helped me access official NPS documents and establish the first list of people to interview. He helped me navigate NPS support, especially with making maps, gathering photographs, and launching the process for transcribing some of the recorded interviews.

Many others contributed. I will mention one or two of their contributions each, although in many cases there were multiple interactions over several topics.

Besides Charlie, the story involves a number of Native Americans. I sent them sections that involved them, and they readily made suggestions to make the story more relevant to their communities. Dr. Kote Lotah, Chumash doctor, and I emailed each other constantly while I was writing sections that involved him. A'lul-koy Lotah added the native women's perspective. John Dawson, Apache, was instrumental in getting the powwow chapter right. Robert Dorame, Tongva, was key in getting the Playa Vista story right. Vince Ibanez, Pechanga, provided insights to Charlie's early days of activism. In addition, Pat Tumamait, Chumash, brought his perspective on Charlie's twenty-first century leadership and monitoring. Ted Garcia, the new Chumash chief (Chumash, Tongva, Tataviam, Vanyume), gave me stories of family dedication to preserving their heritage. His brother, Dennis Garcia, added his stories about Charlie's youth. Dolores Rivera (Mescalero Apache/Pasqua Yaqui/Picuris), Sallie Cuaresma (Cherokee/Creek), and E. Jane Cazabat (Creek/Seminole), provided stories that brought the times alive. Mati Waiya, Chumash, and I sat by a campfire on the Malibu beach, ancient Chumash territory, with the waves roaring behind us as he passionately espoused Charlie's work on behalf of Native Americans and the environment. His wife, Luhui Isha Waiya, helped with story details and photographs.

Many of the SMMNRA and California State Park staff, past and present, gave me their time on Charlie's story. I was so fortunate to talk with Bob Chandler, first superintendent at SMMNRA, before he passed away. He gave me some launching points and cornerstone quotes. Woody Smeck, superintendent of SMMNRA while I was working on this project gave me heartfelt stories and contact suggestions which proved invaluable. One of those, John Reynolds, who ran the gamut from being the deputy at SMMNRA to being the deputy for the entire NPS, took the time to send me a list of additional people I should talk to and then willingly read sections and finally the whole draft, finding detail that mattered and providing big picture comments which made the final work more tuned to the times and the issues. Bill Ehorn and I emailed the Channel Islands sections back and forth, helping me make those sections an experience rather than just words on a page. Nancy Fries Ehorn added her impressions from both her NPS work and general friendship perspectives. Ernie Quintana, Marti Leicester, Bill Redmond, Bill Anderson, and Ruth Kilday shared many early SMMNRA experiences and information about photos.

Dan Preece, the first superintendent of the Angeles District, California State Parks, also read the draft and verified names of parks, made suggestions about plants Charlie discussed on his guided walks, and illuminated Charlie's impact on preserving cultural heritage in the State Park System. Edra Moore, the first staff curator at the Antelope Valley Indian Museum State Historic Park, talked and emailed back and forth over a few weeks about that part of the story. Peggy Ronning, her sucessor, spent quite a bit of time researching photographs. Rosi Dagit, Suzanne Goode, and Barbara Tejada told of other California State Park staff interactions with Charlie. Not part of NPS or State Parks, Dr. Ed Krupp, director of the Griffith

Observatory and expert on ancient astronomy, told of rock art expeditions where Charlie was along. Joe Edmiston, Executive Director of the Santa Monica Mountains Conservancy, and Rorie Skei, also of SMMC staff, gave examples of how Charlie made people aware of Southern California Indians and worked with government agencies in the early days of SMMNRA. Dennis Washburn, founding mayor of Calabasas and president of the Santa Monica Mountains Fund, helped with information about photos and verified Charlie's constant involvement in the mountains. Joan Genter remembered whole scenes from SMMNRA Friends of Satwiwa volunteer days, shared them, and asked her husband, Rodney to send photos from that time.

I contacted several anthropologists. Even though their input conflicted at times, they provided context. Clay Singer and Dr. Alex Kirkish helped me understand Charlie's early involvement with archaeology. Dr. Nancy Desautels Wiley spent time talking with me and sent materials that gave me a better picture of what happened on the Lost Village site in the 1980s. Dr. Wendy Teeter, curator at the UCLA Fowler Museum, helped unravel some of the Lost Village artifacts story and added insights regarding Charlie's importance in Southern California. Dr. Lynn Gamble and Bryn Barabas Potter helped me provide both accuracy and color to the dig at the Talepop site, also back in the 1980s. Al Knight gave me an amusing story that allowed me to write a summary of Charlie's work in an engaging way. Dr. Chester King talked at length with me in the Topanga Canyon wooded area with the birds chirping all around about his long association with Charlie. Then he answered questions by email and sent packets of information many times. Dr. John Johnson gave me input to Charlie's family tree and explained his view of Charlie's ancestry. Dr. Thomas Blackburn further explained the view of some Chumash on verifying Chumash ancestry for themselves and others. Dr. Lowell Bean read the entire draft and encouraged me to publish.

Charlie was an involved citizen of his community. Former Thousand Oaks mayor Bob Lewis, developer Rad Sutnar, and citizen activist Vicki Goldschleger gave me civic vignettes for the story.

I would like to acknowledge Dr. Frederick F. York, Regional Anthropologist, National Park Service, Pacific West Region, who looked at my research plans, helped with initial forms, and answered questions along the way. Thanks to Kevin Feeney, curator at the San Fernando Mission, for showing me mission records, helping me understand the issues about them, reading the mission section, and giving me information that helped me round out that part of the story. Also, thanks to Dr. Jay Phelan, UCLA life sciences professor, who helped me understand the DNA aspect of the story.

Appreciation to additional NPS staff: James Mansfield and Brendan Clarke, NPS cartographers, for their patience making and remaking maps, Darren Davis for helping me find photos in the SMMNRA Archives, Ann Huston for helping me search for photos in the Channel Islands National Park archives, Yvonne Menard who gave me access to Channel Islands documents, Melanie Beck who verified some NPS acquisition dates, Jean Bray, retired public affairs officer who took time to check files and identify people in photos, Ranger Sheila Baden who read a draft and made some overarching suggestions, Linda Valois, program assistant at SMMNRA, who oversaw the transcription process for NPS, and Marilyn Medina and Deanna Jones, historical research assistants and college students, who transcribed long and involved interviews. Also, thanks to the Thousand Oaks Library whose student interns helped me find newspaper articles and to Jeanette Benard from Special Collections who helped search and find historical photographs.

Crystal Barker, a good friend and professional colleague, who is a technical writer, read one of my early drafts, marked it up, and encouraged me onward. Bob Golkowski, who understands English grammar better than anyone I know, made well-honed suggestions. I asked a few people to read some chapters to see how the approach I was taking worked. Thanks to Connie Tunick, Tim O'Connor, Susan Roche Wolf, Rick Kerner, and Bryn Potter for their insights on those chapters.

Charlie's story is one of relationships so it is natural that my work on it would involve connecting with many people, all gracious. So there are a few more to mention: Karen Malatesta (CFF), Manuel Medeiros (NAHC), and Larry Myers (NAHC), looked for minutes from meetings in the 1980s and then let me know they probably had been purged. With their phone and email communications, several people rounded out parts of the story. Thank you to: Dave Brown, Mitzi Chandler, Beverly Folkes, Margo Feuer, Dan Larson, Dr. Rebecca Lubitz, Francis Prince, Reggie Pagaling, Theo Radic, Bob Reynolds, and Dr. Andrew Weil.

Thank you to Sherry Matlack, my editor, who certainly has the eye of an eagle.

And finally thank you to my mother, Rosaria Contini, who inspired my approach to this story and who allowed me to stay at her home in the SMMNRA area so many times while I was working on it.

Table of Maps

Table of Photos and Illustrations

Index: People, Places, Organizations, Laws in the Story

About the Author

Dr. Mary Contini Gordon crosswalks between the analytical and the creative. Her background makes her a thorough researcher and an engaging writer. Mary has written stories, plays, and poems since childhood usually for private audiences, but with Charlie's book, as she calls it, Mary has stepped out into the public sector.

Dr. Gordon holds advanced degrees in theater, TV production, and educational psychology. For a time she produced and developed educational media and hosted a local TV talk show in Thousand Oaks, California. She encountered Charlie Cooke as a guest on one of her shows. Not long after, she became the executive director of the Hughes Institute for Professional Development, overseeing executive education. Around the same time, Mary volunteered at a national park site where Charlie was a central figure. She observed him in action and was struck by his effective leadership style. She thought to herself then that she would write about him one day.

Mary managed large ethnographic research projects for major corporations, including a book on business anthropology. So she took in stride that Charlie's book required acquiring, managing, and analyzing massive amounts of narrative data—always with the goals of not losing the spirit that is TIQ SLO'W and immersing the reader in varied scenes across decades and causes. In addition to writing, Mary enjoys nature trips with the families of her four children, Greg, Dan, Sara, and Rebecca, who beckon from their homes in different places across North America.

For more information about Dr. Gordon's leadership development work, go to www.ampubbooks.com/authors/authorgordon.html.

SIA information can be obtained at www.ICGtesting.com
in the USA
0455091013
V00003B/14/P

9 781938 714177